MATLAB Machine Learning

Michael Paluszek
Stephanie Thomas

Apress®

MATLAB Machine Learning

Michael Paluszek and Stephanie Thomas
New Jersey
USA

ISBN-13 (pbk): 978-1-4842-2249-2
DOI 10.1007/978-1-4842-2250-8

ISBN-13 (electronic): 978-1-4842-2250-8

Library of Congress Control Number: 2016963347

Managing Director: Welmoed Spahr
Lead Editor: Steve Anglin
Technical Reviewers: Jonah Lissner, Joseph Mueller, and Derek Surka
Editorial Board: Steve Anglin, Pramila Balan, Laura Berendson, Aaron Black, Louise Corrigan, Jonathan Gennick, Robert Hutchinson, Celestin Suresh John, Nikhil Karkal, James Markham, Susan McDermott, Matthew Moodie, Natalie Pao, Gwenan Spearing
Coordinating Editor: Mark Powers
Copy Editor: Kristen Cassereau Ng
Compositor: SPi Global
Indexer: SPi Global
Artist: SPi Global

Distributed to the book trade worldwide by Springer Science+Business Media New York, 233 Spring Street, 6th Floor, New York, NY 10013. Phone 1-800-SPRINGER, fax (201) 348-4505, e-mail orders-ny@springer-sbm.com, or visit www.springeronline.com. Apress Media, LLC is a California LLC and the sole member (owner) is Springer Science + Business Media Finance Inc (SSBM Finance Inc). SSBM Finance Inc is a Delaware corporation.

For information on translations, please e-mail rights@apress.com, or visit www.apress.com.

Apress and friends of ED books may be purchased in bulk for academic, corporate, or promotional use. eBook versions and licenses are also available for most titles. For more information, reference our Special Bulk Sales-eBook Licensing web page at www.apress.com/bulk-sales.

Any source code or other supplementary materials referenced by the author in this text are available to readers at www.apress.com. For detailed information about how to locate your book's source code, go to www.apress.com/source-code/. Readers can also access source code at SpringerLink in the Supplementary Material section for each chapter.

Printed on acid-free paper

For Marilyn and Matt.

Contents at a Glance

Contents

About the Authors

Michael Paluszek is president of Princeton Satellite Systems, Inc. (PSS) in Plainsboro, New Jersey. Mr. Paluszek founded PSS in 1992 to provide aerospace consulting services. He used MATLAB to develop the control system and simulation for the Indostar-1 geosynchronous communications satellite, resulting in the launch of Princeton Satellite Systems' first commercial MATLAB toolbox, the Spacecraft Control Toolbox, in 1995. Since then he has developed toolboxes and software packages for aircraft, submarines, robotics, and nuclear fusion propulsion, resulting in Princeton Satellite Systems' current extensive product line. He is currently leading a U.S. Army research contract for precision attitude control of small satellites and working with the Princeton Plasma Physics Laboratory on a compact nuclear fusion reactor for energy generation and space propulsion.

Prior to founding PSS, Mr. Paluszek was an engineer at GE Astro Space in East Windsor, NJ. At GE he designed the Global Geospace Science Polar despun platform control system and led the design of the GPS IIR attitude control system, the Inmarsat-3 attitude control systems, and the Mars Observer Delta-V control system, leveraging MATLAB for control design. Mr. Paluszek also worked on the attitude determination system for the DMSP meteorological satellites. Mr. Paluszek flew communication satellites on more than 12 satellite launches, including the GSTAR III recovery, the first transfer of a satellite to an operational orbit using electric thrusters. At Draper Laboratory Mr. Paluszek worked on the Space Shuttle, Space Station, and submarine navigation. His Space Station work included design of control moment gyro-based systems for attitude control.

Mr. Paluszek received his bachelor's degree in electrical engineering and master's and engineer's degrees in aeronautics and astronautics from the Massachusetts Institute of Technology. He is the author of numerous papers and has over a dozen U.S. patents. Mr. Paluszek is the coauthor of "MATLAB Recipes" published by Apress.

Stephanie Thomas is vice president of Princeton Satellite Systems, Inc. in Plainsboro, New Jersey. She received her bachelor's and master's degrees in aeronautics and astronautics from the Massachusetts Institute of Technology in 1999 and 2001, respectively. Ms. Thomas was introduced to PSS' Spacecraft Control Toolbox for MATLAB during a summer internship in 1996 and has been using MATLAB for aerospace analysis ever since. In her nearly 20 years of MATLAB experience, she has developed many software tools including the Solar Sail Module for the Spacecraft Control Toolbox; a proximity satellite operations toolbox for the Air Force; collision monitoring Simulink blocks for the Prisma satellite mission; and launch vehicle analysis tools in MATLAB and Java. She has developed novel methods for space situation assessment such as a numeric approach to assessing the general rendezvous problem between any two satellites implemented in both MATLAB and C++. Ms. Thomas has contributed to PSS' *Attitude and Orbit Control* textbook, featuring examples using the Spacecraft Control Toolbox (SCT), and has written many software user guides. She has conducted SCT training for engineers from diverse locales such as Australia, Canada, Brazil, and Thailand and has performed MATLAB consulting for NASA, the Air Force, and the European Space Agency. Ms. Thomas is the coauthor of *MATLAB Recipes* published by Apress. In 2016, Ms. Thomas was named a NASA NIAC Fellow for the project "Fusion-Enabled Pluto Orbiter and Lander."

About the Technical Reviewer

Jonah Lissner is a Research Scientist advancing PhD and DSc programs, scholarships, applied projects and academic journal publications in Theoretical Physics, Power Engineering, Complex Systems, Meta-materials, Geophysics, and Computation Theory. He has strong cognitive ability in empiricism and scientific reason for the purpose of hypothesis building, theory learning, mathematical and axiomatic modeling and testing for abstract problem-solving. His Dissertations, Research Publications and Projects, CV, Journals, Blog, Novels, System are listed at http://Lissnerresearch.weebly.com.

Dr. Joseph Mueller specializes in control systems and trajectory optimization. For his doctoral thesis, he developed optimal ascent trajectories for stratospheric airships. His active research interests include robust optimal control, adaptive control, applied optimization and planning for decision support systems, and intelligent systems to enable autonomous operations of robotic vehicles.

Prior to joining SIFT in early 2014, Dr. Mueller worked at Princeton Satellite Systems for 13 years. In that time, he served as the principal investigator for eight Small Business Innovative Research contracts for NASA, Air Force, Navy and MDA. He has developed algorithms for optimal guidance and control of both formation flying spacecraft and high altitude airships, and developed a course of action planning tool for DoD communication satellites.

In support of a research study for NASA Goddard Space Flight Center in 2005, Dr. Mueller developed the Formation Flying Toolbox for Matlab, a commercial product that is now used at NASA, ESA, and several universities and aerospace companies around the world.

In 2006, Dr. Mueller developed the safe orbit guidance mode algorithms and software for the Swedish Prisma mission, which has successfully flown a 2-spacecraft formation flying mission since it launch in 2010.

Dr. Mueller also serves as an adjunct professor in the Aerospace Engineering & Mechanics Department at the University of Minnesota, Twin Cities campus.

Derek Surka has over 20 years of professional experience in the aerospace field, specializing in space situational awareness, guidance, navigation, and control, distributed system autonomy, and formation flying. Mr. Surka has applied his expertise in astrodynamics, data fusion, estimation and control systems, and software development to over 20 satellites and payloads for a variety of military, civil, and commercial space customers. Mr. Surka is an active runner and triathlete and is a former National Mixed Curling Champion.

Introduction

Machine learning is becoming important in every discipline. It is used in engineering for autonomous cars. It is used in finance for predicting the stock market. Medical professionals use it for diagnoses. While many excellent packages are available from commercial sources and open-source repositories, it is valuable to understand how these algorithms work. Writing your own algorithms is valuable both because it gives you insight into the commercial and open-source packages and also because it gives you the background to write your own custom Machine Learning software specialized for your application.

MATLAB® had its origins for that very reason. Scientists who needed to do operations on matrices used numerical software written in FORTRAN. At the time, using computer languages required the user to go through the write-compile-link-execute process that was time consuming and error prone. MATLAB presented the user with a scripting language that allowed the user to solve many problems with a few lines of a script that executed instantaneously. MATLAB has built-in visualization tools that helped the user better understand the results. Writing MATLAB was a lot more productive and fun than writing FORTRAN.

The goal of *MATLAB Machine Learning* is to help all users harness the power of MATLAB to do a wide range of learning problems. This book has two parts. The first part, Chapters 1–3, provides background on machine learning including learning control that is not often associated with machine intelligence. We coin the term "autonomous learning" to embrace all of these disciplines.

The second part of the book, Chapters 4–12, shows complete MATLAB machine learning applications. Chapters 4–6 introduce the MATLAB features that make it easy to implement machine learning. The remaining chapters give examples. Each chapter provides the technical background for the topic and ideas on how you can implement the learning algorithm. Each example is implemented in a MATLAB script supported by a number of MATLAB functions.

The book has something for everyone interested in machine learning. It also has material that will allow people with interest in other technology areas to see how machine learning, and MATLAB, can help them solve problems in their areas of expertise.

PART I

■ ■ ■

Introduction to Machine Learning

CHAPTER 1

■ ■ ■

An Overview of Machine Learning

1.1   Introduction

Machine learning is a field in computer science where existing data are used to predict, or respond to, future data. It is closely related to the fields of pattern recognition, computational statistics, and artificial intelligence. Machine learning is important in areas like facial recognition, spam filtering, and others where it is not feasible, or even possible, to write algorithms to perform a task.

For example, early attempts at spam filtering had the user write rules to determine what was spam. Your success depended on your ability to correctly identify the attributes of the message that would categorize an email as spam, such as a sender address or subject keyword, and the time you were willing to spend to tweak your rules. This was only moderately successful as spam generators had little difficulty anticipating people's rules. Modern systems use machine learning techniques with much greater success. Most of us are now familiar with the concept of simply marking a given message as "spam" or "not spam," and we take for granted that the email system can quickly learn which features of these emails identify them as spam and prevent them from appearing in our inbox. This could now be any combination of IP or email addresses and keywords in the subject or body of the email, with a variety of matching criteria. Note how the machine learning in this example is data-driven, autonomous, and continuously updating itself as you receive email and flag it.

In a more general sense, what does machine learning mean? Machine learning can mean using machines (computers and software) to gain meaning from data. It can also mean giving machines the ability to learn from their environment. Machines have been used to assist humans for thousands of years. Consider a simple lever, which can be fashioned using a rock and a length of wood, or the inclined plane. Both of these machines perform useful work and assist people, but neither has the ability to learn. Both are limited by how they are built. Once built, they cannot adapt to changing needs without human interaction. Figure 1.1 shows early machines that do not learn.

© Michael Paluszek, Stephanie Thomas 2017
M. Paluszek and S. Thomas, *MATLAB Machine Learning*, DOI 10.1007/978-1-4842-2250-8_1

Figure 1.1: Simple machines that do not have the capability to learn.

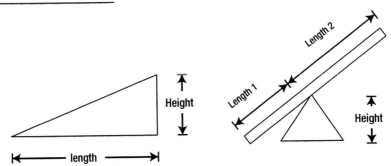

Both of these machines do useful work and amplify the capabilities of people. The knowledge is inherent in their parameters, which are just the dimensions. The function of the inclined plane is determined by its length and height. The function of the lever is determined by the two lengths and the height. The dimensions are chosen by the designer, essentially building in the designer's knowledge.

Machine learning involves memory that can be changed while the machine operates. In the case of the two simple machines described above, knowledge is implanted in them by their design. In a sense they embody the ideas of the builder; thus, they are a form of fixed memory. Learning versions of these machines would automatically change the dimensions after evaluating how well the machines were working. As the loads moved or changed, the machines would adapt. A modern crane is an example of a machine that adapts to changing loads, albeit at the direction of a human being. The length of the crane can be changed depending on the needs of the operator.

In the context of the software we will be writing in this book, *machine learning* refers to the process by which an algorithm converts the input data into parameters it can use when interpreting future data. Many of the processes used to mechanize this learning derive from optimization techniques and in turn are related to the classic field of automatic control. In the remainder of this chapter we will introduce the nomenclature and taxonomy of machine learning systems.

1.2   Elements of Machine Learning

This section introduces key nomenclature for the field of machine learning.

1.2.1 Data

All learning methods are data driven. Sets of data are used to train the system. These sets may be collected by humans and used for training. The sets may be very large. Control systems may collect data from sensors as the systems operate and use that to identify parameters—or train the system.

■ **Note**   When collecting data from training, one must be careful to ensure that the time variation of the system is understood. If the structure of a system changes with time, it may be necessary to discard old data before training the system. In automatic control this is sometimes called a "forgetting factor" in an estimator.

1.2.2 Models

Models are often used in learning systems. A model provides a mathematical framework for learning. A model is human derived and based on human observations and experiences. For example, a model of a car, seen from above, might be that it is rectangular shaped with dimensions that fit within a standard parking spot. Models are usually thought of as human derived and providing a framework for machine learning. However, some forms of machine learning develop their own models without a human-derived structure.

1.2.3 Training

A system that maps an input to an output needs training to do this in a useful way. Just as people need to be trained to perform tasks, machine learning systems need to be trained. Training is accomplished by giving the system an input and the corresponding output and modifying the structure (models or data) in the learning machine so that mapping is learned. In some ways this is like curve fitting or regression. If we have enough training pairs, then the system should be able to produce correct outputs when new inputs are introduced. For example, if we give a face recognition system thousands of cat images and tell it that those are cats, we hope that when it is given new cat images, it will also recognize them as cats. Problems can arise when you don't give it enough training sets or the training data are not sufficiently diverse, that is, do not represent the full range of cats in this example.

1.2.3.1 Supervised Learning

Supervised learning means that specific training sets of data are applied to the system. The learning is supervised in that the "training sets" are human derived. It does not necessarily mean that humans are actively validating the results. The process of classifying the system's outputs for a given set of inputs is called *labeling*. That is, you explicitly say which results are correct or which outputs are expected for each set of inputs.

The process of generating training sets can be time consuming. Great care must be taken to ensure that the training sets will provide sufficient training so that when real-world data are collected the system will produce correct results. They must cover the full range of expected inputs and desired outputs. The training is followed by test sets to validate the results. If the results aren't good, then the test sets are cycled into the training sets and the process repeated.

A human example would be a ballet dancer trained exclusively in classical ballet technique. If she were then asked to dance a modern dance, the results might not be as good as required because the dancer did not have the appropriate training sets; her training sets were not sufficiently diverse.

1.2.3.2 Unsupervised Learning

Unsupervised learning does not utilize training sets. It is often used to discover patterns in data for which there is no "right" answer. For example, if you used unsupervised learning to train a face identification system, the system might cluster the data in sets, some of which might be faces. Clustering algorithms are generally examples of unsupervised learning. The advantage of unsupervised learning is that you can learn things about the data that you might not know in advance. It is a way of finding hidden structures in data.

1.2.3.3 Semisupervised Learning

With the semisupervised approach, some of the data is in the form of labeled training sets and other data are not [1]. In fact, typically only a small amount of the input data is labeled while most is not, as the labeling may be an intensive process requiring a skilled human. The small set of labeled data is leveraged to interpret the unlabeled data.

1.2.3.4 Online Learning

The system is continually updated with new data [1]. This is called "online" because many of the learning systems use data collected online. It could also be called "recursive learning." It can be beneficial to periodically "batch" process data used up to a given time and then return to the online learning mode. The spam filtering systems from the introduction utilize online learning.

1.3   The Learning Machine

Figure 1.2 shows the concept of a learning machine. The machine absorbs information from the environment and adapts. Note that inputs may be separated into those that produce an immediate response and those that lead to learning. In some cases they are completely separate. For example, in an aircraft a measurement of altitude is not usually used directly for control. Instead, it is used to help select parameters for the actual control laws. The data required for learning and regular operation may be the same, but in some cases separate measurements or data will be needed for learning to take place. Measurements do not necessarily mean data collected by a sensor such as radar or a camera. It could be data collected by polls, stock market prices, data in accounting ledgers, or data gathered by any other means. The machine learning is then the process by which the measurements are transformed into parameters for future operation.

Figure 1.2: A learning machine that senses the environment and stores data in memory.

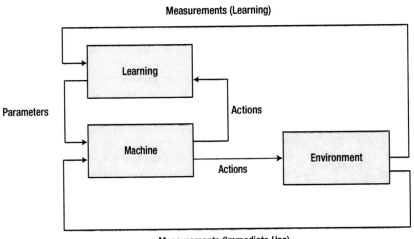

Note that the machine produces output in the form of actions. A copy of the actions may be passed to the learning system so that it can separate the effects of the machine actions from those of the environment. This is akin to a feedforward control system, which can result in improved performance.

A few examples will clarify the diagram. We will discuss a medical example, a security system, and spacecraft maneuvering.

A doctor might want to diagnose diseases more quickly. She would collect data on tests on patients and then collate the results. Patient data might include age, height, weight, historical data like blood pressure readings and medications prescribed, and exhibited symptoms. The machine learning algorithm would detect patterns so that when new tests were performed on a patient the machine learning algorithm would be able to suggest diagnoses or additional tests to narrow down the possibilities. As the machine learning algorithm was used, it would hopefully get better with each success or failure. In this case the environment would be the patients themselves. The machine would use the data to generate actions, which would be new diagnoses. This system could be built in two ways. In the supervised learning process, test data and known correct diagnoses would be used to train the machine. In an unsupervised learning process, the data would be used to generate patterns that might not have been known before, and these could lead to diagnosing conditions that would normally not be associated with those symptoms.

A security system might be put into place to identify faces. The measurements are camera images of people. The system would be trained with a wide range of face images taken from multiple angles. The system would then be tested with these known persons and its success rate validated. Those that are in the database should be readily identified and those that are not should be flagged as unknown. If the success rate were not acceptable, more training might be needed or the algorithm itself might need to be tuned. This type of face recognition is now common, used in Mac OS X's "Faces" feature in Photos and Facebook when "tagging" friends in photos.

For precision maneuvering of a spacecraft, the inertia of the spacecraft needs to be known. If the spacecraft has an inertial measurement unit that can measure angular rates, the inertia matrix can be identified. This is where machine learning is tricky. The torque applied to the spacecraft, whether by thrusters or momentum exchange devices, is only known to a certain degree of accuracy. Thus, the system identification system must sort out, if it can, the torque scaling factor from the inertia. The inertia can only be identified if torques are applied. This leads to the issue of stimulation. A learning system cannot learn if the system to be studied does not have known inputs, and those inputs must be sufficient to stimulate the system so that the learning can be accomplished.

1.4   Taxonomy of Machine Learning

In this book we take a bigger view of machine learning than is normally done. We expand machine learning to include adaptive and learning control. This field started off independently but now is adapting technology and methods from machine learning. Figure 1.3 shows how we organize the technology of machine learning. You will notice that we created a title that encompasses three branches of learning;

Figure 1.3: Taxonomy of machine learning. Optimization is part of the taxonomy because the results of optimization can be new discoveries, such as a new type of spacecraft or aircraft trajectory.

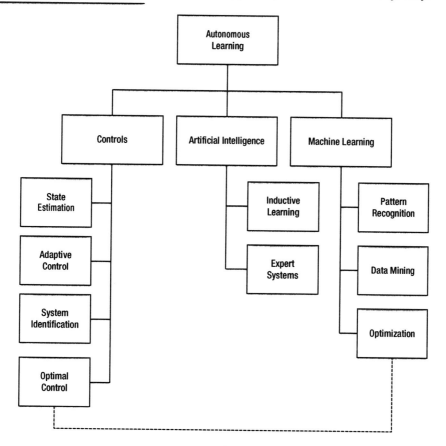

we call the whole subject area "autonomous learning." That means learning without human intervention during the learning process.

There are three categories under autonomous learning. The first is *control*. Feedback control is used to compensate for uncertainty in a system or to make a system behave differently than it would normally behave. If there was no uncertainty, you wouldn't need feedback. For example, if you are a quarterback throwing a football at a running player, assume for a moment that you know everything about the up-coming play. You know exactly where the player should be at a given time, so you can close your eyes, count, and just throw the ball to that spot. Assuming the player has good hands, you would have a 100% reception rate! More realistically, you watch the player, estimate the player's speed, and throw the ball. You are applying feedback to the problem. As stated, this is not a learning system. However, if now you practice the same play repeatedly, look at your success rate and modify the mechanics and timing of your throw using that information, you would have an adaptive control system, the second box from the top of the control list. Learning in control takes place in adaptive control systems and also in the general area of system identification. System identification is learning about a system. Optimal control may not involve any learning. For example, what is known as full state feedback produces an optimal control signal but does involve learning. In full state feedback the combination of model and data tells us everything we need to know about the system. However, in more complex systems we can't measure all the states and don't know the parameters perfectly, so some form of learning is needed to produce "optimal" results.

The second category of autonomous learning is *artificial intelligence*. Machine learning traces some of its origins in artificial intelligence. Artificial intelligence is the area of study whose goal is to make machines reason. While many would say the goal is "think like people," this is not necessarily the case. There may be ways of reasoning that are not similar to human reasoning but are just as valid. In the classic Turing test, Turing proposes that the computer only needs to imitate a human in its output to be a "thinking machine" regardless of how those outputs are generated. In any case, intelligence generally involves learning, and so learning is inherent in many artificial intelligence technologies.

The third category is what many people consider true *machine learning*. This is making use of data to produce behavior that solves problems. Much of its background comes from statistics and optimization. The learning process may be done once in a batch process or continually in a recursive process. For example, in a stock buying package a developer might have processed stock data for several years, say prior to 2008, and used that to decide which stocks to buy. That software might not have worked well during the financial crash. A recursive program would continuously incorporate new data. Pattern recognition and data mining fall into this category. Pattern recognition is looking for patterns in images. For example, the early AI Blocks World software could identify a block in its field of view. It could find one block in a pile of blocks. Data mining is taking large amounts of data and looking for patterns, for example, taking stock market data and identifying companies that have strong growth potential.

1.5 Autonomous Learning Methods

This section introduces you to popular machine learning techniques. Some will be used in the examples in this book. Others are available in MATLAB products and open-source products.

1.5.1 Regression

Regression is a way of fitting data to a model. A model can be a curve in multiple dimensions. The regression process fits the data to the curve, producing a model that can be used to predict future data. Some methods, such as linear regression or least squares, are parametric in that the number of parameters to be fit are known. An example of linear regression is shown in the listing below and in Figure 1.4. This model was created by starting with the line $y = x$ and adding noise to y. The line was recreated using a least-squares fit via MATLAB's `pinv` Pseudoinverse function.

Listing 1.1: Linear Regression

```
%% LinearRegression Script that demonstrates linear regression
% Fit a linear model to linear or quadratic data

%% Generate the data and perform the regression
% Input
x = linspace(0,1,500)';
n = length(x);

% Model a polynomial, y = ax2 + mx + b
a     = 1.0;       % quadratic - make nonzero for larger errors
m     = 1.0;       % slope
b     = 1.0;       % intercept
sigma = 0.1; % standard deviation of the noise
y0    = a*x.^2 + m*x + b;
y     = y0 + sigma*randn(n,1);

% Perform the linear regression using pinv
a     = [x ones(n,1)];
c     = pinv(a)*y;
yR    = c(1)*x + c(2); % the fitted line

%% Generate plots
h = figure('name','Linear_Regression');
h.Name = 'Linear_Regression';
plot(x,y); hold on;
plot(x,yR,'linewidth',2);
grid on
xlabel('x');
ylabel('y');
title('Linear_Regression');
legend('Data','Fit')

figure('Name','Regression_Error')
plot(x,yR-y0);
grid on
```

We can solve the problem

$$Ax = b \qquad (1.1)$$

by taking the inverse of A if the length of x and b are the same:

$$x = A^{-1}b \qquad (1.2)$$

This works because A is a square matrix but only works if A is not singular. That is, it has a valid inverse. If the length of x and that of b are the same, we can still find an approximation to x where $x = \text{pinv}(A)b$. For example, in the first case below A is 2 by 2. In the second case, it is 3 by 2, meaning there are 3 elements of x and 2 of b.

```
>> inv(rand(2,2))

ans =

    1.4518   -0.2018
   -1.4398    1.2950

>> pinv(rand(2,3))

ans =

    1.5520   -1.3459
   -0.6390    1.0277
    0.2053    0.5899
```

Figure 1.4: Learning with linear regression.

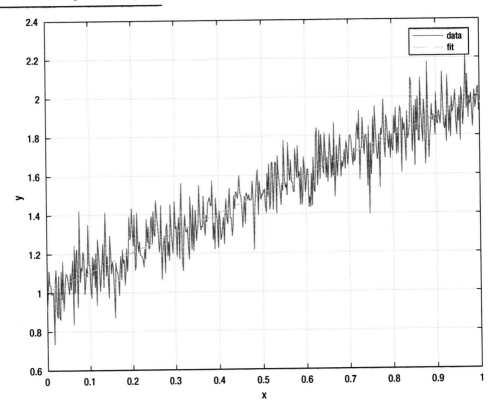

The system learns the parameters, slope and y-intercept, from the data. The more data, the better the fit. As it happens, our model

$$y = mx + b \qquad (1.3)$$

is correct. However, if it were wrong, the fit would be poor. This is an issue with model-based learning. The quality of the results is highly dependent on the model. If you are sure of your model, then it should be used. If not, other methods, such as unsupervised learning, may produce better results. For example, if we add the quadratic term x^2 we get the fit in Figure 1.5. Notice how the fit is not as good as we might like.

Figure 1.5: Learning with linear regression for a quadratic.

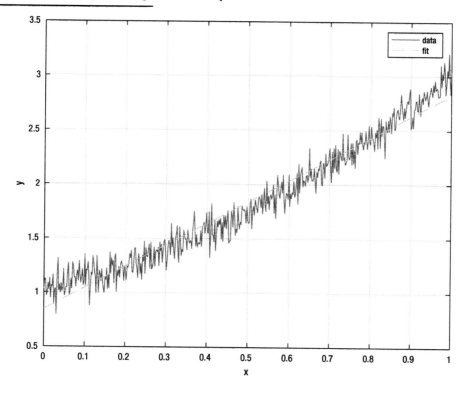

1.5.2 Neural Nets

A neural net is a network designed to emulate the neurons in a human brain. Each "neuron" has a mathematical model for determining its output from its input; for example, if the output is a step function with a value of 0 or 1, the neuron can be said to be "firing" if the input stimulus results in a 1 output. Networks are then formed with multiple layers of interconnected neurons. Neural networks are a form of pattern recognition. The network must be trained using sample data, but no a priori model is required. Networks can be trained to estimate the output of nonlinear processes and the network then becomes the model.

Figure 1.6 displays a simple neural network that flows from left to right, with two input nodes and one output node. There is one "hidden" layer of neurons in the middle. Each node has a set of numeric weights that is tuned during training.

A "deep" neural network is a neural network with multiple intermediate layers between the input and output. Neural nets are an active area of research.

Figure 1.6: A neural net with one intermediate layer between the inputs on the left and the output on the right.

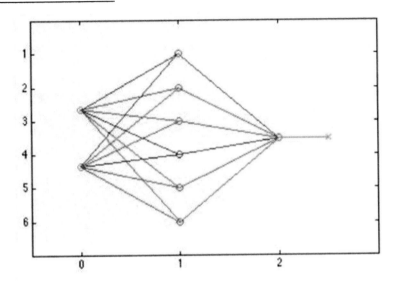

1.5.3 Support Vector Machines

Support vector machines (SVMs) are supervised learning models with associated learning algorithms that analyze data used for classification and regression analysis. An SVM training algorithm builds a model that assigns examples into categories. The goal of an SVM is to produce a model, based on the training data, that predicts the target values.

In SVMs nonlinear mapping of input data in a higher-dimensional feature space is done with kernel functions. In this feature space a separation hyperplane is generated that is the solution to the classification problem. The kernel functions can be polynomials, sigmoidal functions, and radial basis functions. Only a subset of the training data is needed; these are known as the support vectors [2]. The training is done by solving a quadratic program, which can be done with many numerical software programs.

1.5.4 Decision Trees

A decision tree is a tree-like graph used to make decisions. It has three kinds of nodes:

1. Decision nodes

2. Chance nodes

3. End nodes

You follow the path from the beginning to the end node. Decision trees are easy to understand and interpret. The decision process is entirely transparent although very large decision trees may be hard to follow visually. The difficulty is finding an optimal decision tree for a set of training data.

Two types of decision trees are classification trees, which produce categorical outputs, and regression trees, which produce numeric outputs. An example of a classification tree is shown in Figure 1.7. This helps an employee decide where to go for lunch. This tree has only decision nodes.

Figure 1.7: A classification tree.

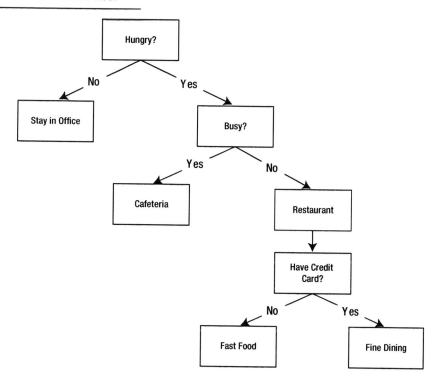

This might be used by management to predict where they could find an employee at lunch time. The decision are Hungry, Busy, and Have a Credit Card. From that the tree could by synthesized. However, if there were other factors in the decision of employees, for example, it's someone's birthday, which would result in the employee's going to a restaurant, then the tree would not be accurate.

1.5.5 Expert System

A system uses a knowledge base to reason and present the user with a result and an explanation of how it arrived at that result. Expert systems are also known as knowledge-based systems. The process of building an expert system is called "knowledge engineering." This involves a knowledge engineer, someone who knows how to build the expert system, interviewing experts for the knowledge needed to build the system. Some systems can induce rules from data, speeding the data acquisition process.

An advantage of expert systems, over human experts, is that knowledge from multiple experts can be incorporated into the database. Another advantage is that the system can explain the process in detail so that the user knows exactly how the result was generated. Even an expert in a domain can forget to check certain things. An expert system will always methodically check its full database. It is also not affected by fatigue or emotions.

Knowledge acquisition is a major bottleneck in building expert systems. Another issue is that the system cannot extrapolate beyond what is programmed into the database. Care must be taken with using an expert system because it will generate definitive answers for problems where there is uncertainty. The explanation facility is important because someone with domain knowledge can judge the results from the explanation.

In cases where uncertainty needs to be considered, a probabilistic expert system is recommended. A Bayesian network can be used as an expert system. A Bayesian network is also known as a belief network. It is a probabilistic graphical model that represents a set of random variables and their dependencies. In the simplest cases, a Bayesian network can be constructed by an expert. In more complex cases, it needs to be generated from data from machine learning.

References

[1] J. Grus. *Data Science from Scratch*. O'Reilly, 2015.

[2] Corinna Cortes and Vladimir Vapnik. Support-Vector Networks. *Machine Learning*, 20:273–297, 1995.

CHAPTER 2

■ ■ ■

The History of Autonomous Learning

2.1   Introduction

In the previous chapter you were introduced to autonomous learning. You saw that autonomous learning could be divided into the areas of machine learning, controls, and artificial intelligence (AI). In this chapter you will learn how each area evolved. Automatic control predates AI. However, we are interested in adaptive or learning control, which is a relatively new development and really began evolving around the time that AI had its foundations. Machine learning is sometimes considered an offshoot of AI. However, many of the methods used in machine learning came from different fields of study such as statistics and optimization.

2.2   Artificial Intelligence

AI research began shortly after World War II [2]. Early work was based on knowledge of the structure of the brain, propositional logic, and Turing's theory of computation. Warren McCulloch and Walter Pitts created a mathematical formulation for neural networks based on threshold logic. This allowed neural network research to split into two approaches. One centered on biological processes in the brain and the other on the application of neural networks to AI. It was demonstrated that any function could be implemented through a set of such neurons and that a neural net could learn. In 1948, Norbert Wiener's book *Cybernetics* was published which described concepts in control, communications, and statistical signal processing. The next major step in neural networks was Donald Hebb's book, *The Organization of Behavior,* connecting connectivity with learning in the brain. His book became a source of learning and adaptive systems. Marvin Minsky and Dean Edmonds built the first neural computer in 1950.

In 1956, Allen Newell and Herbert Simon designed a reasoning program, the Logic Theorist (LT), which worked nonnumerically. The first version was hand simulated using index cards. It could prove mathematical theorems and even improve on human derivations. It solved 38 of the 52 theorems in *Principia Mathematica*. LT employed a search tree with heuristics to limit the search. LT was implemented on a computer using IPL, a programming language that led to Lisp.

Blocks World was one of the first attempts to demonstrate general computer reasoning. The Blocks World was a micro world. A set of blocks would sit on a table, some sitting on other blocks. The AI systems could rearrange blocks in certain ways. Blocks under other blocks could not be moved until the block on top was moved. This is not unlike the Towers of Hanoi problem. The Blocks World was a significant advance as it showed that a machine could reason at least in a limited environment. Computer vision was introduced. Work began on implementing neural networks.

M. Paluszek and S. Thomas, *MATLAB Machine Learning*, DOI 10.1007/978-1-4842-2250-8_2

Figure 2.1: Towers of Hanoi. The disks must be moved from the first peg to the last without ever putting a larger-diameter disk on top of a smaller-diameter disk.

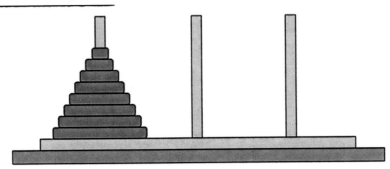

Blocks World and Newell's and Simon's LT was followed up by the General Problem Solver (GPS). It was designed to imitate human problem-solving methods. Within its limited class of puzzles it could solve them much like a human. While GPS solved simple problems such as the Towers of Hanoi, Figure 2.1, it could not solve real-world problems because the search was lost in the combinatorial explosion.

In 1959, Herman Gelernter wrote the Geometry Theorem prover, which could prove theorems that were quite tricky. The first game-playing programs were written at this time. In 1958, John McCarthy invented the language Lisp (LISt Processing), which was to become a major AI language. It is now available as Scheme and Common Lisp. Lisp was implemented only one year after FORTRAN. A typical Lisp expression is

```
(defun sqrt-iter (guess x)
  (if (good-enough-p guess x)
      guess
      (sqrt-iter (improve guess x) x)))
```

This computes a square root through recursion. Eventually, dedicated Lisp machines were built, but they went out of favor when general-purpose processors became faster.

Time sharing was invented at the Massachusetts Institute of Technology (MIT) to facilitate AI research. Professor McCarthy created a hypothetical computer program, Advice Taker, a complete AI system that could embody general-world information. It would have used a formal language such as predicate calculus. For example, it could come up with a route to the airport from simple rules. Marvin Minsky arrived at MIT and began working on micro worlds. Within these limited domains, AI could solve problems, such as closed-form integrals in calculus.

Minsky and Papert wrote the book *Perceptrons*, which was fundamental in the analysis of artificial neural networks. The book contributed to the movement toward symbolic processing in AI. The book noted that single neurons could not implement some logical functions such as exclusive-or and erroneously implied that multilayer networks would have the same issue. It was later found that three-layer networks could implement such functions.

More challenging problems were tried in the 1960s. Limitations in the AI techniques became evident. The first language translation programs had mixed results. Trying to solve problems by working through massive numbers of possibilities (such as in chess) ran into computation problems. Mr. Paluszek (the author) in Patrick Winston's 6.034 class at MIT wrote a paper suggesting the use of pattern recognition in chess to visualize board patterns much as a human player might. As it turned out, this was not the approach taken to produce the champion computer chess programs of today.

As more complex problems were addressed, this approach was not suitable and the number of possibilities grew rapidly with increases in problem complexity. Multilayer neural networks were discovered in the 1960s but were not really studied until the 1980s.

In the 1970s, self-organizing maps using competitive learning were introduced [2]. A resurgence in neural networks happened in the 1980s. Knowledge-based systems were also introduced in the 1980s. According to Jackson [3],

> An expert system is a computer program that represents and reasons with knowledge of some specialized subject with a view to solving problems or giving advice.

This included expert systems that could store massive amounts of domain knowledge. These could also incorporate uncertainty in their processing. Expert systems are applied to medical diagnoses and other problems. Unlike AI techniques up to this time, expert systems could deal with problems of realistic complexity and attain high performance. They also explain their reasoning. This last feature is critical in their operational use. Sometimes these are called knowledge-based systems. A well-known open-source expert system is CLIPS. *write out name*

Back propagation for neural networks was reinvented in the 1980s, leading to renewed progress in this field. Studies began both of human neural networks (i.e., the human brain) and of the creation of algorithms for effective computational neural networks. This eventually led to deep learning networks in machine learning applications.

Advances were made in the 1980s as AI began to apply rigorous mathematical and statistical analysis to develop algorithms. Hidden Markov models were applied to speech. Combined with massive databases, they have resulted in vastly more robust speech recognition. Machine translation has also improved. Data mining, the first form of machine learning as it is known today, was developed. Chess programs improved initially through the use of specialized computers, such as IBM's Deep Blue. With the increase in processing power, powerful chess programs that are better than most human players are now available on personal computers.

The Bayesian network formalism was invented to allow for the rigorous application of uncertainty in reasoning problems. In the late 1990s, intelligent agents were introduced. Search engines, bots, and website aggregators are examples of intelligent agents used on the Internet.

The state of the art of AI includes autonomous cars, speech recognition, planning and scheduling, game playing, robotics, and machine translation. All of these are based on AI technology. They are in constant use today. You can take a PDF document and translate it into any language using Google translate. The translations are not perfect but are adequate for many uses. One certainly would not use them to translate literature!

Recent advances in AI include IBM's Watson. Watson is a question-answering computing system with advanced natural language processing and information retrieval from massive databases. It defeated champion Jeopardy players in 2011. It is currently being applied to medical problems.

2.3 Learning Control

Adaptive or intelligent control was motivated in the 1950s [1] by the problems of aircraft control. Control systems of that time worked very well for linear systems. Aircraft dynamics could be linearized about a particular speed. For example, a simple equation for total velocity in level flight is

$$m\frac{dv}{dt} = T - \frac{1}{2}\rho C_D S v^2 \qquad (2.1)$$

This says the mass m times the change in velocity $\frac{dv}{dt}$ equals the thrust T minus the drag. C_D is the drag coefficient and S is the wetted area (i.e., the area that causes drag). The thrust is used for control. This is a nonlinear equation. We can linearize it around a velocity v_s so that $v = v_\delta + v_s$ and get

$$m\frac{dv_\delta}{dt} = T - \rho C_D S v_s v_\delta \tag{2.2}$$

This equation is linear. We can control velocity with a simple thrust control law

$$T = T_s - c v_\delta \tag{2.3}$$

where $T_s = \frac{1}{2}\rho C_D S v_s^2$. c is the damping coefficient. ρ is the atmospheric density and is a nonlinear function of altitude. For the linear control to work, the control must be adaptive. If we want to guarantee a certain damping value, which is the quantity in parentheses,

$$m\frac{dv_\delta}{dt} = -(c + \rho C_D S v_s) v_\delta \tag{2.4}$$

we need to know ρ, C_D, S, and v_s. This approach leads to a gain-scheduling control system where we measure the flight condition and schedule the linear gains based on where the aircraft is in the gain schedule.

In the 1960s, progress was made on adaptive control. State-space theory was developed, which made it easier to design multiloop control systems, that is, control systems that controlled more than one state at a time with different control loops. The general space-space controller is

$$\dot{x} = Ax + Bu \tag{2.5}$$

$$y = Cx + Du \tag{2.6}$$

$$u = -Ky \tag{2.7}$$

where A, B, C, and D are matrices. If A completely models the system and y contains all of the information about the state vector x, then this system is stable. Full state feedback would be $x = -Kx$, where K can be computed to have guaranteed phase and gain margins (that is, tolerance to delays and tolerance to amplification errors). This was a major advance in control theory. Before this, multiloop systems had to be designed separately and combined very carefully.

Learning control and adaptive control were found to be realizable from a common framework. The Kalman filter, also known as linear quadratic estimation, was introduced.

Spacecraft required autonomous control since they were often out of contact with the ground or the time delays were too long for effective ground supervision. The first digital autopilots were on the Apollo spacecraft. Geosynchronous communications satellites were automated to the point where one operator could fly a dozen satellites.

Advances in system identification, the process of just determining parameters of a system (such as the drag coefficient above), were made. Adaptive control was applied to real problems. The F-111 aircraft had an adaptive control system. Autopilots have progressed from fairly simple mechanical pilot augmentation systems to sophisticated control systems that can take off, cruise, and land under computer control.

In the 1970s, proofs about adaptive control stability were made. Stability of linear control systems was well established, but adaptive systems are inherently nonlinear. Universally stabilizing controllers were studied. Progress was made in the robustness of adaptive control. Robustness is the ability of a system to deal with changes in parameters that were assumed to be known, sometimes because of failures in the systems. It was in the 1970s that digital control became widespread, replacing traditional analog circuits composed of transistors and operational amplifiers.

Adaptive controllers started to appear commercially in the 1980s. Most modern single-loop controllers have some form of adaptation. Adaptive techniques were also found to be useful for tuning controllers.

More recently there has been a melding of AI and control. Expert systems have been proposed that determine what algorithms (not just parameters) to use depending on the environment. For example, during a winged reentry of a glider the control system would use one system in orbit, a second at high altitudes, a third during high Mach (Mach is the ratio of the velocity to the speed of sound) flight, and a fourth at low Mach numbers and during landing.

2.4   Machine Learning

Machine learning started as a branch of AI. However, many techniques are much older. Thomas Bayes created what's known as Bayes' theorem in 1763. Bayes' theorem says

$$P(A_i|B) = \frac{P(B|A_i)P(A_i)}{\sum P(B|A_i)}$$

$$P(A_i|B) = \frac{P(B|A_i)P(A_i)}{P(B)} \tag{2.8}$$

which is just the probability of A_i given B. This assumes that $P(B) \neq 0$. In the Bayesian interpretation, the theorem introduces the effect of evidence on belief. One technique, regression, was discovered by Legendre in 1805 and Gauss in 1809.

As noted in the section on AI, modern machine learning began with data mining, which is the process of getting new insights from data. In the early days of AI, there was considerable work on machine learning from data. However, this lost favor and in the 1990s was reinvented as the field of machine learning. The goal was to solve practical problems of pattern recognition using statistics. This was greatly aided by the massive amounts of data available online along with the tremendous increase in processing power available to developers. Machine learning is closely related to statistics.

In the early 1990s, Vapnik and coworkers invented a computationally powerful class of supervised learning networks known as support vector machines (SVMs). These networks could solve problems of pattern recognition, regression, and other machine learning problems.

A growing application of machine learning is autonomous driving. Autonomous driving makes use of all aspects of autonomous learning including controls, AI, and machine learning. Machine vision is used in most systems as cameras are inexpensive and provide more information than radar or sonar (which are also useful). It isn't possible to build really safe autonomous driving systems without learning through experience. Thus, designers of such systems put their cars on the roads and collect experiences which are used to fine-tune the system.

Other applications include high-speed stock trading and algorithms to guide investments. These are under rapid development and are now available to the consumer. Data mining and machine learning are used to predict events, both human and natural. Searches on the Internet have been used to track disease outbreaks. If there are a lot of data—and the Internet makes gathering massive data easy—then you can be sure that machine learning techniques are being applied to mine the data.

2.5   The Future

Autonomous learning in all its branches is undergoing rapid development today. Many of the technologies are used operationally even in low-cost consumer technology. Virtually every automobile company in the world and many nonautomotive companies are working to perfect autonomous driving. Military organizations are extremely interested in AI and machine learning. Combat aircraft today have systems to take over from the pilot, for example, to prevent planes from crashing into the ground.

While completely autonomous systems are the goal in many areas, the meshing of human and machine intelligence is also an area of active research. Much AI research has been to study how the human mind works. This work will allow machine learning systems to mesh more seamlessly with human beings. This is critical for autonomous control involving people, but may also allow people to augment their own abilities.

This is an exciting time for machine learning! We hope that this book helps you bring your own advances to machine learning!

References

[1] K. J. Åström and B. Wittenmark. *Adaptive Control, Second Edition*. Addison-Wesley, 1995.

[2] S. Haykin. *Neural Networks*. Prentice-Hall, 1999.

[3] P. Jackson. *Introduction to Expert Systems, Third Edition*. Addison-Wesley, 1999.

[4] S. Russell and P. Norvig. *Artificial Intelligence: A Modern Approach, Third Edition*. Prentice-Hall, 2010.

CHAPTER 3

■ ■ ■

Software for Machine Learning

3.1 Autonomous Learning Software

There are many sources for machine learning software. Machine learning encompasses machine learning software to help the user learn from data and software that helps machines learn and adapt to their environment. This book gives you a sampling of software that you can use immediately. However, the software is not designed for industrial applications. This chapter describes software that is available for the MATLAB environment. Both professional and open-source MATLAB software is discussed. The book may not cover every available package, as new packages are continually becoming available while older packages may become obsolete.

This chapter includes software for what is conventionally called "machine learning." These are the statistics functions that help give us insight into data. These are often used in the context of "big data." It also includes descriptions of packages for other branches of autonomous learning systems such as system identification. System identification is a branch of automatic control that learns about the systems under control, allowing for better and more precise control.

The chapter, for completeness, also covers popular software that is MATLAB compatible but requires extra steps to use it from within MATLAB. Examples include R, Python, and SNOPT. In all cases it is straightforward to write MATLAB interfaces to these packages. Using MATLAB as a front end can be very helpful and allow you to create integrated packages that include MATLAB, Simulink, and the machine learning package of your choice.

You will note that we include optimization software. Optimization is a tool used as part of machine learning to find the best or "optimal" parameters. We use it in this book in our decision tree chapter.

Don't be upset if we didn't include your favorite package, or your package! We apologize in advance!

3.2 Commercial MATLAB Software

3.2.1 MathWorks Products

The MathWorks sells several packages for machine learning. These are in the Machine Learning branch of our taxonomy Figure 1.3. The MathWorks products provide high-quality algorithms for data analysis along with graphics tools to visualize the data. Visualization tools are a critical part of any machine learning system. They can be used for data acquisition, for example, for image recognition or as part of systems for autonomous control of vehicles, or for diagnosis and debugging during development. All of these packages can be integrated with each other and with other MATLAB functions to produce powerful systems for machine learning. The most applicable toolboxes that we will discuss are

© Michael Paluszek, Stephanie Thomas 2017
M. Paluszek and S. Thomas, *MATLAB Machine Learning*, DOI 10.1007/978-1-4842-2250-8_3

- Statistics and Machine Learning Toolbox

- Neural Network Toolbox

- Computer Vision System Toolbox

- System Identification Toolbox

3.2.1.1 Statistics and Machine Learning Toolbox

The Statistics and Machine Learning Toolbox provides data analytics methods for gathering trends and patterns from massive amounts of data. These methods do not require a model for analyzing the data. The toolbox functions can be broadly divided into classification tools, regression tools, and clustering tools.

Classification methods are used to place data into different categories. For example, data, in the form of an image, might be used to classify an image of an organ as having a tumor. Classification is used for handwriting recognition, credit scoring, and face identification. Classification methods include support vector machines (SVMs), decision trees, and neural networks.

Regression methods let you build models from current data to predict future data. The models can then be updated as new data become available. If the data are only used once to create the model, then it is a batch method. A regression method that incorporates data as they become available is a recursive method.

Clustering finds natural groupings in data. Object recognition is an application of clustering methods. For example, if you want to find a car in an image, you look for data that are associated with the part of an image that is a car. While cars are of different shapes and sizes, they have many features in common.

The toolbox has many functions to support these areas and many that do not fit neatly into these categories. The Statistics and Machine Learning Toolbox is an excellent place to start for professional tools that are seamlessly integrated into the MATLAB environment.

3.2.1.2 Neural Network Toolbox

The MATLAB Neural Network Toolbox is a comprehensive neural net toolbox that seamlessly integrates with MATLAB. The toolbox provides functions to create, train, and simulate neural networks. The toolbox includes convolutional neural networks and deep learning networks. Neural networks can be computationally intensive because of the large numbers of nodes and associated weights, especially during training. The Neural Network Toolbox allows you to distribute computation across multicore processors and graphical processing units (GPUs) if you have the Parallel Computing Toolbox, another MATLAB add-on. You can extend this even further to a network cluster of computers using MATLAB Distributed Computing Server™. As with all MATLAB products, the Neural Network Toolbox provides extensive graphics and visualization capabilities that make it easier to understand your results.

The Neural Network Toolbox is capable of handling large data sets. This could be gigabytes or terabytes of data. This makes it suitable for industrial-strength problems and complex research. MATLAB also provides videos, webinars, and tutorials, including a full suite of resources for applying deep learning.

3.2.1.3 Computer Vision System Toolbox

The MATLAB Computer Vision System Toolbox provides functions for developing computer vision systems. The toolbox provides extensive support for video processing but also includes functions for feature detection and extraction. It also supports three-dimensional (3D) vision and can process information from stereo cameras. 3D motion detection is supported.

3.2.1.4   System Identification Toolbox

The System Identification Toolbox provides MATLAB functions and Simulink blocks for constructing mathematical models of systems. You can identify transfer functions from input/output data and perform parameter identification for models. Both linear and nonlinear system identification is supported.

3.2.2   Princeton Satellite Systems Products

Several of our own commercial packages provide tools within the purview of autonomous learning.

3.2.2.1   Core Control Toolbox

The Core Control Toolbox provides the control and estimation functions of our Spacecraft Control Toolbox with general industrial dynamics examples including robotics and chemical processing. The suite of Kalman filter routines includes conventional filters, extended Kalman filters, and unscented Kalman filters (UKFs). The unscented filters have a fast sigma-point calculation algorithm. All of the filters can now handle multiple measurement sources that can be changed dynamically. Add-ons for the Core Control Toolbox include imaging and target tracking modules. Imaging includes lens models, image processing, ray tracing, and image analysis tools.

3.2.2.2   Target Tracking

The target tracking module employs track-oriented multiple-hypothesis testing (MHT). Track-oriented MHT is a powerful technique for assigning measurements to tracks of objects when the number of objects is unknown or changing. It is absolutely essential for accurate tracking of multiple objects.

In many situations a sensor system must track multiple targets, like in rush-hour traffic. This leads to the problem of associating measurements with objects, or tracks. This is a crucial element of any practical tracking system.

The track-oriented approach recomputes the hypotheses using the newly updated tracks after each scan of data is received. Rather than maintaining, and expanding, hypotheses from scan to scan, the track-oriented approach discards the hypotheses formed on scan $k - 1$. The tracks that survive pruning are propagated to the next scan k, where new tracks are formed, using the new observations, and reformed into hypotheses. The hypothesis formation step is formulated as a mixed-integer linear program and solved using GNU Linear Programming Kit (GLPK). Except for the necessity to delete some tracks based upon low probability, no information is lost because the track scores, which are maintained, contain all the relevant statistical data.

The MHT module uses a powerful track-pruning algorithm that does the pruning in one step. Because of its speed, ad hoc pruning methods are not required, leading to more robust and reliable results. The track management software is, as a consequence, quite simple.

The toolbox includes Kalman filters, extended Kalman filters, and UKFs. All of the Kalman filters use a common code format with separate prediction and update functions. This allows the two steps to be used independently. Each Kalman filter can handle multiple measurement sources and measurements arriving at different times. All three Kalman filters can be used independently or as part of the MHT system. The UKF automatically uses sigma points and does not require derivatives to be taken of the measurement functions or linearized versions of the measurement models.

Interactive multiple-model (IMM) systems can also be used as part of the MHT system. IMM employs multiple dynamic models to facilitate tracking maneuvering objects. One model might involve maneuvering while another models constant motion. Measurements are assigned to all of the models. The IMM systems are based on jump Markovian systems.

3.3 MATLAB Open-Source Resources

MATLAB open-source tools are a great resource for implementing state-of-the-art machine learning. Machine learning and convex optimization packages are available.

3.3.1 Deep Learn Toolbox

The Deep Learn Toolbox by Rasmus Berg Palm is a MATLAB toolbox for deep learning. It includes deep belief nets, stacked autoencoders, convolutional neural nets, and other neural net functions. It is available through the MathWorks File Exchange.

3.3.2 Deep Neural Network

The Deep Neural Network by Masayuki Tanaka provides deep learning tools of deep belief networks of stacked restricted Boltzmann machines. It has functionality for both unsupervised and supervised learning. It is available through the MathWorks File Exchange.

3.3.3 MatConvNet

MatConvNet implements convolutional neural networks for image processing. It includes a range of pretrained networks for image processing functions.

3.4 Products for Machine Learning

There are many products, both open-source and commercial, for machine learning. We cover some of the more popular open-source products. Both machine learning and convex optimization packages are discussed.

3.4.1 R

R is open-source software for statistical computing. It compiles on MacOS, UNIX, and Windows. It is similar to the Bell Labs S language developed by John Chambers and colleagues. It includes many statistical functions and graphics techniques.

You can use R in batch mode from MATLAB using the `system` command. Write

```
system('R_CMD_BATCH_inputfile_outputfile');
```

This runs the code in `inputfile` and puts it into `outputfile`. You can then read the `outputfile` into MATLAB.

3.4.2 scikit-learn

scikit-learn is a machine learning library for use in Python. It includes a wide variety of tools, including

1. Classification

2. Regression

3. Clustering

4. Dimensionality reduction

5. Model selection

6. Preprocessing

scikit-learn is well suited to a wide variety of data mining and data analysis.

MATLAB supports the reference implementation of Python, CPython. Mac and Linux users already have Python installed. Windows users need to install a distribution.

3.4.3 LIBSVM

LIBSVM [3] is a library for SVMs. It has an extensive collection of tools for SVMs including extensions by many users of LIBSVM. LIBSVM tools include distributed processing and multicore extensions.

3.5   Products for Optimization

Optimization tools often are used as part of machine learning systems. Optimizers minimize a cost given a set of constraints on the variables that are optimized. The maximum or minimum value for a variable is one type of constraint. Constraints and costs may be linear or nonlinear.

3.5.1 LOQO

LOQO [6] is a system for solving smooth constrained optimization problems available from Princeton University. The problems can be linear or nonlinear, convex or nonconvex, constrained or unconstrained. The only real restriction is that the functions defining the problem be smooth (at the points evaluated by the algorithm). If the problem is convex, LOQO finds a globally optimal solution. Otherwise, it finds a locally optimal solution near a given starting point.

Once you compile the mex-file interface to LOQO, you must pass it an initial guess and sparse matrices for the problem definition variables. You may also pass in a function handle to provide animation of the algorithm at each iteration of the solution.

3.5.2 SNOPT

SNOPT [4] is a software package for solving large-scale optimization problems (linear and nonlinear programs) hosted at the University of California, San Diego. It is especially effective for nonlinear problems whose functions and gradients are expensive to evaluate. The functions should be smooth but need not be convex. SNOPT is designed to take advantage of the sparsity of the Jacobian matrix, effectively reducing the size of the problem being solved. For optimal control problems, the Jacobian is very sparse because you have a matrix with rows and columns that span a large number of time points, but only adjacent time points can have nonzero entries.

SNOPT makes use of nonlinear function and gradient values. The solution obtained will be a local optimum (which may or may not be a global optimum). If some of the gradients are unknown, they will be estimated by finite differences. Infeasible problems are treated methodically via elastic bounds. SNOPT allows the nonlinear constraints to be violated and minimizes the sum of such violations. Efficiency is improved in large problems if only some of the variables are nonlinear, or if the number of active constraints is nearly equal to the number of variables.

3.5.3 GLPK

GLPK solves a variety of linear programming problems. It is part of the GNU project (https://www.gnu.org/software/glpk/). The most well-known one solves the linear program

$$Ax = b \qquad\qquad (3.1)$$

$$y = cx \qquad\qquad (3.2)$$

where it is desired to find x that when multiplied by A equals b. c is the cost vector that when multiplied by x gives the scalar cost of applying x. If x is the same length as b, the solution is

$$x = A^{-1}b \qquad\qquad (3.3)$$

Otherwise, we can use GLPK to solve for x that minimizes y. GLPK can solve this problem and others where x has to be an integer or even just 0 or 1.

3.5.4 CVX

CVX [2] is a MATLAB-based modeling system for convex optimization. CVX turns MATLAB into a modeling language, allowing constraints and objectives to be specified using standard MATLAB expression syntax.

In its default mode, CVX supports a particular approach to convex optimization that we call disciplined convex programming. Under this approach, convex functions and sets are built up from a small set of rules from convex analysis, starting from a base library of convex functions and sets. Constraints and objectives that are expressed using these rules are automatically transformed to a canonical form and solved. CVX can be used for free with solvers like SeDuMi or with a license from CVX Research with commercial solvers.

3.5.5 SeDuMi

SeDuMi [5] is MATLAB software for optimization over second-order cones, currently hosted at Lehigh University. It can handle quadratic constraints. SeDuMi was used in Acikmese [1]. SeDuMi stands for Self-Dual Minimization. It implements the *self-dual* embedding technique over *self-dual* homogeneous cones. This makes it possible to solve certain optimization problems in one phase. SeDuMi is available as part of YALMIP and as a standalone package.

3.5.6 YALMIP

YALMIP is free MATLAB software by Johan Lofberg that provides an easy-to-use interface to other solvers. It interprets constraints and can select the solver based on the constraints. SeDuMi and MATLAB's *fmincon* from the Optimization Toolbox are available solvers.

References

[1] Behcet Acikmese and Scott R. Ploen. Convex programming approach to powered descent guidance for Mars landing. *Journal of Guidance, Control, and Dynamics*, 30(5):1353–1366, 2007.

[2] S. Boyd. CVX: MATLAB software for disciplined convex programming. `http://cvxr.com/cvx/`, 2015.

[3] Chih-Chung Chang and Chih-Jen Lin. LIBSVM – A library for support vector machines. `https://www.csie.ntu.edu.tw/~cjlin/libsvm/`, 2015.

[4] Philip Gill, Walter Murray, and Michael Saunders. SNOPT 6.0 description. `http://www.sbsi-sol-optimize.com/asp/sol_products_snopt_desc.htm`, 2013.

[5] Jos F. Sturm. Using SeDuMi 1.02, a MATLAB toolbox for optimization over symmetric cones. `http://sedumi.ie.lehigh.edu/wp-content/sedumi-downloads/usrguide.ps`, 1998.

[6] R. J. Vanderbvei. LOQO user's manual version 4.05. `http://www.princeton.edu/~rvdb/tex/loqo/loqo405.pdf`, September 2013.

PART II

■ ■ ■

MATLAB Recipes for Machine Learning

CHAPTER 4

■ ■ ■

Representation of Data for Machine Learning in MATLAB

4.1 Introduction to MATLAB Data Types

4.1.1 Matrices

By default, all variables in MATLAB are double-precision matrices. You do not need to declare a type for these variables. Matrices can be multidimensional and are accessed using 1-based indices via parentheses. You can address elements of a matrix using a single index, taken column-wise, or one index per dimension. To create a matrix variable, simply assign a value to it, like this 2×2 matrix a:

```
>> a = [1 2; 3 4];
>> a(1,1)
    1

>> a(3)
    2
```

You can simply add, subtract, multiply, and divide matrices with no special syntax. The matrices must be the correct size for the linear algebra operation requested. A transpose is indicated using a single quote suffix, A', and the matrix power uses the operator ^.

```
>> b = a'*a;
>> c = a^2;
>> d = b + c;
```

By default, every variable is a numerical variable. You can initialize matrices to a given size using the zeros, ones, eye, or rand functions, which produce zeros, ones, identity matrices (ones on the diagonal), and random numbers, respectively. Use isnumeric to identify numeric variables.

Table 4.1 summarizes some key functions for interacting with matrices.

© Michael Paluszek, Stephanie Thomas 2017
M. Paluszek and S. Thomas, *MATLAB Machine Learning*, DOI 10.1007/978-1-4842-2250-8_4

Table 4.1: Key Functions for Matrices

Function	Purpose
zeros	Initialize a matrix to zeros
ones	Initialize a matrix to ones
eye	Initialize an identity matrix
rand, randn	Initialize a matrix of random numbers
isnumeric	Identify a matrix or scalar numeric value
isscalar	Identify a scalar value (a 1 × 1 matrix)
size	Return the size of the matrix

4.1.2 Cell Arrays

One variable type unique to MATLAB is cell arrays. This is really a list container, and you can store variables of any type in elements of a cell array. Cell arrays can be multidimensional, just like matrices, and are useful in many contexts.

Cell arrays are indicated by curly braces, {}. They can be of any dimension and contain any data, including string, structures, and objects. You can initialize them using the `cell` function, recursively display the contents using `celldisp`, and access subsets using parentheses just like for a matrix. A short example is below.

```
>> c = cell(3,1);
>> c{1} = 'string';
>> c{2} = false;
>> c{3} = [1 2; 3 4];
>> b = c(1:2);
>> celldisp(b)
b{1} =
string

b{2} =
    0
```

Using curly braces for access gives you the element data as the underlying type. When you access elements of a cell array using parentheses, the contents are returned as another cell array, rather than the cell contents. MATLAB help has a special section called *Comma-Separated Lists* that highlights the use of cell arrays as lists. The code analyzer will also suggest more efficient ways to use cell arrays. For instance,

Replace

```
a = {b{:} c};
```
with
```
a = [b {c}];
```

Cell arrays are especially useful for sets of strings, with many of MATLAB's string search functions optimized for cell arrays, such as `strcmp`.

Use `iscell` to identify cell array variables. Use `deal` to manipulate structure array and cell array contents.

Table 4.2 summarizes some key functions for interacting with cell arrays.

36

Table 4.2: Key Functions for Cell Arrays

Function	Purpose
cell	Initialize a cell array
cellstr	Create cell array from a character array
iscell	Identify a cell array
iscellstr	Identify a cell array containing only strings
celldisp	Recursively display the contents of a cell array

4.1.3 Data Structures

Data structures in MATLAB are highly flexible, leaving it up to the user to enforce consistency in fields and types. You are not required to initialize a data structure before assigning fields to it, but it is a good idea to do so, especially in scripts, to avoid variable conflicts.

Replace

```
d.fieldName = 0;
```

with

```
d = struct;
d.fieldName = 0;
```

In fact, we have found it generally a good idea to create a special function to initialize larger structures that are used throughout a set of functions. This is similar to creating a class definition. Generating your data structure from a function, instead of typing out the fields in a script, means you always start with the correct fields. Having an initialization function also allows you to specify the types of variables and provide sample or default data. Remember, since MATLAB does not require you to declare variable types, doing so yourself with default data makes your code that much clearer.

■ **TIP**   Create an initialization function for data structures.

You make a data structure into an array simply by assigning an additional copy. The fields must be in the same order, which is yet another reason to use a function to initialize your structure. You can nest data structures with no limit on depth.

```
d = MyStruct;
d(2) = MyStruct;

function d = MyStruct

d = struct;
d.a = 1.0;
d.b = 'string';
```

MATLAB now allows for *dynamic field names* using variables, that is, structName.(dynamic Expression). This provides improved performance over getfield, where the field name is passed as a string. This allows for all sorts of inventive structure programming. Take our data structure array in the previous code snippet, and let's get the values of field a using a dynamic field name; the values are returned in a cell array.

```
>> field = 'a';
>> values = {d.(field)}
```

```
values =

    [1]      [1]
```

Use `isstruct` to identify structure variables and `isfield` to check for the existence of fields. Note that `isempty` will return *false* for a struct initialized with `struct`, even if it has no fields.

Table 4.3 provides key functions for structs.

Table 4.3: Key Functions for Structs

Function	Purpose
struct	Initialize a structure with or without fields
isstruct	Identify a structure
isfield	Determine if a field exists in a structure
fieldnames	Get the fields of a structure in a cell array
rmfield	Remove a field from a structure
deal	Set fields in a structure to a value

4.1.4 Numerics

While MATLAB defaults to doubles for any data entered at the command line or in a script, you can specify a variety of other numeric types, including `single`, `uint8`, `uint16`, `uint32`, `uint64`, `logical` (i.e., an array of booleans). Use of the integer types is especially relevant to using large data sets such as images. Use the minimum data type you need, especially when your data sets are large.

4.1.5 Images

MATLAB supports a variety of formats, including GIF, JPG, TIFF, PNG, HDF, FITS, and BMP. You can read in an image directly using `imread`, which can determine the type automatically from the extension, or `fitsread`. (FITS stands for Flexible Image Transport System and the interface is provided by the CFITSIO library.) `imread` has special syntaxes for some image types, such as handling alpha channels for PNG, so you should review the options for your specific images. `imformats` manages the file format registry and allows you to specify handling of new user-defined types if you can provide read and write functions.

You can display an image using either `imshow`, `image`, or `imagesc`, which scales the colormap for the range of data in the image.

For example, we use a set of images of cats in Chapter 7, Face Recognition. If we look at the image info for one of these sample images using `imfinfo`,

```
>> imfinfo('IMG_4901.JPG')
ans =
              Filename: 'MATLAB/Cats/IMG_4901.JPG'
           FileModDate: '28-Sep-2016 12:48:15'
              FileSize: 1963302
                Format: 'jpg'
         FormatVersion: ''
                 Width: 3264
                Height: 2448
              BitDepth: 24
             ColorType: 'truecolor'
       FormatSignature: ''
```

```
     NumberOfSamples: 3
        CodingMethod: 'Huffman'
       CodingProcess: 'Sequential'
             Comment: {}
                Make: 'Apple'
               Model: 'iPhone_6'
         Orientation: 1
         XResolution: 72
         YResolution: 72
      ResolutionUnit: 'Inch'
            Software: '9.3.5'
            DateTime: '2016:09:17_22:05:08'
    YCbCrPositioning: 'Centered'
       DigitalCamera: [1x1 struct]
             GPSInfo: [1x1 struct]
        ExifThumbnail: [1x1 struct]
```

and we view this image using imshow, it will publish a warning that the image is too big to fit on the screen and that it is displayed at 33%. If we view it using image, there will be a visible set of axes. image is useful for displaying other two-dimensional matrix data as individual elements per pixel. Both functions return a handle to an image object; only the axes' properties are different. Figure 4.1 shows the resulting figures. Note the labeled axes on the right figure.

```
>> figure; hI = image(imread('IMG_2398_Zoom.png'))
hI =
  Image with properties:

           CData: [680x680x3 uint8]
     CDataMapping: 'direct'

  Show all properties
```

Figure 4.1: Image display options. A figure created using imshow is on the left and a figure using image is on the right.

Table 4.4 provides key images for interacting with images.

Table 4.4: Key Functions for Images

Function	Purpose
imread	Read an image in a variety of formats
imfinfo	Gather information about an image file
imformats	Determine if a field exists in a structure
imwrite	Write data to an image file
image	Display image from array
imagesc	Display image data scaled to the current colormap
imshow	Display an image, optimizing figure, axes, and image object properties, and taking an array or a filename as an input
rgb2gray	Write data to an image file
ind2rgb	Convert index data to RGB
rgb2ind	Convert RGB data to indexed image data
fitsread	Read a FITS file
fitswrite	Write data to a FITS file
fitsinfo	Information about a FITS file returned in a data structure
fitsdisp	Display FITS file metadata for all Header Data Units (HDUs) in the file

4.1.6 Datastore

Datastores allow you to interact with files containing data that are too large to fit in memory. There are different types of datastores for tabular data, images, spreadsheets, databases, and custom files. Each datastore provides functions to extract smaller amounts of data that do fit in memory for analysis. For example, you can search a collection of images for those with the brightest pixels or maximum saturation values. We will use our directory of cat images as an example.

```
>> location = pwd
location =
/Users/Shared/svn/Manuals/MATLABMachineLearning/MATLAB/Cats
>> ds = datastore(location)
ds =
  ImageDatastore with properties:

      Files: {
              '.../Shared/svn/Manuals/MATLABMachineLearning/MATLAB/Cats/
                IMG_0191.png';
              '.../Shared/svn/Manuals/MATLABMachineLearning/MATLAB/Cats/
                IMG_1603.png';
              '.../Shared/svn/Manuals/MATLABMachineLearning/MATLAB/Cats/
                IMG_1625.png'
              ... and 19 more
             }
     Labels: {}
    ReadFcn: @readDatastoreImage
```

Once the datastore is created, you use the applicable class functions to interact with it. Datastores have standard container-style functions like `read`, `partition`, and `reset`. Each type of datastore has different properties. The `DatabaseDatastore` requires the Database Toolbox and allows you to use SQL queries.

MATLAB provides the MapReduce framework for working with out-of-memory data in datastores. The input data can be any of the datastore types, and the output is a key-value datastore. The map function processes the datastore input in chunks and the reduce function calculates the output values for each key. mapreduce can be sped up by using it with the MATLAB Parallel Computing Toolbox, Distributed Computer Server, or Compiler. Table 4.5 gives key functions for using datastores.

Table 4.5: Key Functions for Datastore

Function	Purpose
datastore	
read	Read a subset of data from the datastore
readall	Read all of the data in the datastore
hasdata	Check to see if there is more data in the datastore
reset	Check to see if there is more data in the datastore
partition	Excerpt a portion of the datastore
numpartitions	Estimate a reasonable number of partitions
ImageDatastore	Datastore of a list of image files
TabularTextDatastore	A collection of one or more tabular text files
SpreadsheetDatastore	Datastore of spreadsheets
FileDatastore	Datastore for files with a custom format, for which you provide a reader function
KeyValueDatastore	Datastore of key-value pairs
DatabaseDatastore	Database connection, provides Database Toolbox

4.1.7 Tall Arrays

Tall arrays are new to release R2016b of MATLAB. They are allowed to have more rows than will fit in memory. You can use them to work with datastores that might have millions of rows. Tall arrays can use almost any MATLAB type as a column variable, including numeric data, cell arrays, strings, datetimes, and categoricals. The MATLAB documentation provides a list of functions that support tall arrays. Results for operations on the array are only evaluated when they are explicitly requested using the gather function. The histogram function can be used with tall arrays and will execute immediately.

The MATLAB Statistic and Machine Learning Toolbox™, Database Toolbox, Parallel Computing Toolbox, Distributed Computing Server, and Compiler all provide additional extensions for working with tall arrays. For more information about this new feature, use the following topics in the documentation:

- Tall Arrays

- Analysis of Big Data with Tall Arrays

- Functions That Support Tall Arrays (AZ)

- Index and View Tall Array Elements

- Visualization of Tall Arrays

- Extend Tall Arrays with Other Products

- Tall Array Support, Usage Notes, and Limitations

Table 4.6 gives key functions for using Tall Arrays.

Table 4.6: Key Functions for Tall Arrays

Function	Purpose
tall	Initialize a tall array
gather	Execute the requested operations
summary	Display summary information to the command line
head	Access first rows of a tall array
tail	Access last rows of a tall array
istall	Check the type of the array to determine if it is tall
write	Write the tall array to disk

4.1.8 Sparse Matrices

Sparse matrices are a special category of matrix in which most of the elements are zero. They appear commonly in large optimization problems and are used by many such packages. The zeros are "squeezed" out and MATLAB stores only the nonzero elements along with index data such that the full matrix can be recreated. Many regular MATLAB functions, such as `chol` or `diag`, preserve the sparseness of an input matrix. Table 4.7 gives key functions for sparse matrices.

Table 4.7: Key Functions for Sparse Matrices

Function	Purpose
sparse	Create a sparse matrix from a full matrix or from a list of indices and values
issparse	Determine if a matrix is sparse
nnz	Number of nonzero elements in a sparse matrix
spalloc	Allocate nonzero space for a sparse matrix
spy	Visualize a sparsity pattern
spfun	Selectively apply a function to the nonzero elements of a sparse matrix
full	Convert a sparse matrix to full form

4.1.9 Tables and Categoricals

Tables were introduced in release R2013 of MATLAB and allow tabular data to be stored with metadata in one workspace variable. It is an effective way to store and interact with data that one might put in, or import from, a spreadsheet. The table columns can be named, assigned units and descriptions, and accessed as one would fields in a data structure, that is, `T.DataName`. See `readtable` on creating a table from a file, or try out the Import Data button from the command window.

Categorical arrays allow for storage of discrete nonnumeric data, and they are often used within a table to define groups of rows. For example, time data may have the day of the week, or geographic data may be organized by state or county. They can be leveraged to rearrange data in a table using `unstack`.

You can also combine multiple data sets into single tables using `join`, `innerjoin`, and `outerjoin`, which will be familiar to you if you have worked with databases.

Table 4.8 lists key functions for using tables.

Table 4.8: Key Functions for Tables

Function	Purpose
table	Create a table with data in the workspace
readtable	Create a table from a file
join	Merge tables by matching up variables
innerjoin	Join tables A and B retaining only the rows that match
outerjoin	Join tables including all rows
stack	Stack data from multiple table variables into one variable
unstack	Unstack data from a single variable into multiple variables
summary	Calculate and display summary data for the table
categorical	Arrays of discrete categorical data
iscategorical	Create a categorical array
categories	List of categories in the array
iscategory	Test for a particular category
addcats	Add categories to an array
removecats	Remove categories from an array
mergecats	Merge categories

4.1.10 Large MAT-Files

You can access parts of a large MAT-file without loading the entire file into memory by using the `matfile` function. This creates an object that is connected to the requested MAT-file without loading it. Data are only loaded when you request a particular variable, or part of a variable. You can also dynamically add new data to the MAT-file.

For example, we can load a MAT-file of neural net weights generated in a later chapter.

```
>> m = matfile('PitchNNWeights','Writable',true)
m =
  matlab.io.MatFile

  Properties:
      Properties.Source: '/Users/Shared/svn/Manuals/MATLABMachineLearning/
         MATLAB/PitchNNWeights.mat'
    Properties.Writable: true
                      w: [1x8 double]
```

We can access a portion of the previously unloaded w variable, or add a new variable name, all using this object m.

```
>> y = m.w(1:4)
y =
     1     1     1     1
>> m.name = 'Pitch_Weights'
m =
  matlab.io.MatFile

  Properties:
      Properties.Source: '/Users/Shared/svn/Manuals/MATLABMachineLearning/
         MATLAB/PitchNNWeights.mat'
    Properties.Writable: true
```

```
                 name:  [1x13 char]
                    w:  [1x8  double]
>> d = load('PitchNNWeights')
d =
        w:  [1 1 1 1 1 1 1 1]
     name:  'Pitch_Weights'
```

There are some limits to the indexing into unloaded data, such as struct arrays and sparse arrays. Also, `matfile` requires MAT-files using version 7.3, which is not the default for a generic `save` operation as of R2016b. You must either create the MAT-file using `matfile` to take advantage of these features or use the `-v7.3'` flag when saving the file.

4.2 Initializing a Data Structure Using Parameters

4.2.1 Problem

It's always a good idea to use a special function to define a data structure you are using as a type in your codebase, similar to writing a class but with less overhead. Users can then overload individual fields in their code, but there is an alternative way to set many fields at once: an initialization function, which can handle a parameter-pair input list. This allows you to do additional processing in your initialization function. Also, your parameter string names can be more descriptive than you would choose to make your field names.

4.2.2 Solution

The simplest way to implement the parameter pairs is using `varargin` and a switch statement. Alternatively, you could write an `inputParser`, which allows you to specify required and optional inputs as well as named parameters. In that case, you have to write separate or anonymous functions for validation that can be passed to the `inputParser`, rather than just write out the validation in your code.

4.2.3 How It Works

We will use the data structure developed for the automobile simulation in Chapter 12 as an example. The header lists the input parameters along with the input dimensions and units, if applicable.

```
%% AUTOMOBILEINITIALIZE Initialize the automobile data structure.
%
%% Form:
%   d = AutomobileInitialize( varargin )
%
%% Description
% Initializes the data structure using parameter pairs.
%
%% Inputs
% varargin:   ('parameter',value,...)
%
% 'mass'                             (1,1)  (kg)
% 'steering angle'                   (1,1)  (rad)
% 'position tires'                   (2,4)  (m)
% 'frontal drag coefficient'         (1,1)
% 'side drag coefficient'            (1,1)
% 'tire friction coefficient'        (1,1)
% 'tire radius'                      (1,1)  (m)
% 'engine torque'                    (1,1)  (Nm)
```

```
% 'rotational inertia'                    (1,1)  (kg-m^2)
% 'state'                                 (6,1)  [m;m;m/s;m/s;rad;rad/s]
```

The function first creates the data structure using a set of defaults and then handles the parameter pairs entered by a user. After the parameters have been processed, two areas are calculated using the dimensions and the height.

```
function d = AutomobileInitialize( varargin )

% Defaults
d.mass          = 1513;
d.delta         = 0;
d.r             = [  1.17 1.17 -1.68 -1.68;...
                    -0.77 0.77 -0.77  0.77];
d.cDF           = 0.25;
d.cDS           = 0.5;
d.cF            = 0.01; % Ordinary car tires on concrete
d.radiusTire    = 0.4572; % m
d.torque        = d.radiusTire*200.0; % N
d.inr           = 2443.26;
d.x             = [0;0;0;0;0;0];
d.fRR           = [0.013 6.5e-6];
d.dim           = [1.17+1.68 2*0.77];
d.h             = 2/0.77;
d.errOld        = 0;
d.passState     = 0;


n = length(varargin);


for k = 1:2:length(varargin)
  switch lower(varargin{k})
    case 'mass'
      d.mass        = varargin{k+1};
    case 'steering angle'
      d.delta       = varargin{k+1};
    case 'position tires'
      d.r           = varargin{k+1};
    case 'frontal drag coefficient'
      d.cDF         = varargin{k+1};
    case 'side drag coefficient'
      d.cDS         = varargin{k+1};
    case 'tire friction coefficient'
      d.cF          = varargin{k+1};
    case 'tire radius'
      d.radiusTire    = varargin{k+1};
    case 'engine torque'
      d.torque      = varargin{k+1};
    case 'rotational inertia'
      d.inertia     = varargin{k+1};
    case 'state'
      d.x           = varargin{k+1};
    case 'rolling resistance coefficients'
      d.fRR         = varargin{k+1};
```

```
  case 'height_automobile'
    d.h             = varargin{k+1};
  case 'side_and_frontal_automobile_dimensions'
    d.dim           = varargin{k+1};
  end
end

% Processing
d.areaF      = d.dim(2)*d.h;
d.areaS      = d.dim(1)*d.h;
```

To perform the same tasks with inputParser, you add a addRequired, addOptional, or addParameter call for every item in the switch statement. The named parameters require default values. You can optionally specify a validation function; in the example below we use isNumeric to limit the values to numeric data.

```
p = inputParser('FunctionName','AutomobileInitialize',... % throw errors as
    from AutomobileInitialize
               'PartialMatching',false);   % disallow partial matches
cDF_Default        = 0.25;
mass_Default       = 1513;
addParameter(p,'mass',mass_Default,@isnumeric);
addParameter(p,'cDF',cDF_Default,@isnumeric);
parse(p,varargin{:});
d = p.Results;
```

In this case, the results of the parsed parameters are stored in a Results substructure.

4.3   Performing mapreduce on an Image Datastore

4.3.1 Problem

We discussed the datastore class in the introduction to the chapter. Now let's use it to perform analysis on the full set of cat images using mapreduce, which is scalable to very large numbers of images.

4.3.2 Solution

We create the datastore by passing in the path to the folder of cat images. We also need to create a map function and a reduce function, to pass into mapreduce. If you are using additional toolboxes like the Parallel Computing Toolbox, you would specify the reduce environment using mapreducer.

4.3.3 How It Works

First, create the datastore using the path to the images.

```
>> imds = imageDatastore('MATLAB/Cats');
imds =
  ImageDatastore with properties:

      Files: {
              '_.../Shared/svn/Manuals/MATLABMachineLearning/MATLAB/Cats/
                IMG_0191.png';
```

```
'␣.../Shared/svn/Manuals/MATLABMachineLearning/MATLAB/Cats/
    IMG_1603.png';
'␣.../Shared/svn/Manuals/MATLABMachineLearning/MATLAB/Cats/
    IMG_1625.png'
... and 19 more
}
Labels: {}
ReadFcn: @readDatastoreImage
```

Second, we write the map function. This must generate and store the intermediate values that will be processed by the reduce function. Each intermediate value must be stored as a key in the intermediate key-value datastore using add. In this case, the map function will receive one image each time it is called.

```
function catColorMapper(data, info, intermediateStore)

add(intermediateStore, 'Avg_Red', struct('Filename', info.Filename, 'Val',
    mean(mean(data(:,:,1)))) );
add(intermediateStore, 'Avg_Blue', struct('Filename', info.Filename, 'Val',
    mean(mean(data(:,:,2)))) );
add(intermediateStore, 'Avg_Green', struct('Filename', info.Filename, 'Val',
    mean(mean(data(:,:,3)))) );
```

The reduce function will then receive the list of the image files from the datastore once for each key in the intermediate data. It receives an iterator to the intermediate datastore as well as an output datastore. Again, each output must be a key-value pair. The hasnext and getnext functions used are part of the mapreduce ValueIterator class.

```
function catColorReducer(key, intermediateIter, outputStore)

% Iterate over values for each key
minVal = 255;
minImageFilename = '';
while hasnext(intermediateIter)
  value = getnext(intermediateIter);

  % Compare values to find the minimum
  if value.Val < minVal
     minVal = value.Val;
     minImageFilename = value.Filename;
  end
end

% Add final key-value pair
add(outputStore, ['Maximum_' key], minImageFilename);
```

Finally, we call `mapreduce` using function handles to our two helper functions.

```
maxRGB = mapreduce(imds, @catColorMapper, @hueSaturationValueReducer);
```

```
* * * * * * * * * * * * * * * * * * * * * * * * * * * *
*       MAPREDUCE PROGRESS       *
* * * * * * * * * * * * * * * * * * * * * * * * * * * *
Map    0%  Reduce    0%
Map   13%  Reduce    0%
Map   27%  Reduce    0%
Map   40%  Reduce    0%
Map   50%  Reduce    0%
Map   63%  Reduce    0%
Map   77%  Reduce    0%
Map   90%  Reduce    0%
Map  100%  Reduce    0%
Map  100%  Reduce   33%
Map  100%  Reduce   67%
Map  100%  Reduce  100%
```

The results are stored in a MAT-file, for example, `results_1_28-Sep-2016_16-28-38_347`. The store returned is a key-value store to this MAT-file, which in turn contains the store with the final key-value results.

```
>> output = readall(maxRGB)
output =
            Key                          Value
    _____         _____

    'Maximum_Avg_Red'           '/MATLAB/Cats/IMG_1625.png'
    'Maximum_Avg_Blue'          '/MATLAB/Cats/IMG_4866.JPG'
    'Maximum_Avg_Green'         '/MATLAB/Cats/IMG_4866.JPG'
```

4.4   Creating a Table from a File

Summary

There are a variety of data containers in MATLAB to assist you in analyzing your data for machine learning. If you have access to a computer cluster of one of the specialized computing toolboxes, you have even more options. Table 4.9 gives a listing of the code presented in this chapter.

Table 4.9: Chapter Code Listing

File	Description
AutomobileInitialize	Data structure initialization example from Chapter 12
catReducer	Image datastore used with `mapreduce`

CHAPTER 5

MATLAB Graphics

Plotting is used extensively in machine learning problems. MATLAB plots can be two or three dimensional. The same data can be represented using many different types of plots.

5.1 Two-Dimensional Line Plots

5.1.1 Problem

You want a single function to generate two-dimensional (2D) line graphs, avoiding a long list of code for the generation of each graphic.

5.1.2 Solution

Write a single function to take the data and *parameter pairs* to encapsulate the functionality of MATLAB's 2D line-plotting functions. An example of a plot created with a single line of code is shown in Figure 5.1.

© Michael Paluszek, Stephanie Thomas 2017
M. Paluszek and S. Thomas, *MATLAB Machine Learning*, DOI 10.1007/978-1-4842-2250-8_5

Figure 5.1: PlotSet's built-in demo.

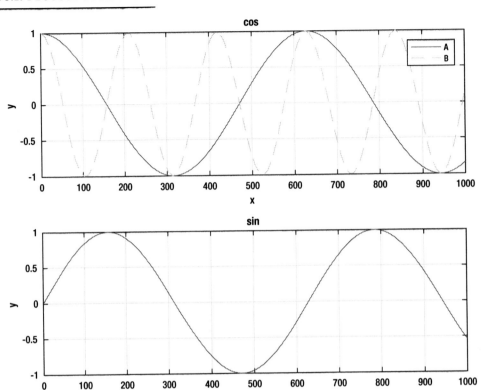

5.1.3 How It Works

PlotSet generates 2D plots, including multiple plots on a page. This code processes varargin as parameter pairs to set options. This makes it easy to expand the options.

```
%% PLOTSET Create two-dimensional plots from a data set.
%% Form
%   h = PlotSet( x, y, varargin )
%
%% Decription
% Plot y vs x in one figure.
% If x has the same number of rows as y then each row of y is plotted
% against the corresponding row of x. If x has one row then all of the
% y vectors are plotted against those x variables.
%
% Accepts optional arguments that modify the plot parameters.
%
% Type PlotSet for a demo.
%
%% Inputs
%   x           (:,:)   Independent variables
%   y           (:,:)   Dependent variables
%   varargin    {}      Optional arguments with values
```

```
%                    'x label', 'y label', 'plot title', 'plot type'
%                    'figure title', 'plot set', 'legend'
%
%% Outputs
%   h           (1,1)   Figure handle
```

The function code is shown below. We supply default values for the *x*- and *y*-axis labels and the figure name. The parameter pairs are handled in a switch statement. We are careful to use `lower` to compare the parameter name in lowercase. The plotting is done in a subfunction called `plotXY`.

```matlab
function h = PlotSet( x, y, varargin )

% Demo
if( nargin < 1 )
  Demo;
  return;
end

% Defaults
nCol       = 1;
n          = size(x,1);
m          = size(y,1);

yLabel     = cell(1,m);
xLabel     = cell(1,n);
plotTitle  = cell(1,n);
for k = 1:m
  yLabel{k} = 'y';
end
for k = 1:n
  xLabel{k}      = 'x';
  plotTitle{k}   = '';
end
figTitle = 'PlotSet';
plotType = 'plot';

plotSet = cell(1,m);
leg     = cell(1,m);
for k = 1:m
  plotSet{k} = k;
  leg{k} = {};
end

% Handle input parameters
for k = 1:2:length(varargin)
  switch lower(varargin{k} )
    case 'x_label'
      for j = 1:n
        xLabel{j} = varargin{k+1};
      end
    case 'y_label'
      temp = varargin{k+1};
      if( ischar(temp) )
```

```matlab
        yLabel{1} = temp;
      else
        yLabel      = temp;
      end
    case 'plot_title'
      if( iscell(varargin{k+1}) )
        plotTitle     = varargin{k+1};
      else
        plotTitle{1} = varargin{k+1};
      end
    case 'figure_title'
      figTitle      = varargin{k+1};
    case 'plot_type'
      plotType      = varargin{k+1};
    case 'plot_set'
      plotSet       = varargin{k+1};
      m             = length(plotSet);
    case 'legend'
      leg           = varargin{k+1};
    otherwise
      fprintf(1,'%s_is_not_an_allowable_parameter\n',varargin{k});
  end
end

h = figure('name',figTitle);
% First path is for just one row in x
if( n == 1 )
  for k = 1:m
    subplot(m,nCol,k);
    j = plotSet{k};
    plotXY(x,y(j,:),plotType);
    xlabel(xLabel{1});
    ylabel(yLabel{k});
    if( length(plotTitle) == 1 )
      title(plotTitle{1})
    else
      title(plotTitle{k})
    end
    if( ~isempty(leg{k}) )
      legend(leg{k});
    end
    grid on
  end
else
  for k = 1:n
    subplot(n,nCol,k);
    j = plotSet{k};
    plotXY(x(j,:),y(j,:),plotType);
    xlabel(xLabel{k});
    ylabel(yLabel{k});
    if( length(plotTitle) == 1 )
      title(plotTitle{1})
    else
```

```matlab
      title(plotTitle{k})
    end
    if( ~isempty(leg{k}) )
      legend(leg{k},'location','best');
    end
    grid on
  end
end


%%% PlotSet>plotXY Implement different plot types
% log and semilog types are supported.
%
%    plotXY(x,y,type)
function plotXY(x,y,type)

h = [];
switch type
  case 'plot'
    h = plot(x,y);
  case {'log' 'loglog' 'log_log'}
    h = loglog(x,y);
  case {'xlog' 'semilogx' 'x_log'}
    h = semilogx(x,y);
  case {'ylog' 'semilogy' 'y_log'}
    h = semilogy(x,y);
  otherwise
    error('%s_is_not_an_available_plot_type',type);
end

if( ~isempty(h) )
  color   = 'rgbc';
  lS      = {'-' '--' ':' '-.'};
  j       = 1;
  for k = 1:length(h)
    set(h(k),'col',color(j),'linestyle',lS{j});
    j = j + 1;
    if( j == 5 )
      j = 1;
    end
  end
end

%%% PlotSet>Demo
function Demo

x = linspace(1,1000);
y = [sin(0.01*x);cos(0.01*x);cos(0.03*x)];
disp('PlotSet:_One_x_and_two_y_rows')
PlotSet( x, y, 'figure_title', 'PlotSet_Demo',...
    'plot_set',{[2 3], 1},'legend',{{'A' 'B'},{}},'plot_title',{'cos','sin'
        });
```

The example in Figure 5.1 is generated by a dedicated demo function at the end of the `PlotSet` function. This demo shows several of the features of the function. These include

1. Multiple lines per graph

2. Legends

3. Plot titles

4. Default axis labels

Using a dedicated demo subfunction is a clean way to provide a built-in example of a function, and it is especially important in graphics functions to provide an example of what the plot should look like. The code is shown below.

```
j        = 1;
for k = 1:length(h)
  set(h(k),'col',color(j),'linestyle',lS{j});
  j = j + 1;
  if( j == 5 )
    j = 1;
  end
end
end
```

5.2 General 2D Graphics

5.2.1 Problem

You want to represent a 2D data set in different ways.

5.2.2 Solution

Write a script to show MATLAB's different 2D plot types. In our example we use subplots within one figure to help reduce figure proliferation.

5.2.3 How It Works

Use the `NewFigure` function to create a new figure window with a suitable name. Then run the following script.

```
NewFigure('Plot_Types')
x = linspace(0,10,10);
y = rand(1,10);

subplot(4,1,1);
plot(x,y);
subplot(4,1,2);
bar(x,y);
subplot(4,1,3);
barh(x,y);
subplot(4,1,4);
pie(y)
```

Four plot types are shown that are helpful in displaying 2D data. One is the 2D line plot, the same as is used in `PlotSet`. The middle two are bar charts. The final is a pie chart. Each gives you different insight into the data. Figure 5.2 shows the plot types.

Figure 5.2: Four different types of MATLAB 2D plots.

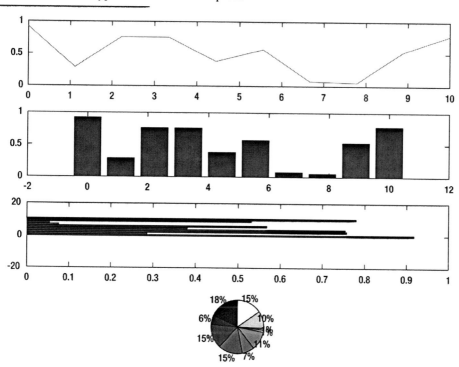

There are many MATLAB functions for making these plots more informative. You can

- Add labels.
- Add grids.
- Change font types and sizes.
- Change the thickness of lines.
- Add legends.
- Change axis limits.

The last item requires looking at the axis properties. Here are the properties for the last plot—the list is very long! gca is the handle to the current axis.

```
>> get(gca)
                        ALim: [0 1]
                    ALimMode: 'auto'
      ActivePositionProperty: 'position'
          AmbientLightColor: [1 1 1]
                BeingDeleted: 'off'
                         Box: 'off'
                    BoxStyle: 'back'
                  BusyAction: 'queue'
               ButtonDownFcn: ''
                        CLim: [1 10]
```

```
              CLimMode: 'auto'
        CameraPosition: [0 0 19.6977]
    CameraPositionMode: 'auto'
          CameraTarget: [0 0 0]
      CameraTargetMode: 'auto'
        CameraUpVector: [0 1 0]
    CameraUpVectorMode: 'auto'
        CameraViewAngle: 6.9724
    CameraViewAngleMode: 'auto'
              Children: [20x1 Graphics]
              Clipping: 'on'
          ClippingStyle: '3dbox'
                 Color: [1 1 1]
            ColorOrder: [7x3 double]
        ColorOrderIndex: 1
             CreateFcn: ''
          CurrentPoint: [2x3 double]
        DataAspectRatio: [1 1 1]
    DataAspectRatioMode: 'manual'
             DeleteFcn: ''
             FontAngle: 'normal'
              FontName: 'Helvetica'
              FontSize: 10
         FontSmoothing: 'on'
             FontUnits: 'points'
            FontWeight: 'normal'
             GridAlpha: 0.1500
         GridAlphaMode: 'auto'
             GridColor: [0.1500 0.1500 0.1500]
         GridColorMode: 'auto'
         GridLineStyle: '-'
      HandleVisibility: 'on'
               HitTest: 'on'
          Interruptible: 'on'
 LabelFontSizeMultiplier: 1.1000
                 Layer: 'bottom'
         LineStyleOrder: '-'
    LineStyleOrderIndex: 1
             LineWidth: 0.5000
         MinorGridAlpha: 0.2500
     MinorGridAlphaMode: 'auto'
         MinorGridColor: [0.1000 0.1000 0.1000]
     MinorGridColorMode: 'auto'
     MinorGridLineStyle: ':'
              NextPlot: 'replace'
          OuterPosition: [0 0.0706 1 0.2011]
                Parent: [1x1 Figure]
          PickableParts: 'visible'
      PlotBoxAspectRatio: [1.2000 1.2000 1]
  PlotBoxAspectRatioMode: 'manual'
              Position: [0.1300 0.1110 0.7750 0.1567]
            Projection: 'orthographic'
```

```
                 Selected: 'off'
        SelectionHighlight: 'on'
                SortMethod: 'childorder'
                       Tag: ''
                   TickDir: 'in'
               TickDirMode: 'auto'
     TickLabelInterpreter: 'tex'
                TickLength: [0.0100 0.0250]
                TightInset: [0 0.0405 0 0.0026]
                     Title: [1x1 Text]
   TitleFontSizeMultiplier: 1.1000
           TitleFontWeight: 'bold'
                      Type: 'axes'
            UIContextMenu: [0x0 GraphicsPlaceholder]
                     Units: 'normalized'
                  UserData: []
                      View: [0 90]
                   Visible: 'off'
                     XAxis: [1x1 NumericRuler]
             XAxisLocation: 'bottom'
                    XColor: [0.1500 0.1500 0.1500]
                XColorMode: 'auto'
                      XDir: 'normal'
                     XGrid: 'off'
                    XLabel: [1x1 Text]
                      XLim: [-1.2000 1.2000]
                  XLimMode: 'manual'
                XMinorGrid: 'off'
                XMinorTick: 'off'
                    XScale: 'linear'
                     XTick: [-1 0 1]
                XTickLabel: {3x1 cell}
            XTickLabelMode: 'auto'
        XTickLabelRotation: 0
                 XTickMode: 'auto'
                     YAxis: [1x1 NumericRuler]
             YAxisLocation: 'left'
                    YColor: [0.1500 0.1500 0.1500]
                YColorMode: 'auto'
                      YDir: 'normal'
                     YGrid: 'off'
                    YLabel: [1x1 Text]
                      YLim: [-1.2000 1.2000]
                  YLimMode: 'manual'
                YMinorGrid: 'off'
                YMinorTick: 'off'
                    YScale: 'linear'
                     YTick: [-1 0 1]
                YTickLabel: {3x1 cell}
            YTickLabelMode: 'auto'
        YTickLabelRotation: 0
                 YTickMode: 'auto'
```

```
            ZAxis: [1x1 NumericRuler]
           ZColor: [0.1500 0.1500 0.1500]
       ZColorMode: 'auto'
             ZDir: 'normal'
            ZGrid: 'off'
           ZLabel: [1x1 Text]
             ZLim: [-1 1]
         ZLimMode: 'auto'
       ZMinorGrid: 'off'
       ZMinorTick: 'off'
           ZScale: 'linear'
            ZTick: [-1 0 1]
       ZTickLabel: ''
   ZTickLabelMode: 'auto'
ZTickLabelRotation: 0
        ZTickMode: 'auto'
```

Every single one of these can be changed by using the set function:

```
set(gca,'YMinorGrid','on','YGrid','on')
```

This uses parameter pairs just like PlotSet. In this list children are pointers to the children of the axes. You can access those using get and change their properties using set.

5.3   Custom 2D Diagrams

5.3.1 Problem

Many machine learning algorithms benefit from 2D diagrams such as tree diagrams, to help the user understand the results and the operation of the software. Such diagrams, automatically generated by the software, are an essential part of learning systems. This section gives an example of how to write MATLAB code for a tree diagram.

5.3.2 Solution

Our solution is to use MATLAB patch function to automatically generate the blocks, and use line to generate connecting lines. Figure 5.3 shows the resulting hierarchical tree diagram. The circles are in rows and each row is labeled.

Figure 5.3: A custom tree diagram.

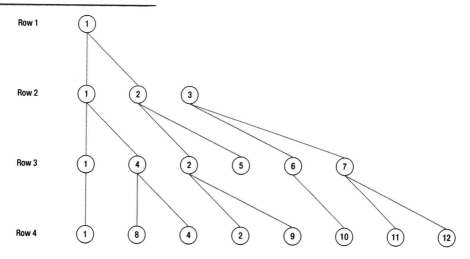

5.3.3 How It Works

Tree diagrams are very useful for machine learning. This function generates a hierarchical tree diagram with the nodes as circles with text within each node. The graphics functions used in this function are

1. `line`

2. `patch`

3. `text`

The data needed to draw the tree are contained in a data structure, which is documented in the header. Each node has a parent field. This information is sufficient to make the connections. The node data are entered as a cell array.

```
%% TreeDiagram Tree diagram plotting function.
%% Description
% Generates a tree diagram from hierarchical data.
%
% Type TreeDiagram for a demo.
%
% w is optional the defaults are:
%
%   .name      = 'Tree';
%   .width     = 400;
%   .fontName  = 'Times';
%   .fontSize  = 10;
%   .linewidth = 1;
%   .linecolor = 'r';
%
%-----------------------------------------------------------------
%% Form:
%   TreeDiagram( n, w, update )
%
%% Inputs
```

```
%    n          {:}      Nodes
%                        .parent       (1,1) Parent
%                        .name         (1,1) Number of observation
%                        .row          (1,1) Row number
%    w          (.)      Diagram data structure
%                        .name         (1,:) Tree name
%                        .width        (1,1) Circle width
%                        .fontName     (1,:) Font name
%                        .fontSize     (1,1) Font size
%    update     (1,1)    If entered and true update an existing plot
```

The code is shown below. The function stores a figure handle in a persistent variable so that the same figure can be updated with subsequent calls, if desired. The last input, a boolean, enables this behavior to be turned on and off.

```
function TreeDiagram( n, w, update )

persistent figHandle

% Demo
%-----
if( nargin < 1 )
  Demo
  return;
end

% Defaults
%---------
if( nargin < 2 )
  w = [];
end
if( nargin < 3 )
  update = false;
end

if( isempty(w) )
  w.name      = 'Tree';
  w.width     = 1200;
  w.fontName  = 'Times';
  w.fontSize  = 10;
  w.linewidth = 1;
  w.linecolor = 'r';
end

% Find row range
%---------------
m      = length(n);
rowMin = 1e9;
rowMax = 0;
```

```matlab
for k = 1:m
  rowMin = min([rowMin n{k}.row]);
  rowMax = max([rowMax n{k}.row]);
end

nRows = rowMax - rowMin + 1;
row   = rowMin:rowMax;
rowID = cell(nRows,1);

% Determine which nodes go with which rows
%-------------------------------------------
for k = 1:nRows
  for j = 1:m
    if( n{j}.row == row(k) )
      rowID{k} = [rowID{k} j];
    end
  end
end

% Determine the maximum number of circles at the last row
%---------------------------------------------------------
width = 3*length(rowID{nRows})*w.width;

% Draw the tree
%--------------
if( ~update )
  figHandle = NewFigure(w.name);
else
  clf(figHandle)
end

figure(figHandle);
set(figHandle,'color',[1 1 1]);
dY = width/(nRows+2);
y  = (nRows+2)*dY;
set(gca,'ylim',[0 (nRows+1)*dY]);
set(gca,'xlim',[0 width]);
for k = 1:nRows

        label = sprintf('Row_%d',k);

  text(0,y,label,'fontname',w.fontName,'fontsize',w.fontSize);
  x = 4*w.width;
  for j = 1:length(rowID{k})
    node            = rowID{k}(j);
    [xC,yCT,yCB]    = DrawNode( x, y, n{node}.name, w );
    n{node}.xC      = xC;
    n{node}.yCT     = yCT;
    n{node}.yCB     = yCB;
    x               = x + 3*w.width;
  end
```

```
  y = y - dY;
end
% Connect the nodes
%-----------------
for k = 1:m
  if( ~isempty(n{k}.parent) )
    ConnectNode( n{k}, n{n{k}.parent},w );
  end
end

axis off
axis image

%--------------------------------------------------------------------
%        Draw a node. This is a circle with a number in the middle.
%--------------------------------------------------------------------
function [xC,yCT,yCB] = DrawNode( x0, y0, k, w )

n = 20;
a = linspace(0,2*pi*(1-1/n),n);

x = w.width*cos(a)/2 + x0;
y = w.width*sin(a)/2 + y0;
patch(x,y,'w');
text(x0,y0,sprintf('%d',k),'fontname',w.fontName,'fontsize',w.fontSize,
    'horizontalalignment','center');

xC  = x0;
yCT = y0 + w.width/2;
yCB = y0 - w.width/2;

%-----------------------------------------------------------------------
%        Connect a node to its parent
%-----------------------------------------------------------------------
function ConnectNode( n, nP, w )

x = [n.xC nP.xC];
y = [n.yCT nP.yCB];

line(x,y,'linewidth',w.linewidth,'color',w.linecolor);
```

The demo shows how to use the function. In this case, it takes more lines of code to write out the hierarchical information than it does to plot the tree!

```
%-----------------------------------------------------------------------
%        Create the demo data structure
%-----------------------------------------------------------------------
function Demo

k = 1;
%--------------
row        = 1;
d.parent         = [];
```

```
d.name      = 1;
d.row       = row;
n{k}        = d; k = k + 1;

%---------------
row         = 2;

d.parent    = 1;
d.name      = 1;
d.row       = row;
n{k}        = d; k = k + 1;

d.parent    = 1;
d.name      = 2;
d.row       = row;
n{k}        = d; k = k + 1;

d.parent    = [];
d.name      = 3;
d.row       = row;
n{k}        = d; k = k + 1;

%---------------
row         = 3;

d.parent    = 2;
d.name      = 1;
d.row       = row;
n{k}        = d; k = k + 1;

d.parent    = 2;
d.name      = 4;
d.row       = row;
n{k}        = d; k = k + 1;

d.parent    = 3;
d.name      = 2;
d.row       = row;
n{k}        = d; k = k + 1;

d.parent    = 3;
d.name      = 5;
d.row       = row;
n{k}        = d; k = k + 1;

d.parent    = 4;
d.name      = 6;
d.row       = row;
n{k}        = d; k = k + 1;

d.parent    = 4;
d.name      = 7;
```

```
d.row        = row;
n{k}         = d; k = k + 1;
%---------------
row          = 4;

d.parent     = 5;
d.name       = 1;
d.row        = row;
n{k}         = d; k = k + 1;

d.parent     = 6;
d.name       = 8;
d.row        = row;
n{k}         = d; k = k + 1;

d.parent     = 6;
d.name       = 4;
d.row        = row;
n{k}         = d; k = k + 1;

d.parent     = 7;
d.name       = 2;
d.row        = row;
n{k}         = d; k = k + 1;

d.parent     = 7;
d.name       = 9;
d.row        = row;
n{k}         = d; k = k + 1;

d.parent     = 9;
d.name       = 10;
d.row        = row;
n{k}         = d; k = k + 1;

d.parent     = 10;
d.name       = 11;
d.row        = row;
n{k}         = d; k = k + 1;

d.parent     = 10;
d.name       = 12;
d.row        = row;
n{k}         = d;

%---------------
% Call the function with the demo data
TreeDiagram( n )
```

5.4 Three-Dimensional Box

There are two broad classes of three-dimensional (3D) graphics. One is to draw an object, like the earth. The other is to draw large data sets. This recipe plus the following one will show you how to do both.

5.4.1 Problem

We want to draw a 3D box.

5.4.2 Solution

Use the `patch` function to draw the object. An example is shown in Figure 5.4.

Figure 5.4: A box drawn with `patch`.

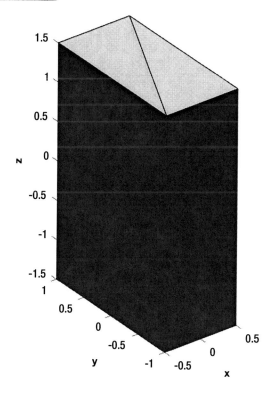

5.4.3 How It Works

Three-dimensional objects are created from vertices and faces. A vertex is a point in space. You create a list of vertices that are the corners of your 3D object. You then create faces that are lists of vertices. A face with two vertices is a line, while one with three vertices is a triangle. A polygon can have as many vertices as you would like. However, at the lowest level graphics processors deal with triangles, so you are best off making all patches triangles. Figure 5.5 shows a triangle and the outward normal. You will notice the normal vector. This is the outward vector. Your vertices in your patches should be ordered using the "right-hand rule"; that is, if the normal is in the direction of your thumb, then the faces are ordered in the direction of your fingers. In this figure the order for the two triangles would be

Figure 5.5: A patch. The normal is toward the camera or the "outside" of the object.

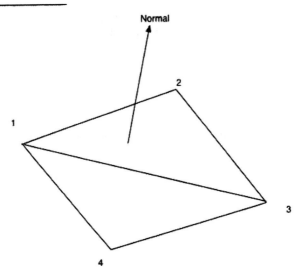

```
[3 2 1]
[1 4 3]
```

MATLAB lighting is not very picky about vertex ordering, but if you export a model then you will need to follow this convention. Otherwise, you can end up with inside-out objects!

The following code creates a box composed of triangle patches. The face and vertex arrays are created by hand.

```
function [v, f] = Box( x, y, z )

% Demo
if( nargin < 1 )
  Demo
  return
end

% Faces
f    = [2 3 6;3 7 6;3 4 8;3 8 7;4 5 8;4 1 5;2 6 5;2 5 1;1 3 2;1 4 3;5 6 7;5 7
     8];

% Vertices
v = [-x   x   x -x -x   x   x -x;...
     -y -y   y   y -y -y   y   y;...
     -z -z -z -z   z   z   z   z]'/2;

% Default outputs
if( nargout == 0 )
        DrawVertices( v, f, 'Box' );
  clear v
end
```

```
function Demo
x = 1;
y = 2;
z = 3;
Box( x, y, z );
```

The box is drawn using `path` in the function `DrawVertices`. There is just one call to `patch`. `patch` accepts parameter pairs to specify face and edge coloring and many other characteristics of the patch. Only one color can be specified for a patch. If you wanted a box with different colors on each side, you would need multiple patches.

```
function DrawVertices( v, f, name )

% Demo
if( nargin < 1 )
  Demo
  return
end

if( nargin < 3 )
  name = 'Vertices';
end

NewFigure(name)
patch('vertices',v,'faces',f,'facecolor',[0.8 0.1 0.2]);
axis image
xlabel('x')
ylabel('y')
zlabel('z')
view(3)
grid on
rotate3d on
s = 10*max(Mag(v'));
light('position',s*[1 1 1])

function Demo

[v,f] = Box(2,3,4);
DrawVertices( v, f, 'box' )
```

We use only the most basic lighting. You can add all sorts of lights in your drawing using `light`.

5.5   Draw a 3D Object with a Texture

5.5.1 Problem

We want to draw a planet.

5.5.2 Solution

Use a surface and overlay a texture onto the surface. Figure 5.6 shows an example with a recent image of Pluto.

Figure 5.6: A three-dimensional globe of Pluto.

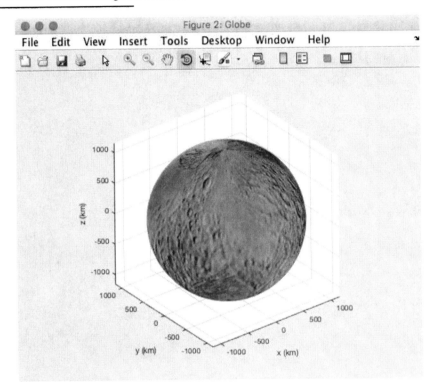

5.5.3 How It Works

We generate the picture by first creating x, y, z points on the sphere and then overlaying a texture that is read in from an image file. The texture map can be read from a file using `imread`. If this is color, it will be a 3D matrix. The third element will be an index to the color, red, blue, or green. However, if it is a grayscale image, you must create the 3D matrix by replicating the image.

```
p = imread('PlutoGray.png');
p3(:,:,1) = p;
p3(:,:,2) = p;
p3(:,:,3) = p;
```

The starting p is a 2D matrix.

You first generate the surface using the coordinates generated from the `sphere` function. This is done with `surface`. You then apply the texture

```
set(hSurf,'edgecolor', 'none',...
          'EdgeLighting', 'phong','FaceLighting', 'phong',...
          'specularStrength',0.1,'diffuseStrength',0.9,...
          'SpecularExponent',0.5,'ambientStrength',0.2,...
          'BackFaceLighting','unlit');
```

Phong is a type of shading. It takes the colors at the vertices and interpolates the colors at the pixels on the polygon based on the interpolated normals. The complete code is shown below. Diffuse and specular refer to different types of reflections of light. They aren't too important when you apply a texture to the surface.

```
% Defaults
if( nargin < 1 )
  planet = 'Pluto.png';
  radius = 1151;
end

if( ischar(planet) )
  planetMap = imread(planet);
else
  planetMap = planet;
end

NewFigure('Globe')

[x,y,z] = sphere(50);
x        = x*radius;
y        = y*radius;
z        = z*radius;
hSurf    = surface(x,y,z);
grid on;
for i= 1:3
  planetMap(:,:,i)=flipud(planetMap(:,:,i));
end
set(hSurf,'Cdata',planetMap,'Facecolor','texturemap');
set(hSurf,'edgecolor', 'none',...
          'EdgeLighting', 'phong','FaceLighting', 'phong',...
          'specularStrength',0.1,'diffuseStrength',0.9,...
          'SpecularExponent',0.5,'ambientStrength',0.2,...
          'BackFaceLighting','unlit');

view(3);
xlabel('x_(km)')
ylabel('y_(km)')
zlabel('z_(km)')
rotate3d on
axis image
```

5.6   General 3D Graphics

5.6.1 Problem

We want to use 3D graphics to study a 2D data set.

5.6.2 Solution

Use MATLAB surface, mesh, bar, and contour functions. An example of a random data set with different visualizations is shown in Figure 5.7.

Figure 5.7: Two-dimensional data shown with six different plot types.

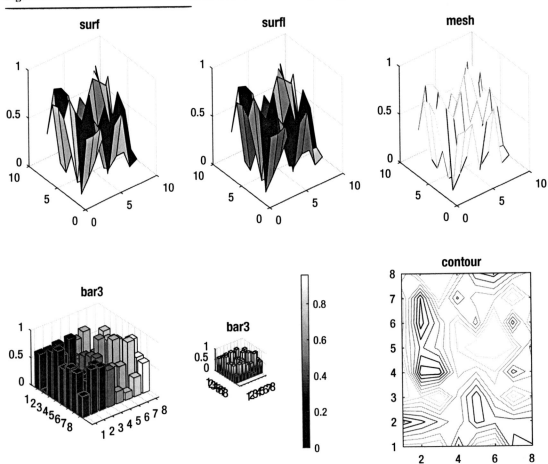

5.6.3 How It Works

We generate a random 2D data set that is 8×8 using `rand`. We display it in several ways in a figure with subplots. In this case, we create two rows and three columns of subplots. Figure 5.7 shows six types of 2D plots. `surf`, `mesh` and `surfl` (3D shaded surface with lighting) are very similar. The surface plots are more interesting when lighting is applied. The two `bar3` plots show different ways of coloring the bars. In the second bar plot, the color varies with length. This requires a bit of code, changing the `CData` and `FaceColor`.

```
m = rand(8,8);

NewFigure('Two_Dimensional_Data');

subplot(2,3,1)
surf(m)
title('surf')

subplot(2,3,2)
surfl(m,'light')
title('surfl')

subplot(2,3,3)
mesh(m)
title('mesh')

subplot(2,3,4)
bar3(m)
title('bar3')

subplot(2,3,5)
h = bar3(m);
title('bar3')

colorbar
for k = 1:length(h)
        zdata = h(k).ZData;
        h(k).CData = zdata;
        h(k).FaceColor = 'interp';
end

subplot(2,3,6)
contour(m);
title('contour')
```

5.7   Building a Graphical User Interface

5.7.1 Problem

We want a graphical user interface (GUI) to provide a second-order system simulation.

5.7.2 Solution

We will use the MATLAB GUIDE to build a GUI that will allow us to

1. Set the damping constant.

2. Set the end time for the simulation.

3. Set the type of input (pulse, step, or sinusoid).

4. Display the inputs and outputs plot.

5.7.3 How It Works

We want to build a GUI to interface with SecondOrderSystemSim shown below.

```matlab
function [xP, t, tL] = SecondOrderSystemSim( d )

if( nargin < 1 )
  xP   = DefaultDataStructure;
  return
end

omega    = max([d.omega d.omegaU]);
dT       = 0.1*2*pi/omega;
n        = floor(d.tEnd/dT);
xP       = zeros(2,n);
x        = [0;0];
t        = 0;

for k = 1:n
  [~,u]   = RHS(t,x,d);
  xP(:,k) = [x(1);u];
  x       = RungeKutta( @RHS, t, x, dT, d );
  t       = t + dT;
end

[t,tL] = TimeLabel((0:n-1)*dT);

if( nargout == 0 )
  PlotSet(t,xP,'x_label',tL,'y_label', {'x' 'u'}, 'figure_title','Filter');
end
```

```
%% SecondOrderSystemSim>>RHS
function [xDot,u] = RHS( t, x, d )

u = 0;

switch( lower(d.input) )
  case 'pulse'
    if( t > d.tPulseBegin && t < d.tPulseEnd )
      u = 1;
    end

  case 'step'
    u = 1;

  case 'sinusoid'
    u = sin(d.omegaU*t);
end

f = u - 2*d.zeta*d.omega*x(2) - d.omega^2*x(1);

xDot = [x(2);f];

%% SecondOrderSystemSim>>DefaultDataStructure
function d = DefaultDataStructure

d                = struct();
d.omega          = 0.1;
d.zeta           = 0.4;
d.omegaU         = 0.3;
d.input          = 'step';
```

Running it gives the following plot Figure 5.8. The function has the simulation loop built in.

Figure 5.8: Second-order system simulation.

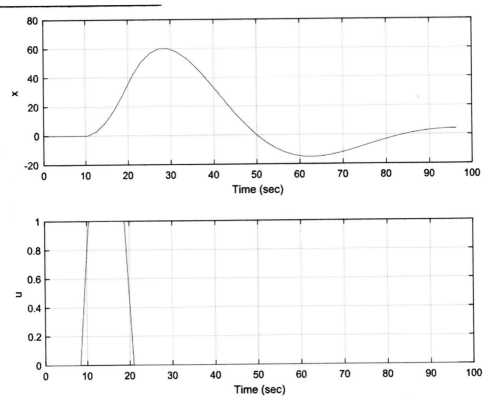

The MATLAB GUI building system, GUIDE, is invoked by typing `guide` at the command line. There are several options for GUI templates, or a blank GUI. We will start from a blank GUI. First, let's make a list of the controls we will need from our desired features list above:

- Edit boxes for

  - Simulation duration

  - Damping ratio

  - Undamped natural frequency

  - Sinusoid input frequency

  - Pulse start and stop time

- Radio button for the type of input

- Run button for starting a simulation

- Plot axes

We type "guide" in the command window and it asks us to either pick an existing GUI or create a new one. We choose blank GUI. Figure 5.9 shows the template GUI in GUIDE before we make any changes to it. You add elements by dragging and dropping from the table at the left.

Figure 5.9: Blank GUI.

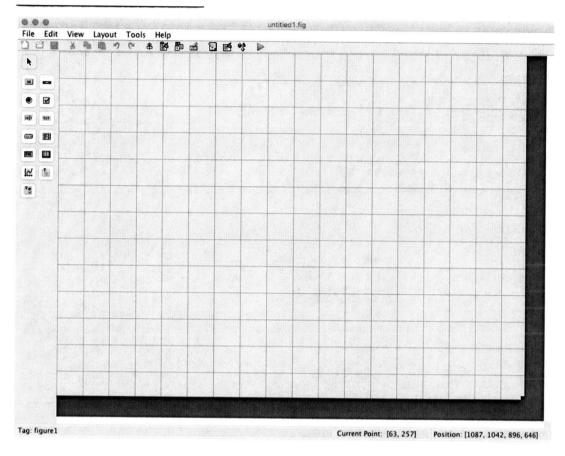

Figure 5.10 shows the GUI inspector. You edit GUI elements here. You can see that the elements have a lot of properties. We aren't going to try and make this GUI really slick, but with some effort you can make it a work of art. The ones we will change are the tag and text properties. The tag gives the software a name to use internally. The text is just what is shown on the device.

We then add all the desired elements by dragging and dropping. We choose to name our GUI GUI. The resulting initial GUI is shown in Figure 5.11. In the inspector for each element you will see a field for "tag." Change the names from things like `edit1` to names you can easily identify. When you save them and run the GUI from the .fig file, the code in GUI.m will automatically change.

We create a radio button group and add the radio buttons. This handles disabling all but the selected radio button. When you hit the green arrow in the layout box, it saves all changes to the m-file and also simulates it. It will warn you about bugs.

At this point, we can start work on the GUI code itself. The template GUI stores its data, calculated from the data the user types into the edit boxes, in a field called `simdata`. The entire function is shown below. We've removed the repeated comments to make it more compact.

```
gui_Singleton = 1;
gui_State = struct('gui_Name',          mfilename, ...
                   'gui_Singleton',  gui_Singleton, ...
                   'gui_OpeningFcn', @SimGUI_OpeningFcn, ...
                   'gui_OutputFcn',  @SimGUI_OutputFcn, ...
                   'gui_LayoutFcn',  [] , ...
                   'gui_Callback',   []);
if nargin && ischar(varargin{1})
    gui_State.gui_Callback = str2func(varargin{1});
end

if nargout
    [varargout{1:nargout}] = gui_mainfcn(gui_State, varargin{:});
else
```

Figure 5.10: The GUI inspector.

Figure 5.11: Snapshot of the GUI in the editing window after adding all the elements.

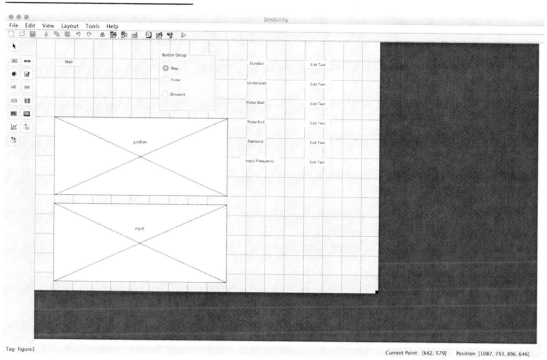

```
      gui_mainfcn(gui_State, varargin{:});
end
% End initialization code - DO NOT EDIT

% --- Executes just before SimGUI is made visible.
function SimGUI_OpeningFcn(hObject, eventdata, handles, varargin)

% Choose default command line output for SimGUI
handles.output = hObject;

% Get the default data
handles.simData = SecondOrderSystemSim;

% Set the default states
set(handles.editDuration,'string',num2str(handles.simData.tEnd));
set(handles.editUndamped,'string',num2str(handles.simData.omega));
set(handles.editPulseStart,'string',num2str(handles.simData.tPulseBegin));
set(handles.editPulseEnd,'string',num2str(handles.simData.tPulseEnd));
set(handles.editDamping,'string',num2str(handles.simData.zeta));
set(handles.editInputFrequency,'string',num2str(handles.simData.omegaU));

% Update handles structure
guidata(hObject, handles);
```

```matlab
% UIWAIT makes SimGUI wait for user response (see UIRESUME)
% uiwait(handles.figure1);

% --- Outputs from this function are returned to the command line.
function varargout = SimGUI_OutputFcn(hObject, eventdata, handles)

varargout{1} = handles.output;

% --- Executes on button press in step.
function step_Callback(hObject, eventdata, handles)

if( get(hObject,'value') )
  handles.simData.input = 'step';
  guidata(hObject, handles);
end

% --- Executes on button press in pulse.
function pulse_Callback(hObject, eventdata, handles)

if( get(hObject,'value') )
  handles.simData.input = 'pulse';
        guidata(hObject, handles);
end

% --- Executes on button press in sinusoid.
function sinusoid_Callback(hObject, eventdata, handles)

if( get(hObject,'value') )
  handles.simData.input = 'sinusoid';
        guidata(hObject, handles);
end

% --- Executes on button press in start.
function start_Callback(hObject, eventdata, handles)

[xP, t, tL] = SecondOrderSystemSim(handles.simData);

axes(handles.position)
plot(t,xP(1,:));
ylabel('Position')
grid

axes(handles.input)
plot(t,xP(2,:));
xlabel(tL);
ylabel('input');
grid

function editDuration_Callback(hObject, eventdata, handles)

handles.simData.tEnd = str2double(get(hObject,'String'));
guidata(hObject, handles);
```

```matlab
% --- Executes during object creation, after setting all properties.
function editDuration_CreateFcn(hObject, eventdata, handles)
if ispc && isequal(get(hObject,'BackgroundColor'), get(0,'
    defaultUicontrolBackgroundColor'))
    set(hObject,'BackgroundColor','white');
end


function editUndamped_Callback(hObject, eventdata, handles)

handles.simData.omega = str2double(get(hObject,'String'));
guidata(hObject, handles);

% --- Executes during object creation, after setting all properties.
function editUndamped_CreateFcn(hObject, eventdata, handles)
if ispc && isequal(get(hObject,'BackgroundColor'), get(0,'
    defaultUicontrolBackgroundColor'))
    set(hObject,'BackgroundColor','white');
end


function editPulseStart_Callback(hObject, eventdata, handles)

handles.simData.tPulseStart = str2double(get(hObject,'String'));
guidata(hObject, handles);

% --- Executes during object creation, after setting all properties.
function editPulseStart_CreateFcn(hObject, eventdata, handles)

if ispc && isequal(get(hObject,'BackgroundColor'), get(0,'
    defaultUicontrolBackgroundColor'))
    set(hObject,'BackgroundColor','white');
end


function editPulseEnd_Callback(hObject, eventdata, handles)

handles.simData.tPulseEnd = str2double(get(hObject,'String'));
guidata(hObject, handles);

% --- Executes during object creation, after setting all properties.
function editPulseEnd_CreateFcn(hObject, eventdata, handles)
if ispc && isequal(get(hObject,'BackgroundColor'), get(0,'
    defaultUicontrolBackgroundColor'))
    set(hObject,'BackgroundColor','white');
end


function editDamping_Callback(hObject, eventdata, handles)

handles.simData.zeta = str2double(get(hObject,'String'));
guidata(hObject, handles);

% --- Executes during object creation, after setting all properties.
function editDamping_CreateFcn(hObject, eventdata, handles)
```

79

```
if ispc && isequal(get(hObject,'BackgroundColor'), get(0,'
    defaultUicontrolBackgroundColor'))
    set(hObject,'BackgroundColor','white');
end


function editInput_Callback(hObject, eventdata, handles)

% --- Executes during object creation, after setting all properties.
function editInput_CreateFcn(hObject, eventdata, handles)

if ispc && isequal(get(hObject,'BackgroundColor'), get(0,'
    defaultUicontrolBackgroundColor'))
    set(hObject,'BackgroundColor','white');
end

% --- If Enable == 'on', executes on mouse press in 5 pixel border.
% --- Otherwise, executes on mouse press in 5 pixel border or over step.
function step_ButtonDownFcn(hObject, eventdata, handles)

% --- If Enable == 'on', executes on mouse press in 5 pixel border.
% --- Otherwise, executes on mouse press in 5 pixel border or over pulse.
function pulse_ButtonDownFcn(hObject, eventdata, handles)

% --- If Enable == 'on', executes on mouse press in 5 pixel border.
% --- Otherwise, executes on mouse press in 5 pixel border or over sinusoid.
function sinusoid_ButtonDownFcn(hObject, eventdata, handles)


function editInputFrequency_Callback(hObject, eventdata, handles)

handles.simData.omegaU = str2double(get(hObject,'String'));
guidata(hObject, handles);


% --- Executes during object creation, after setting all properties.
function editInputFrequency_CreateFcn(hObject, eventdata, handles)
% hObject      handle to editInputFrequency (see GCBO)
% eventdata    reserved - to be defined in a future version of MATLAB
% handles      empty - handles not created until after all CreateFcns called

% Hint: edit controls usually have a white background on Windows.
%        See ISPC and COMPUTER.
if ispc && isequal(get(hObject,'BackgroundColor'), get(0,'
    defaultUicontrolBackgroundColor'))
    set(hObject,'BackgroundColor','white');
end
```

When the GUI loads, we initialize the text fields with the data from the default data structure. Make sure that the initialization corresponds to what is seen in the GUI. You need to be careful about radio buttons and button states.

```matlab
function SimGUI_OpeningFcn(hObject, eventdata, handles, varargin)

% Choose default command line output for SimGUI
handles.output = hObject;

% Get the default data
handles.simData = SecondOrderSystemSim;

% Set the default states
set(handles.editDuration,'string',num2str(handles.simData.tEnd));
set(handles.editUndamped,'string',num2str(handles.simData.omega));
set(handles.editPulseStart,'string',num2str(handles.simData.tPulseBegin));
set(handles.editPulseEnd,'string',num2str(handles.simData.tPulseEnd));
set(handles.editDamping,'string',num2str(handles.simData.zeta));
set(handles.editInputFrequency,'string',num2str(handles.simData.omegaU));

% Update handles structure
guidata(hObject, handles);
```

When the start button is pushed, we run the simulation and plot the results. This essentially is the same as the demo code in the second-order simulation.

```matlab
function start_Callback(hObject, eventdata, handles)

[xP, t, tL] = SecondOrderSystemSim(handles.simData);

axes(handles.position)
plot(t,xP(1,:));
ylabel('Position')
grid

axes(handles.input)
plot(t,xP(2,:));
xlabel(tL);
ylabel('input');
grid
```

The callbacks for the edit boxes require a little code to set the data in the stored data. All data are stored in the GUI handles. guidata must be called to store new data in the handles.

```matlab
function editDuration_Callback(hObject, eventdata, handles)

handles.simData.tEnd = str2double(get(hObject,'String'));
guidata(hObject, handles);
```

One simulation is shown in Figure 5.12. Another simulation in the GUI is shown in Figure 5.13.

81

Figure 5.12: Snapshot of the GUI in simulation.

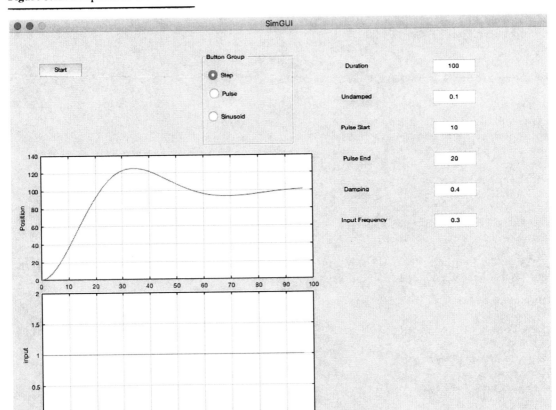

Figure 5.13: Snapshot of the GUI in simulation.

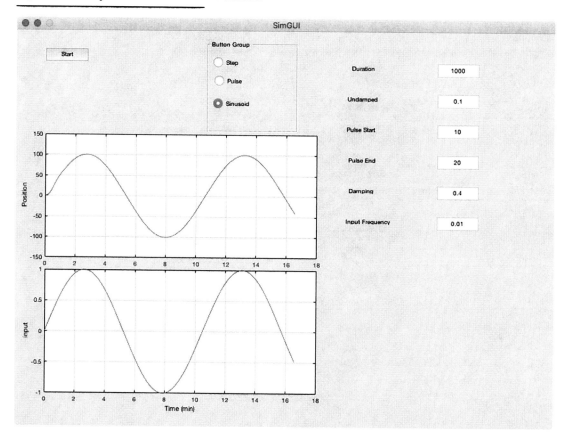

Summary

This chapter has demonstrated graphics that can help understand the results of machine learning software. Two- and three-dimensional graphics were demonstrated. The chapter also showed how to build a GUI to help automate functions. Table 5.1 lists the files used in this chapter.

Table 5.1: Chapter Code Listing

File	Description
Box	Draw a box.
DrawVertices	Draw a set of vertices and faces
Globe	Draw a texture mapped globe
PlotSet	2D line plots
SecondOrderSystemSim	Simulates a second-order system
SimGUI	Code for the simulation GUI
SimGUI.fig	The figure
TreeDiagram	Draw a tree diagram
TwoDDataDisplay	A script to display 2D data in 3D graphics

CHAPTER 6

■ ■ ■

Machine Learning Examples in MATLAB

6.1 Introduction

The remainder of the book provides machine learning examples in MATLAB that span the technologies discussed. Each example provides a useful application in its own right. Full source code is provided. In each case the theory behind the code is provided. References for further study are provided. Each example is self-contained and addresses one of the autonomous learning technologies discussed earlier in the book. You can jump around and try the examples that interest you the most.

As we explained earlier, autonomous learning is a huge field. There are many benefits from knowing all aspects of the field. Those with experience in any one of the applications may find the examples to be straightforward. Topics outside your area of expertise will be more challenging. Much like cross-training in the gym, working in other areas will help you in your own area of expertise.

6.2 Machine Learning

We present three types of machine learning algorithms. In each case we present a simple algorithm to achieve the desired results.

6.2.1 Neural Networks

This example will use a neural network to classify digits. We will start with a set of six digits and create a training set by adding noise to the digital images. We will then see how well our learning network performs at identifying a single digit, and then add more nodes and outputs to identify multiple digits with one network. Classifying digits is one of the oldest uses of machine learning. The U.S. Post Office introduced zip code reading years before machine learning started hitting the front pages of all the newspapers! Earlier digit readers required block letters written in well-defined spots on a form. Reading digits off any envelope is an example of learning in an unstructured environment.

© Michael Paluszek, Stephanie Thomas 2017
M. Paluszek and S. Thomas, *MATLAB Machine Learning*, DOI 10.1007/978-1-4842-2250-8_6

6.2.2 Face Recognition

Face recognition is available in almost every photo application. Many social media sites, such as Facebook and Google Plus, also use face recognition. Cameras have built-in face recognition, though not identification, to help with focusing when taking portraits. Our goal is to get the algorithm to match faces, not classify them. Data classification is covered in the next chapter.

There are many algorithms for face identification, and commercial software can use multiple algorithms. In this application, we pick a single algorithm and use it to identify one face in a set of photographs—of cats.

Face recognition is a subset of general image recognition. The chapter on neural networks, Chapter 9, gives another example. Our example of face recognition works within a structured environment. The pictures are all taken from the front and the picture only shows the head. This makes the problem much easier to solve.

6.2.3 Data Classification

This example uses a decision tree to classify data. Classifying data is one of the most widely used areas of machine learning. In this example, we assume that two data points are sufficient to classify a sample and determine to which group it belongs. We have a training set of known data points with membership in one of three groups. We then use a decision tree to classify the data. We'll introduce a graphical display to make understanding the process easier.

With any learning algorithm it is important to know why the algorithm made its decision. Graphics can help you explore large data sets when columns of numbers aren't terribly helpful.

6.3 Control

Feedback control algorithms inherently learn about the environment through measurements used for control. These chapters show how control algorithms can be extended to effectively design themselves using measurements. The measurements may be the same as used for control but the adaptation, or learning, happens more slowly than the control response time. An important aspect of control design is stability. A stable controller will produce bounded outputs for bounded inputs. It will also produce smooth, predictable behavior of the system that is controlled. An unstable controller will typically experience growing oscillations in the quantities (such as speed or position) that are controlled. In these chapters we explore both the performance of learning control and the stability of such controllers.

6.3.1 Kalman Filters

The Kalman filters chapter, Chapter 10, shows how Kalman filters allow you to learn about dynamical systems for which we already have a model. This chapter provides an example of a variable-gain Kalman filter for a spring system. That is a system with a mass connected to its base via a spring and a damper. This is a linear system. We write the system in discrete time. This provides an introduction to Kalman filtering. We show how Kalman filters can be derived from Bayesian statistics. This ties it into many machine learning algorithms. Originally, the Kalman filter, developed by R. E. Kalman, C. Bucy, and R. Battin, was not derived in this fashion.

The second section adds a nonlinear measurement. A linear measurement is a measurement proportional to the state (in this case position) it measures. Our nonlinear measurement will be the angle of a tracking device that points at the mass from a distance from the line of movement. One way is to use an unscented Kalman filter (UKF) for state estimation. The UKF lets us use a nonlinear measurement model easily.

The last part of the chapter describes the UKF configured for parameter estimation. This system learns the model, albeit one that has an existing mathematical model. As such, it is an example of model-based learning. In this example the filter estimates the oscillation frequency of the spring-mass system. It will demonstrate how the system needs to be stimulated to identify the parameters.

6.3.2 Adaptive Control

Adaptive control is a branch of control systems in which the gains of the control system change based on measurements of the system. A gain is a number that multiplies a measurement from a sensor to produce a control action such as driving a motor or other actuator. In a nonlearning control system, the gains are computed prior to operation and remain fixed. This works very well most of the time since we can usually pick gains so that the control system is tolerant of parameter changes in the system. Our gain "margins" tell us how tolerant we are to uncertainties in the system. If we are tolerant to big changes in parameters, we say that our system is robust.

Adaptive control systems change the gain based on measurements during operation. This can help a control system perform even better. The better we know a system's model, the tighter we can control the system. This is much like driving a new car. At first you have to be cautious driving a new car because you don't know how sensitive the steering is to turning the wheel or how fast it accelerates when you depress the gas pedal. As you learn about the car you can maneuver it with more confidence. If you didn't learn about the car, you would need to drive every car in the same fashion.

This chapter starts with a simple example of adding damping to a spring using a control system. Our goal is to get a specific damping time constant. For this we need to know the spring constant. Our learning system uses a fast Fourier transform to measure the spring constant. We'll compare it to a system that does know the spring constant. This is an example of tuning a control system.

The second example is model reference adaptive control of a first-order system. This system automatically adapts so that the system behaves like the desired model. This is a very powerful method and applicable to many situations.

The third example is longitudinal control of an aircraft. We can control the pitch angle using the elevators. We have five nonlinear equations for the pitch rotational dynamics, velocity in the x-direction, velocity in the z-direction, and change in altitude. The system adapts to changes in velocity and altitude. Both change the drag and lift forces and the moments on the aircraft and also change the response to the elevators. We use a neural net as the learning element of our control system. This is a practical problem applicable to all types of aircraft ranging from drones to high-performance commercial aircraft.

Our last example will be ship steering control. Ships use adaptive control because it is more efficient than conventional control. This example demonstrates how the control system adapts and how it performs better than its nonadaptive equivalent. This is an example of gain scheduling.

6.4   Artificial Intelligence

Only one example of artificial intelligence is included in the book. This is really a blending of Bayesian estimation and controls. Machine learning is an offshoot of artificial intelligence so all the machine learning examples could also be considered examples of artificial intelligence.

6.4.1 Autonomous Driving and Target Tracking

Autonomous driving is an area of great interest to automobile manufacturers and to the general public. Autonomous cars are driving the streets today but are not yet ready for general use by the public. There are many technologies involved in autonomous driving. These include

1. Machine vision: turning camera data into information useful for the autonomous control system

2. Sensing: using many technologies including vision, radar, and sound to sense the environment around the car

3. Control: using algorithms to make the car go where it is supposed to go as determined by the navigation system

4. Machine learning: using massive data from test cars to create databases of responses to situations

5. GPS navigation: blending GPS measurements with sensing and vision to figure out where to go

6. Communications/ad hoc networks: talking with other cars to help determine where they are and what they are doing

All of the areas overlap. Communications and ad hoc networks are used with GPS navigation to determine both absolute location (what street and address correspond to your location) and relative navigation (where you are with respect to other cars).

This example explores the problem of a car being passed by multiple cars and needing to compute tracks for each one. We are really addressing just the control and collision avoidance problem. A single-sensor version of track-oriented multiple-hypothesis testing is demonstrated for a single car on a two-lane road. The example includes MATLAB graphics that make it easier to understand the thinking of the algorithm. The demo assumes that the optical or radar preprocessing has been done and that each target is measured by a single "blip" in two dimensions. An automobile simulation is included. It involves cars passing the car that is doing the tracking. The passing cars use a passing control system that is in itself a form of machine intelligence.

This chapter uses a UKF for the estimation of the state. This is the underlying algorithm that propagates the state (that is, advances the state in time in a simulation) and adds measurements to the state. A Kalman filter, or other estimator, is the core of any target tracking system.

The section will also introduce graphics aids to help you understand the tracking decision process. When you implement a learning system, you want to make sure it is working the way you think it should, or understand why it is working the way it does.

CHAPTER 7

■ ■ ■

Face Recognition with Deep Learning

A general neural net is shown in Figure 7.1. This is a "deep learning" neural net because it has multiple internal layers.

Figure 7.1: Deep learning neural net.

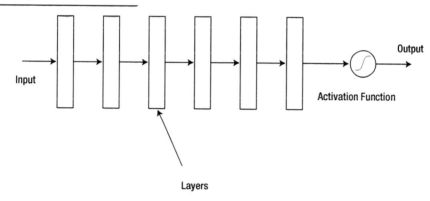

A convolutional neural network is a pipeline with multiple stages. The images go into one end and the probability that the image is a cat comes out the other. There are three types of layers:

- Convolutional layers (hence the name)
- Pooling layers
- Fully connected layers

A convolutional neural net is shown in Figure 7.2. This is also a "deep learning" neural net because it has multiple internal layers, but now the layers are of the three types described above.

© Michael Paluszek, Stephanie Thomas 2017
M. Paluszek and S. Thomas, *MATLAB Machine Learning*, DOI 10.1007/978-1-4842-2250-8_7

Figure 7.2: Deep learning convolutional neural net [1].

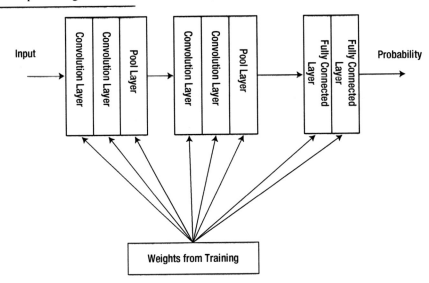

We can have as many layers as we want. A neuron in a neural net is

$$y = \sigma(wx + b) \tag{7.1}$$

where w is a weight, b is a bias, and $\sigma()$ is the nonlinear function that operates on the input $wx + b$. This is the activation function. There are many possible sigmoid functions.

A sigmoid or hyperbolic tangent is often used as the activation function. The function `Activation` generates activation functions.

```
%% ACTIVATION - Implement activation functions

%% Format
% s = Activation( type, x, k )
%
%% Description
% Generates an activation function
%
%% Inputs
%
% type (1,:) Type 'sigmoid', 'tanh', 'rlo'
% x    (1,:) Input
% k    (1,1) Scale factor
%
%% Outputs
%
% s   (1,:) Output
%
```

```
function s = Activation( type, x, k )

% Demo
if( nargin < 1 )
  Demo
  return
end

if( nargin < 3 )
  k = 1;
end

switch lower(type)
  case 'elo'
    j = x > 0;
    s = zeros(1,length(x));
    s(j) = 1;
  case 'tanh'
    s = tanh(k*x);
  case 'sigmoid'
    s = (1-exp(-k*x))./(1+exp(-k*x));
end

function Demo
%% Demo

x         = linspace(-2,2);
s         = [ Activation('elo',x);...
        Activation('tanh',x);...
        Activation('sigmoid',x)];

PlotSet(x,s,'x_label','x','y_label','\sigma(x)',...
        'figure_title','Activation_Functions',...
        'legend',{{'ELO' 'tanh' 'Sigmoid'}},'plot_set',{1:3});
```

Figure 7.3 shows the three activation functions with $k=1$. A third is the rectified linear output function or

Figure 7.3: Activation function.

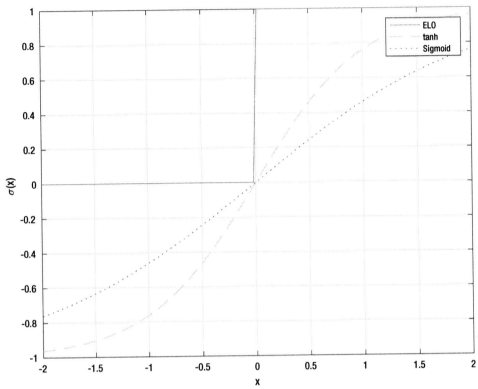

$$f(x) = \begin{cases} x & x > 0 \\ 0 & x \leq 0 \end{cases} \tag{7.2}$$

This seems a bit strange for an image processing network where the inputs are all positive. However, the bias term can make the argument negative and previous layers may also change the sign.

The following recipes will detail each step in the chain. We will start with gathering image data. We will then describe the convolution process. The next recipe will implement pooling. We will show a recipe for Softmax. We will then demonstrate the full network using random weights. Finally, we will train the network using a subset of the images and see if we can identify the other images.

7.1 Obtain Data Online: For Training a Neural Network

7.1.1 Problem

We want to find photographs online for training a face recognition neural net.

7.1.2 Solution

Go to ImageNet to find images.

7.1.3 How It Works

ImageNet, http://www.image-net.org, is an image database organized according to the WordNet hierarchy. Each meaningful concept in WordNet is called a "synonym set." There are more than 100,000 sets and 14 million images in ImageNet. For example, type in "Siamese cat." Click on the link. You will see 445 images. You'll notice that there are a wide variety of shots from many angles and a wide range of distances.

```
Synset: Siamese cat, Siamese
Definition: a slender, short-haired, blue-eyed breed of cat having a pale
    coat with dark ears, paws, face, and tail tip.
Popularity percentile:: 57%
Depth in WordNet: 8
```

This is a great resource! However, we are going to instead use pictures of our cats for our test to avoid copyright issues.

7.2 Generating Data for Training a Neural Net

7.2.1 Problem

We want grayscale photographs for training a face recognition neural net.

7.2.2 Solution

Take photographs using a digital camera.

7.2.3 How It Works

We first take pictures of several cats. We'll use them to train the net. The photos are taken using an iPhone 6. We take just facial photos; to make the problem easier, we limit the photos to facial shots of the cats. We then frame the shots so that they are reasonably consistent in size and minimize the background. We then convert them to grayscale.

We use the function `ImageArray` to read in the images. It takes a path to a folder containing the images to be processed.

```
%% IMAGEARRAY Read in an array of images
%
%% Form:
%   s = ImageArray( folderPath, scale )
%
%% Description
% Creates a cell array of images. scale will scale by 2^scale
%
%% Inputs
%   folderPath    (1,:)   Path to the folder
%   scale         (1,1)   Integer.
%
%% Outputs
%   s        {:}   Image array
%   sName    {:}   Names
```

```matlab
function [s, sName] = ImageArray( folderPath, scale )

% Demo
if( nargin < 1 )
  folderPath = './Cats1024/';
  ImageArray( folderPath, 4 );
  return;
end

c = cd;
cd(folderPath)

d = dir;

n = length(d);

j = 0;
s     = cell(n-2,1);
sName = cell(1,n);
for k = 1:n
  sName{k} = d(k).name;
  if( ~strcmp(sName{k},'.') && ~strcmp(sName{k},'..') )
    j   = j + 1;
    t   = ScaleImage(flipud(imread(d(k).name)),scale);
    s{k} = (t(:,:,1)+ t(:,:,2) + t(:,:,3))/3;
  end
end

del   = size(s{k},1);
lX    = 3*del;

% Draw the images
NewFigure(folderPath);
colormap(gray);
n = length(s);
x = 0;
y = 0;
for k = 1:n
  image('xdata',[x;x+del],'ydata',[y;y+del],'cdata', s{k} );
  hold on
  x = x + del;
  if ( x == lX );
    x = 0;
    y = y + del;
  end
end
axis off
axis image
```

```
for k = 1:length(s)
  s{k} = double(s{k})/256;
end
```

```
cd(c)
```

The function has a demo with our local folder of cat images.

```
function [s, sName] = ImageArray( folderPath, scale )

% Demo
if( nargin < 1 )
  folderPath = './Cats1024/';
  ImageArray( folderPath, 4 );
  return;
end

c = cd;
cd(folderPath)

d = dir;

n = length(d);

j = 0;
s     = cell(n-2,1);
sName = cell(1,n);
for k = 1:n
  sName{k} = d(k).name;
  if( ~strcmp(sName{k},'.') && ~strcmp(sName{k},'..') )
    j    = j + 1;
    t    = ScaleImage(flipud(imread(d(k).name)),scale);
    s{k} = (t(:,:,1)+ t(:,:,2) + t(:,:,3))/3;
  end
end

del   = size(s{k},1);
lX    = 3*del;

% Draw the images
NewFigure(folderPath);
colormap(gray);
n = length(s);
x = 0;
y = 0;
for k = 1:n
  image('xdata',[x;x+del],'ydata',[y;y+del],'cdata', s{k} );
  hold on
  x = x + del;
  if ( x == lX );
    x = 0;
    y = y + del;
```

ImageArray uses averages the three colors to convert the color images to grayscale. It flips them upside down since the image coordinates are opposite that of MATLAB. We used GraphicConverter

10^{TM} to crop the images around the cat's face and make them all 1024 x 1024 pixels. One of the challenges of image matching is to do this process automatically. Also, training typically uses thousands of images. We are using just a few to see if our neural net can determine if the test image is a cat, or even one we have used in training! ImageArray scales the image using the function ScaleImage

```
%% SCALEIMAGE - Scale an image by powers of 2.

%% Format
% s2 = ScaleImage( s1, n )
%
%% Description
% Scales an image by powers of 2. The scaling will be 2^n.
% Takes the mean of the neighboring pixels. Only works with RGB images.
%
%% Inputs
%
% s1 (:,:,3)  Image
% n  Scale     Integer
%
%% Outputs
%
% s1 (:,:,3)  Scaled image
%

function s2 = ScaleImage( s1, q )

% Demo
if( nargin < 1 )
  Demo
  return
end

n = 2^q;

[mR,~,mD] = size(s1);

m = mR/n;

s2 = zeros(m,m,mD,'uint8');

for i = 1:mD
      for j = 1:m
    r = (j-1)*n+1:j*n;
    for k = 1:m
      c        = (k-1)*n+1:k*n;
      s2(j,k,i) = mean(mean(s1(r,c,i)));
    end
        end
end

function Demo
%% Demo
```

```
s1 = flipud(imread('Cat.png'));
n  = 2;

s2 = ScaleImage( s1, n );

n  = 2^n;

NewFigure('ScaleImage')

x = 0;
y = 0;

del = 1024;

sX = image('xdata',[x;x+del],'ydata',[y;y+del],'cdata', s1 );
x = x + del;
s = image('xdata',[x;x+del/n],'ydata',[y;y+del/n],'cdata', s2 );

axis image
axis off
```

Notice that it creates the new image array as `uint8`. Figure 7.4 shows the results of scaling. The images are shown in Figure 7.5.

7.3 Convolution

7.3.1 Problem

We want to implement convolution to reduce the number of weights in the network.

Figure 7.4: Image scaled from 1024×1024 to 256×256.

97

Figure 7.5: (64×64)-pixel grayscale cat images.

7.3.2 Solution

Implement convolution using MATLAB matrix operations.

7.3.3 How It Works

We create an *n-x-n* mask that we apply to the input matrix. The matrix dimensions are *m* x *m*, where *m* is greater than *n*. We start in the upper left corner of the matrix. We multiply the mask times the corresponding elements in the input matrix and do a double sum. That is the first element of the convolved output. We then move it column by column until the highest column of the mask is aligned with the highest column of the input matrix. We then return it to the first column and increment the row. We continue until we have traversed the entire input matrix and our mask is aligned with the maximum row and maximum column.

The mask represents a feature. In effect, we are seeing if the feature appears in different areas of the image. We can have multiple masks. There are one bias and one weight for each element of the mask for each feature. In this case, instead of 16 sets of weights and biases, we only have 4. For large images, the savings can be substantial. In this case the convolution works on the image itself. Convolutions can also be applied to the output of other convolutional layers or pooling layers, as shown in Figure 7.6.

Convolution is implemented in `Convolve.m`.

```
%% Convolve
%
%% Format
% c = Convolve( a, b )
%
%% Description
% Convolves a with b.
% a should be smaller than b.
%
% This is a a way to extract features.
%
% nC = nB - nA + 1;
% mC = mB - mA + 1;
%
%% Inputs
%
% a   (nA,mA)   Matrix to convolve with b
% b   (nB,mB)   Matrix to be convolved
```

Figure 7.6: Convolution process showing the mask at the beginning and end of the process.

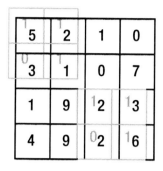

Input Matrix

Convolution Matrix

Mask

```
%
%% Outputs
%
%   c   (nC,mB)   Convolution result with one feature result per element
%

function c = Convolve( a, b )

% Demo
if( nargin < 1 )
  a = [1 0 1;0 1 0;1 0 1]
  b = [1 1 1 0 0 0;0 1 1 1 0 1;0 0 1 1 1 0;0 0 1 1 0 1;0 1 1 0 0 1;0 1 1 0 0
      1]
  c = Convolve( a, b );
  return
end

[nA,mA]  = size(a);
[nB,mB]  = size(b);
nC       = nB - nA + 1;
mC       = mB - mA + 1;
c        = zeros(nC,mC);
for j = 1:mC
  jR = j:j+nA-1;
  for k = 1:nC
    kR = k:k+mA-1;
```

```
    c(j,k) = sum(sum(a.*b(jR,kR)));
  end
end
```

The demo produces the following results.

```
>> Convolve

a =

     1     0     1
     0     1     0
     1     0     1

b =

     1     1     1     0     0     0
     0     1     1     1     0     1
     0     0     1     1     1     0
     0     0     1     1     0     1
     0     1     1     0     0     1
     0     1     1     0     0     1

ans =

     4     3     4     1
     2     4     3     5
     2     3     4     2
     3     3     2     3
```

7.4   Convolution Layer

7.4.1 Problem

We want to implement a convolution connected layer.

7.4.2 Solution

Use code from `Convolve` to implement the layer.

7.4.3 How It Works

The "convolution" neural net scans the input with the mask. Each input to the mask passes through an activation function that is identical for a given mask. This reduces the number of weights.

```
%% CONVOLUTIONLAYER
%
%% Format
% y = ConvolutionLayer( x, d )
%
%% Description
% Implements a fully connected neural network
%
```

100

```
%% Inputs
%
%  x  (n,n)  Input
%  d  (.)    Data structure
%            .mask (m,m) Mask values
%            .w    (m,m) Weights
%            .b    (m,m) Biases
%            .aFun (1,:) Activation Function
%
%% Outputs
%
%  y  (p,p)  Outputs
%

function y = ConvolutionLayer( x, d )

% Demo
if( nargin < 1 )
  if( nargout > 0 )
    y = DefaultDataStructure;
  else
    Demo;
  end
  return
end

a         = d.mask;
aFun      = str2func(d.aFun);
[nA,mA]   = size(a);
[nB,mB]   = size(x);
nC        = nB - nA + 1;
mC        = mB - mA + 1;
y         = zeros(nC,mC);
for j = 1:mC
  jR = j:j+nA-1;
  for k = 1:nC
    kR = k:k+mA-1;
    y(j,k) = sum(sum(a.*Neuron(x(jR,kR),d, aFun)));
  end
end

function y = Neuron( x, d, afun )
%% Neuron function
y = afun(x.*d.w + d.b);

function d = DefaultDataStructure
%% Default Data Structure

d = struct('mask',ones(9,9),'w',rand(9,9),'b',rand(9,9),'aFun','tanh');

function Demo
%% Demo
```

```
d        = DefaultDataStructure;
x        = rand(16,16);
y        = ConvolutionLayer( x, d );

NewFigure('Convolution_Layer');

subplot(2,1,1)
surf(x)
title('Input')

subplot(2,1,2)
surf(y)
title('Output')
```

Figure 7.7 shows the inputs and outputs from the demo. The tanh activation function is used in this demo. The weights and biases are random.

Figure 7.7: Inputs and outputs for the convolution layer.

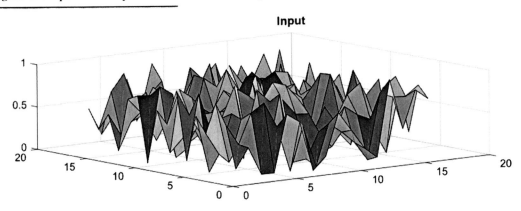

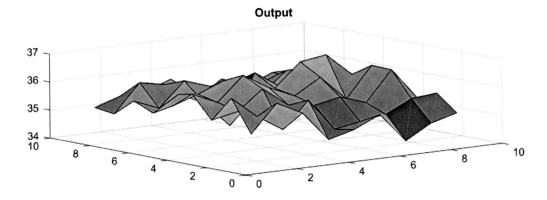

7.5   Pooling

7.5.1   Problem

We want to pool the outputs of the convolution layer to reduce the number of points we need to process.

7.5.2   Solution

Implement a function to take the output of the convolution function.

7.5.3   How It Works

Pooling layers take a subset of the outputs of the convolutional layers and pass that on. They do not have any weights. Pooling layers can use the maximum value of the pool or take the median or mean value. Our pooling function has all there as an option. The pooling function divides the input into n x n subregions and returns an n x n matrix.

Pooling is implemented in `Pool.m`. Notice we use `str2func` instead of a switch statement.

```
%% Pool - pool values from a 2D array
%
%% Format
%  b = Pool( a, n, type )
%
%% Description
%  Creates an nxn matrix from a.
%  a be a power of 2.
%
%% Inputs
%
%  a     (:,:) Matrix to convolve with b
%  n     (1,1) Number of pools
%  type  (1,:) Pooling type
%
%% Outputs
%
%  b     (n,n)  Pool
%

function b = Pool( a, n, type )

% Demo
if( nargin < 1 )
  a = rand(4,4)
  b = Pool( a, 4, type);
  return
end

if( nargin <3 )
  type = 'mean';
end

n = n/2;
p = str2func(type);
```

```
nA = size(a,1);

nPP = nA/n;

b = size(n,n);
for j = 1:n
  r = (j-1)*nPP +1:j*nPP;
  for k = 1:n
    c = (k-1)*nPP +1:k*nPP;
    b(j,k) = p(p(a(r,c)));
  end
end
```

The demo produces the following results.

The built-in demo creates 4 pools from an 4 x 4 matrix.

```
>> Pool

a =

    0.9031    0.7175    0.5305    0.5312
    0.1051    0.1334    0.8597    0.9559
    0.7451    0.4458    0.6777    0.0667
    0.7294    0.5088    0.8058    0.5415

ans =

    0.4648    0.7193
    0.6073    0.5229
```

7.6   Fully Connected Layer

7.6.1 Problem

We want to implement a fully connected layer.

7.6.2 Solution

Use Activation to implement the network.

7.6.3 How It Works

The "fully connected" neural net layer is the traditional neural net where every input is connected to every output as shown in Figure 7.8. We implement the fully connected network with n inputs and m outputs. Each path to an output can have a different weight and bias. FullyConnectedNN can handle any number of inputs or outputs.

```
%% FULLYCONNECTEDNN
%
%% Format
% y = FullyConnectedNN( x, d )
%
```

104

Figure 7.8: Fully connected neural net. This shows only one output.

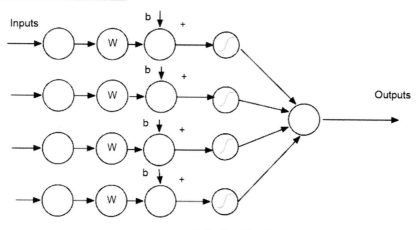

```
%% Description
% Implements a fully connected neural network
%
%% Inputs
%
%   x   (n,1)  Inputs
%   d   (.)    Data structure
%               .w     (n,m)  Weights
%               .b     (n,m)  Biases
%               .aFun  (1,:)  Activation Function
%
%% Outputs
%
%   y   (m,1)  Outputs
%

function y = FullyConnectedNN( x, d )

% Demo
if( nargin < 1 )
  if( nargout > 0 )
    y = DefaultDataStructure;
  else
    Demo;
  end
  return
end

y = zeros(d.m,size(x,2));

aFun = str2func(d.aFun);
```

```
n = size(x,1);
for k = 1:d.m
  for j = 1:n
    y(k,:) = y(k,:) + aFun(d.w(j,k)*x(j,:) + d.b(j,k));
  end
end

function d = DefaultDataStructure
%% Default Data Structure

d = struct('w',[],'b',[],'aFun','tanh','m',1);

function Demo
%% Demo

d       = DefaultDataStructure;
a       = linspace(0,8*pi);
x       = [sin(a);cos(a)];

d.w     = rand(2,2);
d.b     = rand(2,2);
d.aFun  = 'tanh';
d.m     = 2;
n       = length(x);
y       = FullyConnectedNN( x, d );

yL      = {'x_1' 'x_2' 'y_1' 'y_2'};
PlotSet( 1:n, [x;y], 'x_label','step','y_label',yL,'figure_title','FCNN');
```

Figure 7.9 shows the outputs from the demo. The tanh activation function is used in this demo. The weights and biases are random. The change in shape from input to output is the result of the activation function.

7.7 Determining the Probability

7.7.1 Problem

We want to get a probability from neural net outputs.

7.7.2 Solution

Implement the Softmax function. This will be used for the output nodes of our network.

Figure 7.9: The two outputs from the demo function are shown vs. the two inputs.

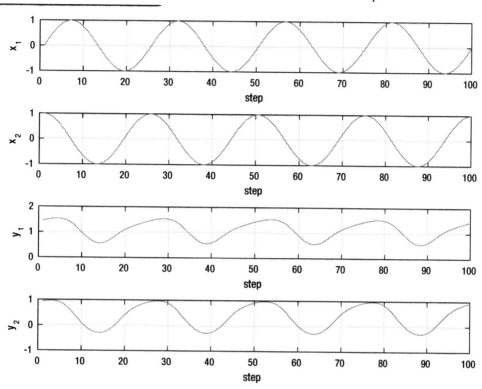

7.7.3 How It Works

Given a set of inputs, the *Softmax* function, a generalization of the logistic function, calculates a set of positive values p that add to 1. It is

$$p_j = \frac{e^{q_j}}{\sum_{k=1}^{N} e^{q_k}} \tag{7.3}$$

where q are the inputs and N is the number of inputs.

The function is implemented in Softmax.m.

```
function [p, pMax, kMax] = Softmax( q )

% Demo
if( nargin == 0 )
  q = [1,2,3,4,1,2,3];
  [p, pMax, kMax] = Softmax( q )
  sum(p)
  clear p
  return
end

q = reshape(q,[],1);
n = length(q);
p = zeros(1,n);
```

```
den = sum(exp(q));

for k = 1:n
  p(k) = exp(q(k))/den;
end
```

The results of the demo are

```
>> Softmax
p =
    0.0236    0.0643    0.1747    0.4748    0.0236    0.0643    0.1747

pMax =
    0.4748

kMax =
    4

ans =
    1.0000
```

The last number is the sum of p, which should be (and is) 1.

7.8   Test the Neural Network

7.8.1 Problem

We want to integrate convolution, pooling, a fully connected layer, and Softmax.

7.8.2 Solution

The solution is write a convolutional neural net. We integrate the convolution, pooling, fully connected net, and Softmax functions. We then test it with randomly generated weights.

7.8.3 How It Works

Figure 7.10 shows the image processing neural network. It has one convolutional layer, one pooling layer, and a fully connected layer, and the final layer is the Softmax.

```
>> TestNN
Image IMG_3886.png has a 13.1% chance of being a cat
```

As expected, the neural net does not identify the cat! The code in ConvolutionNN that performs the test is shown below.

```
function r = NeuralNet( d, t, ~ )
%% Neural net function

% Convolve the image

yCL   = ConvolutionLayer( t, d.cL );
yPool = Pool( yCL, d.pool.n, d.pool.type );
yFC   = FullyConnectedNN( yPool, d.fCNN );
[~,r] = Softmax( yFC );

if( nargin > 1 )
```

Figure 7.10: Neural net for the image processing.

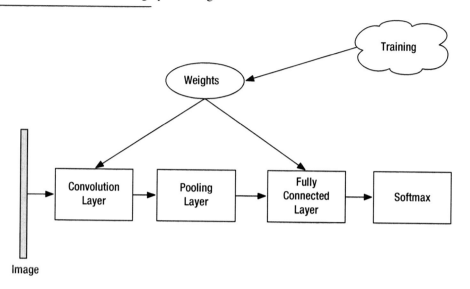

```
NewFigure('ConvolutionNN');
subplot(3,1,1);
mesh(yCL);
title('Convolution␣Layer')
subplot(3,1,2);
      mesh(yPool);
title('Pool␣Layer')
subplot(3,1,3);
      mesh(yFC);
title('Fully␣Connected␣Layer')
end
```

Figure 7.11 shows the output of the various stages.

7.9 Recognizing an Image

7.9.1 Problem

We want to determine if an image is that of a cat.

7.9.2 Solution

We train the neural network with a series of cat images. We then use one picture from the training set and a separate picture and compute the probabilities that they are cats.

Figure 7.11: Stages in the convolutional neural net processing.

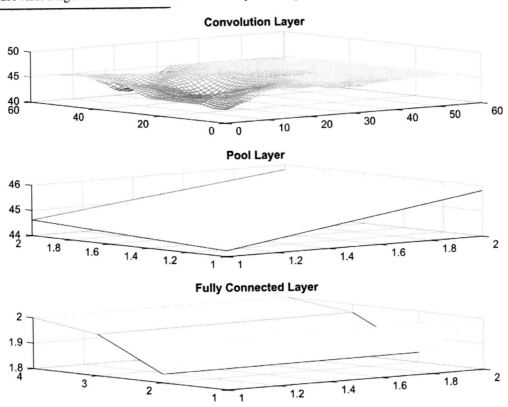

7.9.3 How It Works

We run the script `TrainNN` to see if the input image is a cat.

```
%% Train a neural net
% Trains the net from the images in the folder.

folderPath = './Cat10224';
[s, name]   = ImageArray( folderPath, 4 );
d           = ConvolutionalNN;

% Use all but the last
s           = {s{1:end-1}};

% This may take awhile
d   =   ConvolutionalNN( 'train', d, t );

% Test the net using the last image
[d, r]      = ConvolutionalNN( 'test', d, s{end} );

fprintf(1,'Image_%s_has_a_%4.1f%%_chance_of_being_a_cat\n',name{end},100*r);
```

The script returns that the image is probably a cat.

```
>> TrainNN
Image IMG_3886.png has a 56.0% chance of being a cat
```

We can improve the results with

- More images

- More features (masks)

- Changing the connections in the fully connected layer

- Adding the ability of ConvolutionalNN to handle RGB images directly

- Changing ConvolutionalNN

Summary

This chapter has demonstrated facial recognition using MATLAB. Convolutional neural nets were used to process pictures of cats for learning. When trained, the neural net was asked to identify other pictures to determine if they were pictures of a cat. Table 7.1 lists the code introduced in this chapter.

Table 7.1: Chapter Code Listing

File	Description
Activation	Generate activation functions
ImageArray	Read in images in a folder and convert to grayscale
ConvolutionalNN	Implement a convolutional neural net
ConvolutionLayer	Implement a convolutional layer
Convolve	Convolve a two-dimensional array using a mask
Pool	Pool a two-dimensional array
FullyConnectedNN	Implement a fully connected neural network
ScaleImage	Scale an image
Softmax	Implement the Softmax function
TrainNN	Train the convolutional neural net
TestNN	Test the convolutional neural net
TrainingData.mat	Data from TestNN

Reference

[1] Matthijs Hollemans. Convolutional neural networks on the iPhone with VGGNet. `http://matthijshollemans.com/2016/08/30/vggnet-convolutional-neural-network-iphone/`, 2016.

CHAPTER 8

■ ■ ■

Data Classification

In this chapter we will develop the theory for binary decision trees. Decision trees can be used to classify data. Binary trees are the easiest to implement. We will create functions for the decision trees and to generate sets of data to classify.

8.1 Generate Classification Test Data

8.1.1 Problem

We want to generate a set of training and testing data.

8.1.2 Solution

Write a function using `rand` to generate data.

8.1.3 How It Works

The function `ClassifierSet` generates random data and assigns them to classes. Classes are generated by adding polygons that encompass the data. Any polygon can be used. The function randomly places points on a grid and then adds boundaries for the sets defined by polygons. You specify a set of vertices to be used in the set boundaries and the faces that define the set. The following code generates the sets:

```
function p = ClassifierSets( n, xRange, yRange, name, v, f, setName )

% Demo
if( nargin < 1 )
  v = [0 0;0 4; 4 4; 4 0; 0 2; 2 2; 2 0;2 1;4 1;2 1];
  f = {[5 6 7 1] [5 2 3 9 10 6] [7 8 9 4]};
  ClassifierSets( 5, [0 4], [0 4], {'width', 'length'}, v, f );
  return
end

if( nargin < 7 )
  setName = 'Classifier␣Sets';
end
```

© Michael Paluszek, Stephanie Thomas 2017

M. Paluszek and S. Thomas, *MATLAB Machine Learning*, DOI 10.1007/978-1-4842-2250-8_8

```
p.x     = (xRange(2) - xRange(1))*(rand(n,n)-0.5) + mean(xRange);
p.y     = (yRange(2) - yRange(1))*(rand(n,n)-0.5) + mean(yRange);
p.m     = Membership( p, v, f );

NewFigure(setName);
m = length(f);
c = rand(m,3);
for k = 1:n
  for j = 1:n
    plot(p.x(k,j),p.y(k,j),'marker','o','MarkerEdgeColor','k')
    hold on
  end
end
for k = 1:m
  patch('vertices',v,'faces',f{k},'facecolor',c(k,:),'facealpha',0.1)
end

xlabel(name{1});
ylabel(name{2});
grid

function z = Membership( p, v, f )

n = size(p.x,1);
m = size(p.x,2);
z = zeros(n,m);
for k = 1:n
  for j = 1:m
    for i = 1:length(f)
      vI = v(f{i},:)';
      q  = [p.x(k,j) p.y(k,j)];
      r  = PointInPolygon( q, vI );
      if( r == 1 )
        z(k,j) = i;
        break;
      end
    end
  end
end
end
```

A typical set is shown in Figure 8.1. The function color-codes the points to match the set color. Note that the colors are chosen randomly. The patch function is used to generate the polygons. The code shows a range of graphics coding including the use of graphics parameters.

Figure 8.1: Classifier set.

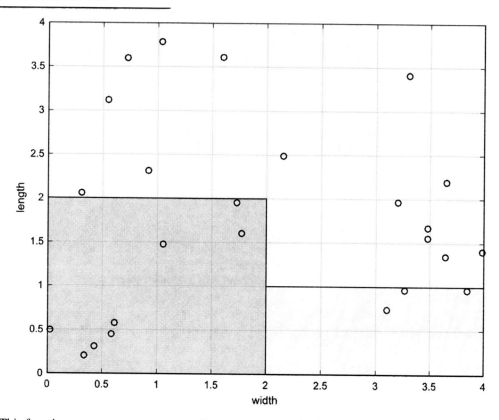

This function can generate test sets or demonstrate the trained decision tree. The drawing shows that the classification regions are boxes. `ClassifierSets` randomly puts points in the regions. It figures out which region each point is in using this code in the function:

```
function r = PointInPolygon( p, v )

m = size(v,2);

% All outside
r = 0;

% Put the first point at the end to simplify the looping
v = [v v(:,1)];

  for i = 1:m
          j    = i + 1;
          v2J  = v(2,j);
          v2I  = v(2,i);
          if (((v2I > p(2)) ~= (v2J > p(2))) && ...
      (p(1) < (v(1,j) - v(1,i)) * (p(2) - v2I) / (v2J - v2I) + v(1,i)))
        r = ~r;
          end
  end
```

This code can determine if a point is inside a polygon defined by a set of vertices. It is used frequently in computer graphics and in games when you need to know if one object's vertex is in another polygon. You could correctly argue that this could replace our decision tree for this type of problem. However, a decision tree can compute membership for more complex sets of data. Our classifier set is simple and makes it easy to validate the results.

8.2 Drawing Decision Trees

8.2.1 Problem

We want to draw a binary decision tree to show decision tree thinking.

8.2.2 Solution

The solution is to use MATLAB graphics functions to draw a tree.

8.2.3 How It Works

The function `DrawBinaryTree` draws any binary tree. You pass it a data structure with the decision criteria in a cell array. The boxes start from the left and go row by row. In a binary tree the number of rows is related to the number of boxes through the formula for a geometric series:

$$m = \log_2(n) \tag{8.1}$$

where m is the number of rows and n is the number of boxes. Therefore, the function can compute the number of rows.

The function starts by checking the number of inputs and either runs the demo or returns the default data structure. The name input is optional. It then steps through the boxes assigning them to rows based on it being a binary tree. The first row has one box, the next two boxes, the following four boxes, etc. As this is a geometric series, it will soon get unmanageable! This points to a problem with decision trees. If they have a depth of more than four, even drawing them is impossible.

As it draws the boxes it computes the bottom and top points that will be the anchors for the lines between the boxes. After drawing all the boxes it draws all the lines.

All of the drawing functionality is in the subfunction `DrawBoxes`. This draws a box using the `patch` function and the text using the `text` function. Notice the extra arguments in `text`. The most interesting is `'HorizontalAlignment'`. This allows you to easily center text in the box.

```
text(x+w/2,y + h/2,t,'fontname',d.font,'fontsize',d.fontSize,
    'HorizontalAlignment','center');
```

Setting `'facecolor'` to [1 1 1] makes the face white and leaves the edges black. As with all MATLAB graphics there are dozens of properties that you can edit to produce beautiful graphics. The following listing shows the code.

```
%% DRAWBINARYTREE - Draw a binary tree in a new figure
%% Forms:
%   DrawBinaryTree( d, name )
%   d = DrawBinaryTree        % default data structure
%
%% Description
%  Draws a binary tree. All branches are drawn. Inputs in d.box go from left
%  to right by row starting with the row with only one box.
%
%% Inputs
%   d     (.)        Data structure
```

116

```
%               .w          (1,1)  Box width
%               .h          (1,1)  Box height
%               .rows       (1,1)  Number of rows in the tree
%               .fontSize   (1,1)  Font size
%               .font       (1,:)  Font name
%               .box        {:}    Text for each box
%   name (1,:)  Figure name
%
%% Outputs
%  d    (.)         Data structure

function d = DrawBinaryTree( d, name )

% Demo
if( nargin < 1 )
  if( nargout == 0 )
    Demo
  else
    d = DefaultDataStructure;
  end
  return
end


if( nargin < 2 )
  name = 'Binary_Tree';
end

NewFigure(name);

m         = length(d.box);
nRows     = ceil(log2(m+1));
w         = d.w;
h         = d.h;
i         = 1;
x         = -w/2;
y         = 1.5*nRows*h;
nBoxes    = 1;
bottom    = zeros(m,2);
top       = zeros(m,2);
rowID     = cell(nRows,1);
for k = 1:nRows
  for j = 1:nBoxes
    bottom(i,:)   = [x+w/2 y ];
    top(i,:)      = [x+w/2 y+h];
    DrawBox(d.box{i},x,y,w,h,d);
    rowID{k}      = [rowID{k} i];
    i             = i + 1;
    x             = x + 1.5*w;
    if( i > length(d.box) )
      break;
    end
  end
end
```

```
  nBoxes    = 2*nBoxes;
  x         = -(0.25+0.5*(nBoxes/2-1))*w - nBoxes*w/2;
  y         = y - 1.5*h;
end

% Draw the lines
for k = 1:length(rowID)-1
  iD = rowID{k};
  i0 = 0;
  % Work from left to right of the current row
  for j = 1:length(iD)
    x(1) = bottom(iD(j),1);
    y(1) = bottom(iD(j),2);
    iDT  = rowID{k+1};
    if( i0+1 > length(iDT) )
      break;
    end
    for i = 1:2
      x(2) = top(iDT(i0+i),1);
      y(2) = top(iDT(i0+i),2);
      line(x,y);
    end
    i0 = i0 + 2;
  end
end
axis off

function DrawBox( t, x, y, w, h, d )
%% Draw boxes and text

v = [x y 0;x y+h 0; x+w y+h 0;x+w y 0];

patch('vertices',v,'faces',[1 2 3 4],'facecolor',[1;1;1]);

text(x+w/2,y + h/2,t,'fontname',d.font,'fontsize',d.fontSize,'
    HorizontalAlignment','center');

function d = DefaultDataStructure
%% Default data structure

d             = struct();
d.fontSize    = 12;
d.font        = 'courier';
d.w           = 1;
d.h           = 0.5;
d.box         = {};

function Demo
%% Demo

d             = DefaultDataStructure;
d.box{1}      = 'a_>_0.1';
d.box{2}      = 'b_>_0.2';
```

```
d.box{3}      = 'b_>_0.3';
d.box{4}      = 'a_>_0.8';
d.box{5}      = 'b_>_0.4';
d.box{6}      = 'a_>_0.2';
d.box{7}      = 'b_>_0.3';

DrawBinaryTree( d );
```

The demo creates three rows. It starts with the default data structure. You only have to add strings for the decision points. You can create them using `sprintf`. For example, for the first box you could write

```
s = sprintf('%s_%s_%3.1f','a','>',0.1);
```

The relationship could be added with an `if-else-end` construct. You can see this done in `DecisionTree`. The following demo draws a binary tree:

```
d.box         = {};
```

```
function Demo
%% Demo

d             = DefaultDataStructure;
d.box{1}      = 'a_>_0.1';
d.box{2}      = 'b_>_0.2';
d.box{3}      = 'b_>_0.3';
d.box{4}      = 'a_>_0.8';
d.box{5}      = 'b_>_0.4';
d.box{6}      = 'a_>_0.2';
d.box{7}      = 'b_>_0.3';
```

The binary tree resulting from the demo is shown in Figure 8.2. The text in the boxes could be anything you want.

Figure 8.2: Binary tree

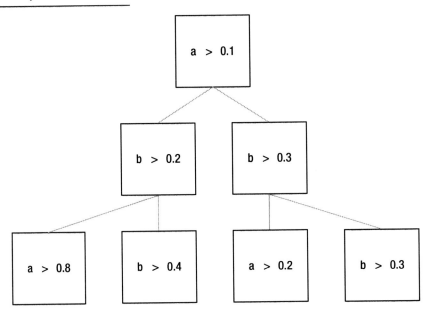

8.3   Decision Tree Implementation

Decision trees are the main focus of this chapter. We'll start by looking at how we determine if our decision tree is working correctly. We'll then hand-build a decision tree and finally write learning code to generate the decisions for each block of the tree.

8.3.1 Problem

We need to measure the homogeneity of a set of data at different nodes on the decision tree.

8.3.2 Solution

The solution is to implement the Gini impurity measure for a set of data.

8.3.3 How It Works

The homogeneity measure is called the information gain (IG).

The IG is defined as the increase in information by splitting at the node. This is

$$\Delta I = I(p) - \frac{N_{c_1}}{N_p}I(c_1) - \frac{N_{c_2}}{N_p}I(c_2) \qquad (8.2)$$

where I is the impurity measure and N is the number of samples at that node. If our tree is working it should go down, eventually to zero or to a very small number. In our training set we know the class of each data point. Therefore, we can determine the IG. Essentially, we have gained information if the mixing decreases in the child nodes. For example, in the first node all the data are mixed. In the two child nodes we expect that each child node will have more of one class than does the other child node. Essentially, we look at the percentages of classes in each node and look for the maximum increase in nonhomogeneity.

There are three impurity measures:

- Gini impurity

- Entropy

- Classification error

The Gini impurity is the criterion to minimize the probability of misclassification. We don't want to push a sample into the wrong category.

$$I_G = 1 - \sum_1^c p(i|t)^2 \tag{8.3}$$

$p(i|t)$ is the proportion of the samples in class c_i at node t. For a binary class, entropy is either zero or one.

$$I_E = 1 - \sum_1^c p(i|t) \log_2 p(i|t) \tag{8.4}$$

The classification error is

$$I_C = 1 - \max p(i|t) \tag{8.5}$$

We will use the Gini impurity in the decision tree. The following code implements the Gini measure.

```
function [i, d] = HomogeneityMeasure( action, d, data )

if( nargin == 0 )
  if( nargout == 1 )
    i = DefaultDataStructure;
  else
    Demo;
  end
  return
end

switch lower(action)
  case 'initialize'
    d = Initialize( d, data );
    i = d.i;
  case 'update'
    d = Update( d, data );
    i = d.i;
  otherwise
    error('%s␣is␣not␣an␣available␣action',action);
end

function d = Update( d, data )
%% Update

newDist = zeros(1,length(d.class));

m = reshape(data,[],1);
c = d.class;
n = length(m);
```

```
if( n > 0 )
  for k = 1:length(d.class)
    j         = find(m==d.class(k));
    newDist(k) = length(j)/n;
  end
end

d.i = 1 - sum(newDist.^2);

d.dist = newDist;

function d = Initialize( d, data )
%% Initialize

m = reshape(data,[],1);

c = 1:max(m);

n = length(m);

d.dist  = zeros(1,c(4));
d.class = c;

if( n > 0 )
  for k = 1:length(c)
    j         = find(m==c(k));
    d.dist(k) = length(j)/n;
  end
end

d.i = 1 - sum(d.dist.^2);

function d = DefaultDataStructure
%% Default data structure
d.dist  = [];
d.data  = [];
d.class = [];
d.i     = 1;
```

The demo is shown below.

```
function d = Demo
%% Demo

data = [ 1 2 3 4 3 1 2 4 4 1 1 1 2 2 3 4]';

d      = HomogeneityMeasure;
[i, d] = HomogeneityMeasure( 'initialize', d, data )

data = [1 1 1 2 2];

[i, d] = HomogeneityMeasure( 'update', d, data )
```

```
data = [1 1 1 1];

[i, d] = HomogeneityMeasure( 'update', d, data )

data = [];

[i, d] = HomogeneityMeasure( 'update', d, data )

>> HomogeneityMeasure
i =

    0.7422
d =

    dist: [0.3125 0.2500 0.1875 0.2500]
    data: []
   class: [1 2 3 4]
       i: 0.7422
i =

    0.4800
d =

    dist: [0.6000 0.4000 0 0]
    data: []
   class: [1 2 3 4]
       i: 0.4800
i =

    0
d =

    dist: [1 0 0 0]
    data: []
   class: [1 2 3 4]
       i: 0
i =

    1
d =
    dist: [0 0 0 0]
    data: []
   class: [1 2 3 4]
       i: 1
```

The second-to-last set has a zero, which is the desired value. If there are no inputs, it returns 1 since by definition for a class to exist it must have members.

8.4   Implementing a Decision Tree

8.4.1 Problem

We want to implement a decision tree for classifying data.

8.4.2 Solution

The solution is to write a binary decision tree function in MATLAB.

8.4.3 How It Works

A decision tree [1] breaks down data by asking a series of questions about the data. Our decision trees will be binary in that there will a yes or no answer to each question. For each feature in the data we ask one question per node. This always splits the data into two child nodes. We will be looking at two parameters that determine class membership. The parameters will be numerical measurements.

At the following nodes we ask additional questions, further splitting the data. Figure 8.3 shows the parent/child structure. We continue this process until the samples at each node are in one of the classes.

Figure 8.3: Parent/child nodes.

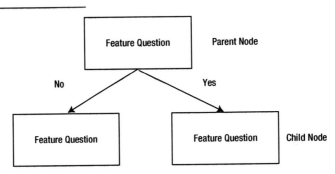

At each node we want to ask the question that provides us with the most information about which class in which our samples reside.

In constructing our decision tree for a two-parameter classification we have two decisions at each node:

- Which parameter to check

- What level to check

For example, for our two parameters we would have either

$$p_1 > a_k \tag{8.6}$$
$$p_2 > b_k \tag{8.7}$$

This can be understood with a very simple case. Suppose we have four sets in a two-dimensional space divided by one horizontal and one vertical line. Our sets can be generated with the following code.

This is done using the Gini values given above. We use `fminbnd` at each node, once for each of the two parameters. There are two actions, "train" and "test." "train" creates the decision tree and "test" runs the generated decision tree. You an also input your own decision tree. `FindOptimalAction` finds the parameter that minimizes the inhomogeneity on both sides of the division. The function called by `fminbnd` is `RHSGT`. We only implement the greater-than action.

The structure of the testing function is very similar to the training function.

```
%% DECISIONTREE - implements a decision tree
%% Form
%   [d, r] = DecisionTree( action, d, t )
%
%% Description
% Implements a binary classification tree.
% Type DecisionTree for a demo using the SimpleClassifierExample
%
%% Inputs
%   action   (1,:) Action 'train', 'test'
%   d        (.) Data structure
%   t        {:} Inputs for training or testing
%
%% Outputs
%   d        (.) Data structure
%   r        (:) Results
%
%% References
%   None

function [d, r] = DecisionTree( action, d, t )

if( nargin < 1 )
  if( nargout > 0 )
    d = DefaultDataStructure;
  else
    Demo;
  end
  return
end

switch lower(action)
  case 'train'
    d = Training( d, t );
  case 'test'
    for k = 1:length(d.box)
      d.box(k).id = [];
    end
    [r, d] = Testing( d, t );
  otherwise
    error('%s is not an available action',action);
end

function d = Training( d, t )
%% Training function
[n,m]   = size(t.x);
nClass  = max(t.m);
box(1)  = AddBox( 1, 1:n*m, [] );
box(1).child = [2 3];
[~, dH] = HomogeneityMeasure( 'initialize', d, t.m );
```

```
class    = 0;
nRow     = 1;
kR0      = 0;
kNR0     = 1;  % Next row;
kInRow   = 1;
kInNRow = 1;
while( class < nClass )
  k   = kR0 + kInRow;
  idK = box(k).id;
  if( isempty(box(k).class) )
    [action, param, val, cMin]  = FindOptimalAction( t, idK, d.xLim, d.yLim,
        dH );
    box(k).value              = val;
    box(k).param              = param;
    box(k).action             = action;
    x                         = t.x(idK);
    y                         = t.y(idK);
    if( box(k).param == 1 )  % x
      id  = find(x >   d.box(k).value );
      idX = find(x <=  d.box(k).value );
    else  % y
      id  = find(y >   d.box(k).value );
      idX = find(y <=  d.box(k).value );
    end
    % Child boxes
    if( cMin < d.cMin)
      class     = class + 1;
      kN        = kNR0 + kInNRow;
      box(k).child = [kN kN+1];
      box(kN)   = AddBox( kN, idK(id), class  );
      class     = class + 1;
      kInNRow   = kInNRow + 1;
      kN        = kNR0 + kInNRow;
      box(kN)   = AddBox( kN, idK(idX), class );
      kInNRow   = kInNRow + 1;
    else
      kN            = kNR0 + kInNRow;
      box(k).child  = [kN kN+1];
      box(kN)       = AddBox( kN, idK(id)  );
      kInNRow       = kInNRow + 1;
      kN            = kNR0 + kInNRow;
      box(kN)       = AddBox( kN, idK(idX) );
      kInNRow       = kInNRow + 1;
    end

    % Update current row
    kInRow   = kInRow + 1;
    if( kInRow > nRow )
      kR0        = kR0 + nRow;
      nRow       = 2*nRow;
```

```
        kNR0      = kNR0 + nRow;
        kInRow    = 1;
        kInNRow   = 1;
      end
    end
end


for k = 1:length(box)
  if( ~isempty(box(k).class) )
    box(k).child = [];
  end
  box(k).id = [];
  fprintf(1,'Box_%d_action_%s_Value_%4.1f_%d\n',k,box(k).action,box(k).value
      ,ischar(box(k).action));
end

d.box = box;

function [action, param, val, cMin] = FindOptimalAction( t, iD, xLim, yLim,
    dH )

c = zeros(1,2);
v = zeros(1,2);

x = t.x(iD);
y = t.y(iD);
m = t.m(iD);
[v(1),c(1)] = fminbnd( @RHSGT, xLim(1), xLim(2), optimset('TolX',1e-16), x,
    m, dH );
[v(2),c(2)] = fminbnd( @RHSGT, yLim(1), yLim(2), optimset('TolX',1e-16), y,
    m, dH );

% Find the minimum
[cMin, j] = min(c);

action = '>';
param  = j;

val = v(j);

function q = RHSGT( v, u, m, dH )
%% RHS greater than function for fminbnd

j  = find( u > v );
q1 = HomogeneityMeasure( 'update', dH, m(j) );
j  = find( u <= v );
q2 = HomogeneityMeasure( 'update', dH, m(j) );
q  = q1 + q2;

function [r, d] = Testing( d, t )
%% Testing function
k      = 1;
```

```
[n,m] = size(t.x);
d.box(1).id = 1:n*m;

class = 0;
while( k <= length(d.box) )
  idK = d.box(k).id;
  v   = d.box(k).value;

  switch( d.box(k).action )
    case '>'
      if( d.box(k).param == 1 )
        id  = find(t.x(idK) >   v );
        idX = find(t.x(idK) <=  v );
      else
        id  = find(t.y(idK) >   v );
        idX = find(t.y(idK) <=  v );
      end
      d.box(d.box(k).child(1)).id = idK(id);
      d.box(d.box(k).child(2)).id = idK(idX);
    case '<='
      if( d.box(k).param == 1 )
        id  = find(t.x(idK) <=  v );
        idX     = find(t.x(idK) >    v );
      else
        id  = find(t.y(idK) <=  v );
        idX     = find(t.y(idK) >       v );
      end
      d.box(d.box(k).child(1)).id = idK(id);
      d.box(d.box(k).child(2)).id = idK(idX);
    otherwise
      class         = class + 1;
      d.box(k).class = class;
  end
  k = k + 1;
end

r = cell(class,1);

for k = 1:length(d.box)
  if( ~isempty(d.box(k).class) )
    r{d.box(k).class,1} = d.box(k).id;
  end
end
```

8.5   Creating a Hand-Made Decision Tree

8.5.1 Problem

We want to test a hand-made decision tree.

8.5.2 Solution

The solution is to write script to test a hand-made decision tree.

8.5.3 How It Works

We write the test script shown below. It uses the 'test' action for DecisionTree.

```
% Create the decision tree
d       = DecisionTree;

% Vertices for the sets
v = [ 0 0; 0 4; 4 4; 4 0; 2 4; 2 2; 2 0; 0 2; 4 2];

% Faces for the sets
f = { [6 5 2 8]  [6 7 4 9]  [6 9 3 5]  [1 7 6 8] };

% Generate the testing set
pTest  = ClassifierSets( 5, [0 4], [0 4], {'width', 'length'}, v, f, '
    Testing_Set' );

% Test the tree
[d, r] = DecisionTree( 'test',  d, pTest  );

q = DrawBinaryTree;
c = 'xy';
for k = 1:length(d.box)
  if( ~isempty(d.box(k).action) )
    q.box{k} = sprintf('%c_%s_%4.1f',c(d.box(k).param),d.box(k).action,d.box
        (k).value);
  else
    q.box{k} = sprintf('Class_%d',d.box(k).class);
  end
end
DrawBinaryTree(q);

m = reshape(pTest.m,[],1);

for k = 1:length(r)
  fprintf(1,'Class_%d\n',k);
  for j = 1:length(r{k})
    fprintf(1,'%d:_%d\n',r{k}(j),m(r{k}(j)));
  end
end
```

`SimpleClassifierDemo` uses the hand-built example in `DecisionTree`.

```
      kN              = kNR0 + kInNRow;
      box(kN)         = AddBox( kN, idK(idX) );
      kInNRow         = kInNRow + 1;
    end

    % Update current row
    kInRow    = kInRow + 1;
    if( kInRow > nRow )
      kR0           = kR0 + nRow;
      nRow          = 2*nRow;
      kNR0          = kNR0 + nRow;
      kInRow        = 1;
      kInNRow       = 1;
    end
  end
end

for k = 1:length(box)
  if( ~isempty(box(k).class) )
    box(k).child = [];
  end
  box(k).id = [];
  fprintf(1,'Box_%d_action_%s_Value_%4.1f_%d\n',k,box(k).action,box(k).value
    ,ischar(box(k).action));
end

d.box = box;

function [action, param, val, cMin] = FindOptimalAction( t, iD, xLim, yLim,
    dH )

c = zeros(1,2);
v = zeros(1,2);

x = t.x(iD);
y = t.y(iD);
m = t.m(iD);
[v(1),c(1)] = fminbnd( @RHSGT, xLim(1), xLim(2), optimset('TolX',1e-16), x,
    m, dH );
[v(2),c(2)] = fminbnd( @RHSGT, yLim(1), yLim(2), optimset('TolX',1e-16), y,
    m, dH );

% Find the minimum
[cMin, j] = min(c);

action = '>';
param  = j;

val = v(j);
```

```
function q = RHSGT( v, u, m, dH )
%% RHS greater than function for fminbnd

j    = find( u > v );
q1   = HomogeneityMeasure( 'update', dH, m(j) );
j    = find( u <= v );
q2   = HomogeneityMeasure( 'update', dH, m(j) );
```

The `action` for the last four box fields as empty strings. This means that no further operations are performed. This happens in the last boxes in the decision tree. In those boxes the `class` field will contain the class of that box. The following shows the testing function in `DecisionTree`.

```
function [r, d] = Testing( d, t )
%% Testing function
k      = 1;

[n,m] = size(t.x);
d.box(1).id = 1:n*m;

class = 0;
while( k <= length(d.box) )
  idK = d.box(k).id;
  v   = d.box(k).value;

  switch( d.box(k).action )
    case '>'
      if( d.box(k).param == 1 )
        id  = find(t.x(idK) >   v );
        idX = find(t.x(idK) <=  v );
      else
        id  = find(t.y(idK) >   v );
        idX = find(t.y(idK) <=  v );
      end
      d.box(d.box(k).child(1)).id = idK(id);
      d.box(d.box(k).child(2)).id = idK(idX);
    case '<='
      if( d.box(k).param == 1 )
        id  = find(t.x(idK) <=  v );
        idX     = find(t.x(idK) >   v );
      else
        id  = find(t.y(idK) <=  v );
        idX     = find(t.y(idK) >      v );
      end
      d.box(d.box(k).child(1)).id = idK(id);
      d.box(d.box(k).child(2)).id = idK(idX);
    otherwise
      class            = class + 1;
      d.box(k).class   = class;
  end
  k = k + 1;
end
```

```
r = cell(class,1);

for k = 1:length(d.box)
  if( ~isempty(d.box(k).class) )
    r{d.box(k).class,1} = d.box(k).id;
  end
end
```

Figure 8.4 shows the results. There are four rectangular areas, which are our sets.

Figure 8.4: Data and classes in the test set.

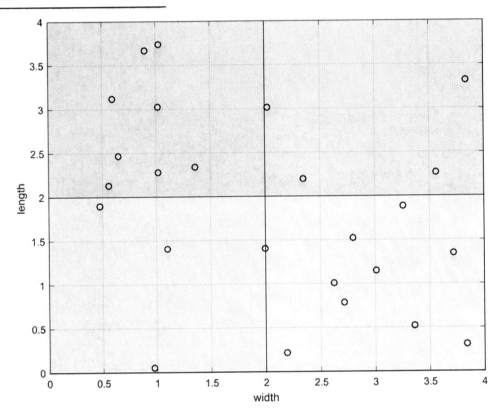

We can create a decision tree by hand as shown Figure 8.5.

Figure 8.5: A manually created decision tree. The drawing is generated by `DecisionTree`. The last row of boxes is the data sorted into the four classes.

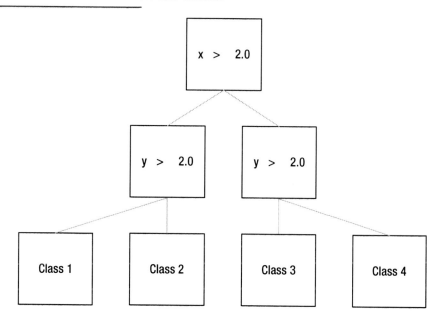

The decision tree sorts the samples into the four sets. In this case we know the boundaries and can use them to write the inequalities. In software we will have to determine what values provide the shortest branches. The following is the output. The decision tree properly classifies all of the data.

```
>> SimpleClassifierDemo
Class 1
7: 3
9: 3
13: 3
15: 3
Class 2
2: 2
3: 2
11: 2
14: 2
16: 2
17: 2
21: 2
23: 2
25: 2
```

```
Class 3
4: 1
8: 1
10: 1
12: 1
18: 1
19: 1
20: 1
22: 1
Class 4
1: 4
5: 4
6: 4
24: 4
```

The class numbers and numbers in the list aren't necessarily the same since the function does know the names of the classes.

8.6 Training and Testing the Decision Tree

8.6.1 Problem

We want to train our decision tree and test the results.

8.6.2 Solution

We replicated the previous recipe only this time we have `DecisionTree` create the decision tree.

8.6.3 How It Works

The following script trains and tests the decision tree. It is very similar to the code for the hand-built decision tree.

```
% Vertices for the sets
v = [ 0 0; 0 4; 4 4; 4 0; 2 4; 2 2; 2 0; 0 2; 4 2];

% Faces for the sets
f = { [6 5 2 8] [6 7 4 9] [6 9 3 5] [1 7 6 8] };

% Generate the training set
pTrain = ClassifierSets( 40, [0 4], [0 4], {'width', 'length'}, v, f, '
    Training_Set' );

% Create the decision tree
d       = DecisionTree;
d       = DecisionTree( 'train', d, pTrain );

% Generate the testing set
pTest   = ClassifierSets( 5, [0 4], [0 4], {'width', 'length'}, v, f, '
    Testing_Set' );

% Test the tree
[d, r] = DecisionTree( 'test',  d, pTest  );

q = DrawBinaryTree;
```

```
c = 'xy';
for k = 1:length(d.box)
  if( ~isempty(d.box(k).action) )
    q.box{k} = sprintf('%c_%s_%4.1f',c(d.box(k).param),d.box(k).action,d.box
      (k).value);
  else
    q.box{k} = sprintf('Class_%d',d.box(k).class);
  end
end
DrawBinaryTree(q);

m = reshape(pTest.m,[],1);

for k = 1:length(r)
  fprintf(1,'Class_%d\n',k);
  for j = 1:length(r{k})
    fprintf(1,'%d:_%d\n',r{k}(j),m(r{k}(j)));
  end
end
```

It uses `ClassifierSets` to generate the training data. The output includes the coordinates and the sets in which they fall. We then create the default data structure and call `DecisionTree` in training mode. The training takes place in this code:

```
function d = Training( d, t )
%% Training function
[n,m]   = size(t.x);
nClass  = max(t.m);
box(1)  = AddBox( 1, 1:n*m, [] );
box(1).child = [2 3];
[~, dH] = HomogeneityMeasure( 'initialize', d, t.m );

class   = 0;
nRow    = 1;
kR0     = 0;
kNR0    = 1; % Next row;
kInRow  = 1;
kInNRow = 1;
while( class < nClass )
  k   = kR0 + kInRow;
  idK = box(k).id;
  if( isempty(box(k).class) )
    [action, param, val, cMin]  = FindOptimalAction( t, idK, d.xLim, d.yLim,
        dH );
    box(k).value                = val;
    box(k).param                = param;
    box(k).action               = action;
    x                           = t.x(idK);
    y                           = t.y(idK);
    if( box(k).param == 1 ) % x
      id  = find(x >   d.box(k).value );
      idX = find(x <=  d.box(k).value );
    else % y
```

```matlab
      id  = find(y >   d.box(k).value );
      idX = find(y <=   d.box(k).value );
    end
    % Child boxes
    if( cMin < d.cMin)
      class     = class + 1;
      kN        = kNR0 + kInNRow;
      box(k).child = [kN kN+1];
      box(kN)    = AddBox( kN, idK(id), class  );
      class     = class + 1;
      kInNRow   = kInNRow + 1;
      kN        = kNR0 + kInNRow;
      box(kN)    = AddBox( kN, idK(idX), class  );
      kInNRow   = kInNRow + 1;
    else
      kN            = kNR0 + kInNRow;
      box(k).child  = [kN kN+1];
      box(kN)       = AddBox( kN, idK(id)  );
      kInNRow       = kInNRow + 1;
      kN            = kNR0 + kInNRow;
      box(kN)       = AddBox( kN, idK(idX) );
      kInNRow       = kInNRow + 1;
    end

    % Update current row
    kInRow    = kInRow + 1;
    if( kInRow > nRow )
      kR0      = kR0 + nRow;
      nRow     = 2*nRow;
      kNR0     = kNR0 + nRow;
      kInRow   = 1;
      kInNRow  = 1;
    end
  end
end

for k = 1:length(box)
  if( ~isempty(box(k).class) )
    box(k).child = [];
  end
  box(k).id = [];
  fprintf(1,'Box_%d_action_%s_Value_%4.1f_%d\n',k,box(k).action,box(k).value
      ,ischar(box(k).action));
end

d.box = box;

function [action, param, val, cMin] = FindOptimalAction( t, iD, xLim, yLim,
    dH )

c = zeros(1,2);
```

```
v = zeros(1,2);

x = t.x(iD);
y = t.y(iD);
m = t.m(iD);
[v(1),c(1)] = fminbnd( @RHSGT, xLim(1), xLim(2), optimset('TolX',1e-16), x,
    m, dH );
[v(2),c(2)] = fminbnd( @RHSGT, yLim(1), yLim(2), optimset('TolX',1e-16), y,
    m, dH );

% Find the minimum
[cMin, j] = min(c);

action = '>';
param  = j;

val = v(j);

function q = RHSGT( v, u, m, dH )
%% RHS greater than function for fminbnd

j   = find( u > v );
q1  = HomogeneityMeasure( 'update', dH, m(j) );
j   = find( u <= v );
q2  = HomogeneityMeasure( 'update', dH, m(j) );
q   = q1 + q2;
```

We use fminbnd to find the optimal switch point. We need to compute the homogeneity on both sides of the switch and sum the values. The sum is minimized by fminbnd. This code is designed for rectangular region classes. Other boundaries won't necessarily work correctly. The code is fairly involved. It needs to keep track of the box numbering to make the parent/child connections. When the homogeneity measure is low enough, it marks the boxes as containing the classes.

The tree is shown in Figure 8.8. The training data are shown in Figure 8.6 and the testing data in Figure 8.7. We need enough testing data to fill the classes. Otherwise, the decision tree generator may draw the lines to encompass just the data in the training set.

Figure 8.6: The training data. A large amount of data is needed to fill the classes.

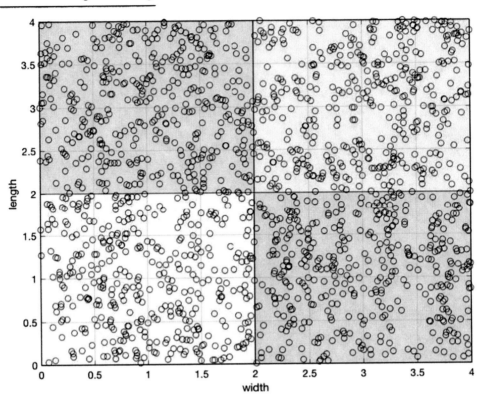

The results are similar to the simple test.

```
Class 1
2: 3
7: 3
9: 3
10: 3
18: 3
19: 3
Class 2
6: 2
11: 2
20: 2
22: 2
24: 2
25: 2
Class 3
3: 1
5: 1
8: 1
12: 1
13: 1
```

Figure 8.7: The testing data.

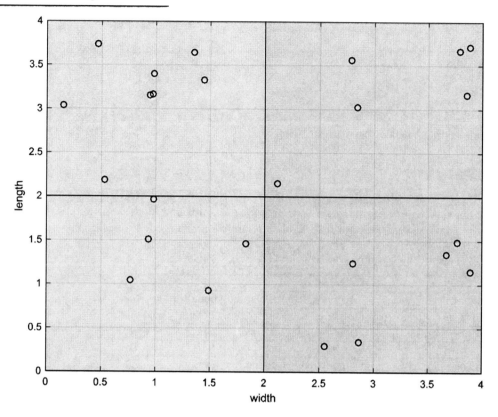

Figure 8.8: The tree derived from the training data. It is essentially the same as the hand-derived tree. The values in the generated tree are not exactly 2.0.

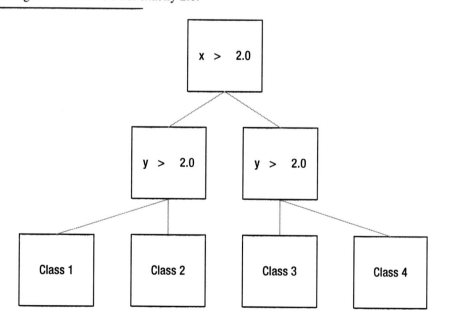

```
14: 1
21: 1
23: 1
Class 4
1: 4
4: 4
15: 4
16: 4
17: 4
```

The generated tree separates the data effectively.

Summary

This chapter has demonstrated data classification using decision trees in MATLAB. We also wrote a new graphics function to draw decision trees. The decision tree software is not general purpose but can serve as a guide to more general-purpose code. Table 8.1 summarizes the code listings from the chapter.

Table 8.1: Chapter Code Listing

File	Description
ClassifierSets	Generates data for classification or training
DecisionTree	Implements a decision tree to classify data
DrawBinaryTree	Generates data for classification or training
HomogeneityMeasure	Computes Gini impurity
SimpleClassifierDemo	Demonstrates decision tree testing
SimpleClassifierExample	Generates data for a simple problem
TestDecisionTree	Tests a decision tree

Reference

[1] Sebastian Raschka. *Python Machine Learning*. [PACKT], 2015.

CHAPTER 9

■ ■ ■

Classification of Numbers Using Neural Networks

Pattern recognition in images is a classic application of neural nets. In this case, we will look at images of computer-generated digits and identify the digits correctly. These images will represent numbers from scanned documents. Attempting to capture the variation in digits with algorithmic rules, considering fonts and other factors, quickly becomes impossibly complex, but with a large number of examples, a neural net can readily perform the task. We allow the weights in the net to perform the job of inferring rules about how each digit may be shaped, rather than codifying them explicitly.

For the purposes of this chapter, we will limit ourselves to images of a single digit. The process of segmenting a series of digits into individual images is one that may be solved by many techniques, not just neural nets.

9.1 Generate Test Images with Defects

9.1.1 Problem

The first step in creating our classification system is to generate sample data. In this case, we want to load in images of numbers for 0–9 and generate test images with defects. For our purposes, defects will be introduced with simple Poisson or shot noise (a random number with a standard deviation of the the the square root of the pixel values).

9.1.2 Solution

We will generate the images in MATLAB by writing a digit to an axis using `text`, then creating an image using `print`. There is an option to capture the pixel data directly from print without creating an interim file, which we will utilize. We will extract the (16 x 16)-pixel area with our digit and then apply the noise. We will also allow the font to be an input. See Figure 9.1 for examples.

© Michael Paluszek, Stephanie Thomas 2017
M. Paluszek and S. Thomas, *MATLAB Machine Learning*, DOI 10.1007/978-1-4842-2250-8_9

Figure 9.1: A sample image of the digits 0 and 1 with noise added.

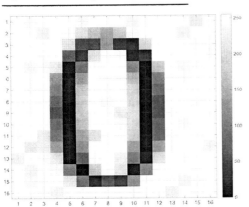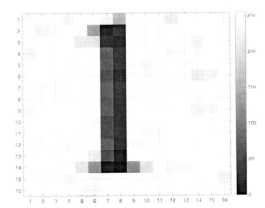

9.1.3 How It Works

The code listing for `CreateDigitImage` is below. It allows for a font to be selected.

```
%% CreateDigitImage Create an image of a single digit.
% Create a 16x16 pixel image of a single digit. The intermediate figure used
    to
% display the digit text is invisible.

function pixels = CreateDigitImage( num, fontname )

if nargin < 1
  num = 1;
if nargin < 2
  fontname = 'times';
end

fonts = listfonts;
avail = strcmp(fontname,fonts);
if ~any(avail)
  error('MachineLearning:CreateDigitImage',...
    'Sorry,_the_font_''%s''_is_not_available.',fontname);
end

f = figure('Name','Digit','visible','off');
a1 = axes( 'Parent', f, 'box', 'off', 'units', 'pixels', 'position', [0 0 16
    16] );

% 20 point font digits are 15 pixels tall (on Mac OS)
text(a1,4,11,num2str(num),'fontsize',20,'fontunits','pixels','unit','pixels'
    ,...
  'fontname','cambria')

% Obtain image data using print and convert to grayscale
cData = print('-RGBImage','-r0');
iGray = rgb2gray(cData);
```

```
% Print image coordinate system starts from upper left of the figure, NOT
    the
% bottom, so our digit is in the LAST 20 rows and the FIRST 20 columns
pixels = iGray(end-15:end,1:16);

% Apply Poisson (shot) noise; must convert the pixel values to double for
    the
% operation and then convert them back to uint8 for the sum. the uint8 type
    will
% automatically handle overflow above 255 so there is no need to apply a
    limit.
noise = uint8(sqrt(double(pixels)).*randn(16,16));
pixels = pixels - noise;

close(f);

if nargout == 0
  h = figure('name','Digit_Image');
  imagesc(pixels);
  colormap(h,'gray');
  grid on
  set(gca,'xtick',1:16)
  set(gca,'ytick',1:16)
  colorbar
end
```

Note that we check that the font exists before trying to use it, and throw an error if it's not found.

Now, we can create the training data using images generated with our new function. In the recipes below we will use data for both a single-digit identification and a multiple-digit identification net. We use a for loop to create a set of images and save them to a MAT-file using the helper function SaveTS. This saves the training sets with their input and output, and indices for training and testing, in a special structure format. Note that we scale the pixels' values, which are nominally integers with a value from 0–255, to have values between 0–1.

```
%% Generate the training data
% Use a for loop to create a set of noisy images for each desired digit
% (between 0 and 9). Save the data along with indices for data to use for
% training.

digits = 0:5;
nImages = 20;
nImages = nDigits*nImages;

input = zeros(256,nImages);
output = zeros(1,nImages);
trainSets = [];
testSets = [];
kImage = 1;
for j = 1:nDigits
  fprintf('Digit_%d\n', digits(j));
  for k = 1:nImages
    pixels = CreateDigitImage( digits(j) );
```

```
% scale the pixels to a range 0 to 1
pixels = double(pixels);
pixels = pixels/255;
input(:,kImage) = pixels(:);
if j == 1
  output(j,kImage) = 1;
end
kImage = kImage + 1;
end
sets = randperm(10);
trainSets = [trainSets (j-1)*nImages+sets(1:5)];
testSets = [testSets (j-1)*nImages+sets(6:10)];
end

% Use 75% of the images for training and save the rest for testing
trainSets = sort(randperm(nImages,floor(0.75*nImages)));
testSets = setdiff(1:nImages,trainSets);

SaveTS( input, output, trainSets, testSets );
```

The helper function will ask for a filename and save the training set. You can load it at the command line to verify the fields. Here's an example with the training and testing sets truncated:

```
>> trainingData = load('Digit0TrainingTS')
trainingData =
  struct with fields:

    Digit0TrainingTS: [1?1 struct]
>> trainingData.Digit0TrainingTS
ans =
  struct with fields:

        inputs: [256?120 double]
    desOutputs: [1?120 double]
     trainSets: [2 8 10 5 4 18 19 12 17 14 30 28 21 27 23 37 34 36 39 38 46
        48 50 41 49 57 53 51 56 54]
      testSets: [1 6 9 3 7 11 16 15 13 20 29 25 26 24 22 35 32 40 33 31 43
          45 42 47 44 58 55 60 52 59]
```

9.2   Create the Neural Net Tool

9.2.1 Problem

We want to create a Neural Net tool that can be trained to identify the digits. In this recipe we will discuss the functions underlying the Neural Net Developer tool. This is a tool we developed in-house in the late 1990s to explore the use of neural nets. It does not use the latest graphical user interface (GUI)-building features of MATLAB, so we will not go into detail about the GUI itself although the full GUI is available in the companion code.

9.2.2 Solution

The solution is to use a multilayer feedforward (MLFF) neural network to classify digits. In this type of network, each neuron depends only on the inputs it receives from the previous layer. We will start with a set of images for each of the 10 digits and create a training set by transforming the digits. We will then see how well our deep learning network performs at identifying the training digits and then other digits similarly transformed.

9.2.3 How It Works

The basis of the neural net is the neuron function. Our neuron function provides six different activation types: sign, sigmoid mag, step, log, tanh, and sum. [2] This can be seen in Figure 9.2.

Figure 9.2: Available neuron activation functions: sign, sigmoid mag, step, log, tanh, and sum.

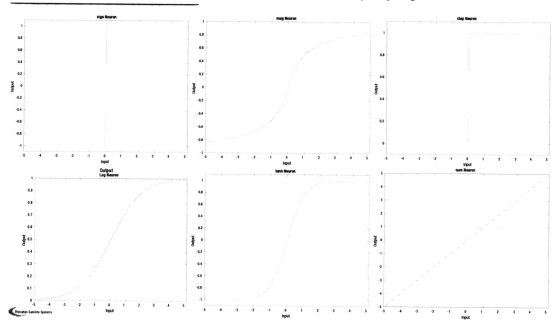

```
function [y, dYDX] = Neuron( x, type, t )

%% NEURON A neuron function for neural nets.
% x may have any dimension. However, if plots are desired x must be 2
% dimensional. The default type is tanh.
%
% The log function is 1./(1 + exp(-x))
% The mag function is x./(1 + abs(x))
%
%% Form:
% [y, dYDX] = Neuron( x, type, t )
%% Inputs
%   x           (:,...)  Input
%   type        (1,:)    'tanh', 'log', 'mag', 'sign', 'step', 'sum'
%   t           (1,1)    Threshold for type = 'step'
```

```
%
%% Outputs
%   y          (:,...) Output
%   dYDX       (:,...) Derivative

%% Reference: Omidivar, O., and D.L. Elliot (Eds) (1997.) "Neural Systems
%              for Control." Academic Press.
%              Russell, S., and P. Norvig. (1995.) Artificial Intelligence-
%              A Modern Approach. Prentice-Hall. p. 583.

% Input processing
%----------------
if( nargin < 1 )
  x = [];
end
if( nargin < 2 )
  type = [];
end
if( nargin < 3 )
  t = 0;
end
if( isempty(type) )
  type = 'log';
end
if( isempty(x) )
  x = sort( [linspace(-5,5) 0 ] );
end

switch lower( deblank(type) )
  case 'tanh'
    yX   = tanh(x);
    dYDX = sech(x).^2;

  case 'log'
    % sigmoid logistic function
    yX   = 1./(1 + exp(-x));
    dYDX = yX.*(1 - yX);

  case 'mag'
    d    = 1 + abs(x);
    yX   = x./d;
    dYDX = 1./d.^2;

  case 'sign'
    yX            = ones(size(x));
    yX(x < 0)     = -1;
    dYDX          = zeros(size(yX));
    dYDX(x == 0)  = inf;

  case 'step'
    yX            = ones(size(x));
    yX(x < t)     = 0;
```

```
   dYDX           = zeros(size(yX));
   dYDX(x == t) = inf;

  case 'sum'
    yX   = x;
    dYDX = ones(size(yX));

  otherwise
    error([type '␣is␣not␣recognized'])
end

% Output processing
%------------------
if( nargout == 0 )
  PlotSet( x, yX, 'x␣label', 'Input', 'y␣label', 'Output',...
          'plot␣title', [type '␣Neuron'] );
  PlotSet( x, dYDX, 'x␣label','Input', 'y␣label','dOutput/dX',...
          'plot␣title',['Derivative␣of␣' type '␣Function'] );
else
  y = yX;
end
```

Neurons are combined into the feedforward neural network using a simple data structure of layers and weights. The input to each neuron is a combination of the signal y, the weight w, and the bias w_0, as in this line:

```
y   = Neuron( w*y - w0, type );
```

The output of the network is calculated by the function `NeuralNetMLFF`. Note that this also outputs the derivatives as obtained from the neuron activation functions, for use in training.

```
%% NEURALNETMLFF - Computes the output of a multilayer feed-forward neural
%    net.
%
%%   Form:
%    [y, dY, layer] = NeuralNetMLFF( x, network )
%
%%  Description
%    Computes the output of a multilayer feed-forward neural net.
%
%    The input layer is a data structure that contains the network data.
%    This data structure must contain the weights and activation functions
%    for each layer.
%
```

```
%    The output layer is the input data structure augmented to include
%    the inputs, outputs, and derivatives of each layer for each run.
%
%% Inputs
%    x            (n,r)       n Inputs, r Runs
%
%    network                  Data structure containing network data
%                             .layer(k,{1,r})   There are k layers to the network
%   which
%                                       includes 1 output and k-1 hidden layers
%
%                             .w(m(j),m(j-1))   w(p,q) is the weight between the
%                                               q-th output of layer j-1 and the
%                                               p-th node of layer j (ie. the
%                                               q-th input to the p-th output of
%                                               layer j)
%                             .w0(m(j))         Biases/Thresholds
%                             .type(1)          'tanh', 'log', 'mag', 'sign',
%                                               'step'
%                                               Only one type is allowed per layer
%
%                             Different weights can be entered for different runs.
%% Outputs
%    y            (m(k),r)    Outputs
%    dY           (m(k),r)    Derivative
%    layer        (k,r)       Information about a desired layer j
%                             .x(m(j-1),1)   Inputs to layer j
%                             .y(m(j),1)     Outputs of layer j
%                             .dYT(m(j),1)   Derivative of layer j
%
%    (:)        Means that the dimension is undefined.
%    (n)      = number of inputs to neural net
%    (r)      = number of runs (ie. sets of inputs)
%    (k)      = number of layers
%    (m(j))   = number of nodes in j-th layer
%
%% References
% Nilsson, Nils J. (1998.) Artificial Intelligence:
% A New Synthesis. Morgan Kaufmann Publishers. Ch. 3.

function [y, dY, layer] = NeuralNetMLFF( x, network )

layer = network.layer;

% Input processing
if( nargin < 2 )
  disp('Will run an example network');
end

if( ~isfield(layer,'w') )
  error('Must input size of neural net.');
end
```

```matlab
if( ~isfield(layer,'w0') )
  layer(1).w0 = [];
end

if( ~isfield(layer,'type') )
  layer(1).type = [];
end

% Generate some useful sizes
nLayers = size(layer,1);
nInputs = size(x,1);
nRuns   = size(x,2);

for j = 1:nLayers
  if( isempty(layer(j,1).w) )
    error('Must_input_weights_for_all_layers')
  end
  if( isempty(layer(j,1).w0) )
    layer(j,1).w0 = zeros( size(layer(j,1).w,1), 1 );
  end
end

nOutputs = size(layer(nLayers,1).w, 1 );

% If there are multiple layers and only one type
% replicate it (the first layer type is the default)
if( isempty(layer(1,1).type) )
  layer(1,1).type = 'tanh';
end

for j = 2:nLayers
  if( isempty(layer(j,1).type) )
    layer(j,1).type = layer(1,1).type;
  end
end

% Set up additional storage
%-------------------------
y0 = zeros(nOutputs,nRuns);
dY = zeros(nOutputs,nRuns);

for k = 1:nLayers
  [outputs,inputs] = size( layer(k,1).w );
  for j = 1:nRuns
    layer(k,j).x  = zeros(inputs,1);
    layer(k,j).y  = zeros(outputs,1);
    layer(k,j).dY = zeros(outputs,1);
  end
end

% Process the network
```

```
%  h = waitbar(0,  'Neural Net Simulation in Progress' );
for j = 1:nRuns
  y = x(:,j);
  for k = 1:nLayers

    % Load the appropriate weights and types for the given run
    if( isempty( layer(k,j).w ) )
      w = layer(k,1).w;
    else
      w = layer(k,j).w;
    end

    if( isempty( layer(k,j).w0 ) )
      w0 = layer(k,1).w0;
    else
      w0 = layer(k,j).w0;
    end

    if( isempty( layer(k,j).type ) )
      type = layer(k,1).type;
    else
      type = layer(k,j).type;
    end

    layer(k,j).x  = y;
        [y, dYT]      = Neuron( w*y - w0, type );
    layer(k,j).y  = y;
    layer(k,j).dY = dYT;

  end
  y0(:,j) = y;
  dY(:,j) = dYT;
%    waitbar(j/nRuns);
end

%  close(h);

if( nargout == 0 )
  PlotSet(1:size(x,2),y0,'x_label','Step','y_label','Outputs',
      'figure_title','Neural_Net');
else
  y = y0;
end
```

Our network will use backpropagation as a training method [1]. This is a gradient descent method and it uses the derivatives output by the network directly. Because of this use of derivatives, any threshold functions such as a step function are substituted with a sigmoid function for the training. The main parameter is the learning rate α, which multiplies the gradient changes applied to the weights in each iteration. This is implemented in NeuralNetTraining.

```
function [w, e, layer] = NeuralNetTraining( x, y, layer )

%% NEURALNETTRAINING Training using back propagation.
% Computes the weights for a neural net using back propagation. If no
% inputs are given it will do a demo for the network
% where node 1 and node 2 use exp functions.
%
%   sin(    x) -- node 1
%                \ /       \
%                 \          ---> Output
%                 / \       /
%   sin(0.2*x) -- node 2
%
%% Form:
%   [w, e, layer] = NeuralNetTraining( x, y, layer )
%% Inputs
%   x          (n,r)      n Inputs, r Runs
%
%   y          (m(k),r)   Desired Outputs
%
%   layer      (k,{1,r})  Data structure containing network data
%                         There are k layers to the network which
%                         includes 1 output and k-1 hidden layers
%
%                         .w(m(j),m(j-1))  w(p,q) is the weight between the
%                                          q-th  output of layer j-1 and the
%                                          p-th nodeof layer j (ie. the q-th
%                                          input to the p-th output of layer
%                                          j)
%                         .w0(m(j))        Biases/Thresholds
%                         .type(1)         'tanh', 'log', 'mag', 'sign',
%                                          'step'
%                         .alpha(1)        Learning rate
%
%                         Only one type and learning rate are allowed per
%                         layer
%
%% Outputs
%   w          (k)        Weights of layer j
%                         .w(m(j),m(j-1))  w(p,q) is the weight between the
%                                          q-th output of layer j-1 and the
%                                          p-th node of layer j (ie. the q-th
%                                          input to the p-th output of layer
%                                          j)
%                         .w0(m(j))        Biases/Thresholds
%
%   e          (m(k),r)   Errors
%
%   layer      (k,r)      Information about a desired layer j
%                         .x(m(j-1),1)   Inputs to layer j
%                         .y(m(j),1)     Outputs of layer j
%                         .dYT(m(j),1)   Derivative of layer j
```

```
%                    .w(m(j),m(j-1)  Weights of layer j
%                    .w0(m(j))       Thresholds of layer j
%
%-------------------------------------------------------------------------
%    (:)        Means that the dimension is undefined.
%    (n)      = number of inputs to neural net
%    (r)      = number of runs (ie. sets of inputs)
%    (k)      = number of layers
%    (m(j))   = number of nodes in j-th layer
%-------------------------------------------------------------------------
%% Reference: Nilsson, Nils J. (1998.) Artificial Intelligence:
%             A New Synthesis. Morgan Kaufmann Publishers. Ch. 3.

% Input Processing
%-----------------
if( ~isfield(layer,'w') )
  error('Must input size of neural net.');
end;

if( ~isfield(layer,'w0') )
  layer(1).w0 = [];
end;

if( ~isfield(layer,'type') )
  layer(1).type = [];
end;

if( ~isfield(layer,'alpha') )
  layer(1).type = [];
end;

% Generate some useful sizes
%---------------------------
nLayers  = size(layer,1);
nInputs  = size(x,1);
nRuns    = size(x,2);

if( size(y,2) ~= nRuns )
  error('The number of input and output columns must be equal.')
end;

for j = 1:nLayers
  if( isempty(layer(j,1).w) )
    error('Must input weights for all layers')
  end;
  if( isempty(layer(j,1).w0) )
    layer(j,1).w0 = zeros( size(layer(j,1).w,1), 1 );
  end;
end;
nOutputs = size(layer(nLayers,1).w, 1 );
```

```
% If there are multiple layers and only one type
% replicate it (the first layer type is the default)
%--------------------------------------------------
if( isempty(layer(1,1).type) )
  layer(1,1).type = 'tanh';
end;

if( isempty(layer(1,1).alpha) )
  layer(1,1).alpha = 0.5;
end;

for j = 2:nLayers
  if( isempty(layer(j,1).type) )
    layer(j,1).type = layer(1,1).type;
  end;
  if( isempty( layer(j,1).alpha) )
    layer(j,1).alpha = layer(1,1).alpha;
  end;
end;

% Set up additional storage
%--------------------------
h     = waitbar(0,'Allocating_Memory');

y0    = zeros(nOutputs,nRuns);
dY    = zeros(nOutputs,nRuns);

for k = 1:nLayers
  [outputs,inputs]    = size( layer(k,1).w );
  temp.layer(k,1).w              = layer(k,1).w;
  temp.layer(k,1).w0             = layer(k,1).w0;
  temp.layer(k,1).type           = layer(k,1).type;

  for j = 1:nRuns
    layer(k,j).w     = zeros(outputs,inputs);
    layer(k,j).w0    = zeros(outputs,1);
    layer(k,j).x     = zeros(inputs,1);
    layer(k,j).y     = zeros(outputs,1);
    layer(k,j).dY    = zeros(outputs,1);
    layer(k,j).delta = zeros(outputs,1);

    waitbar( ((k-1)*nRuns+j) / (nLayers*nRuns) );
  end;
end;

close(h);

% Perform back propagation
%--------------------------
h = waitbar(0, 'Neural_Net_Training_in_Progress' );
for j = 1:nRuns
```

```
        % Work backward from the output layer
        %-------------------------------------
        [yN, dYN,layerT]    = NeuralNetMLFF( x(:,j), temp );
        e(:,j)              = y(:,j) - yN(:,1);

    for k = 1:nLayers
        layer(k,j).w  = temp.layer(k,1).w;
        layer(k,j).w0 = temp.layer(k,1).w0;
        layer(k,j).x  = layerT(k,1).x;
        layer(k,j).y  = layerT(k,1).y;
        layer(k,j).dY = layerT(k,1).dY;
    end;

    layer(nLayers,j).delta = e(:,j).*dYN(:,1);

        for k  = (nLayers-1):-1:1
        layer(k,j).delta = layer(k,j).dY.*(temp.layer(k+1,1).w'*layer(k+1,j).
            delta);
    end

    for k = 1:nLayers
        temp.layer(k,1).w  = temp.layer(k,1).w  + layer(k,1).alpha*layer(k,j).
            delta*layer(k,j).x';
        temp.layer(k,1).w0 = temp.layer(k,1).w0 - layer(k,1).alpha*layer(k,j).
            delta;
    end;

    waitbar(j/nRuns);

end
w = temp.layer;

close(h);

% Output processing
%------------------
if( nargout == 0 )
    PlotSet( 1:size(e,2), e, 'Step', 'Error', 'Neural_Net_Training' );
end
```

9.3 Train a Network with One Output Node

9.3.1 Problem

We want to train the neural network to classify numbers. A good first step is identifying a single number. In this case, we will have a single output node, and our training data will include our desired digit, starting with 0, plus a few other digits.

9.3.2 Solution

We can create this neural network with our GUI, shown in Figure 9.3. We can try training the net with the output node having different types, such as `sign` and `logistic`. In our case, we start with a `sigmoid` function for the hidden layer and a `step` function for the output node.

Figure 9.3: A neural net with 256 inputs, one per pixel, an intermediate layer with 30 nodes, and one output.

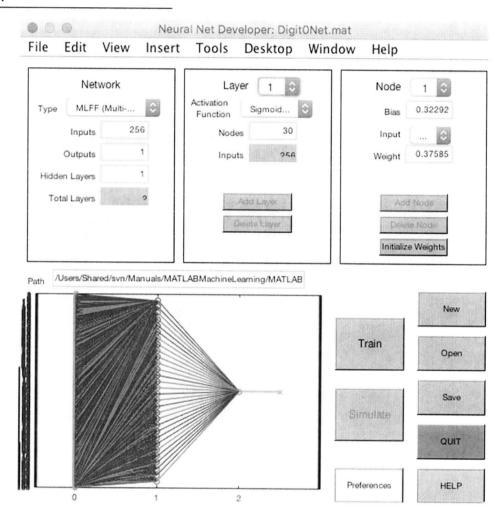

Figure 9.4: The Neural Net Training GUI.

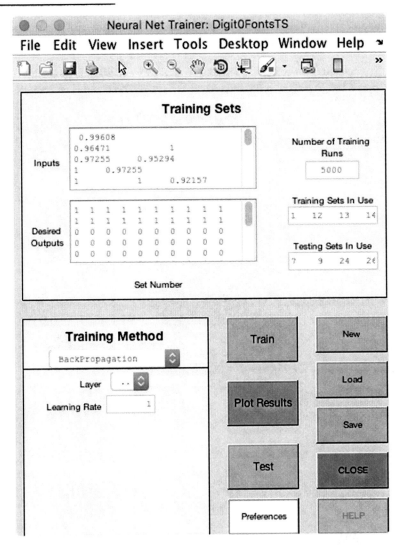

Our GUI has a separate training window, Figure 9.4. It has buttons for loading and saving training sets, training, and testing the trained neural net. It will plot results automatically based on preferences selected.

9.3.3 How It Works

Then we build the network with 256 inputs, 1 for each pixel; 30 nodes in 1 hidden layer; and 1 output node. We load the training data from the first recipe into the Trainer GUI, and we must select the number of training runs. Two thousand runs should be sufficient if our neuron functions are selected properly. We have an additional parameter to select, the learning rate for the backpropagation; it is reasonable to start with a value of 1.0. Note that our training data script assigned 75% of the images for training and

Figure 9.5: Layer 2 node weights and biases evolution.

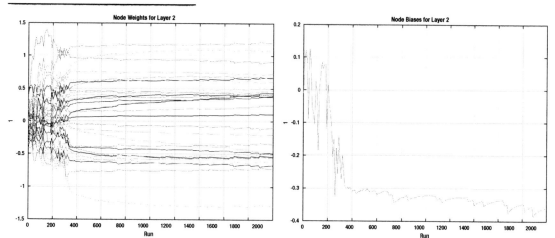

Figure 9.6: Single-digit training error and RMS error.

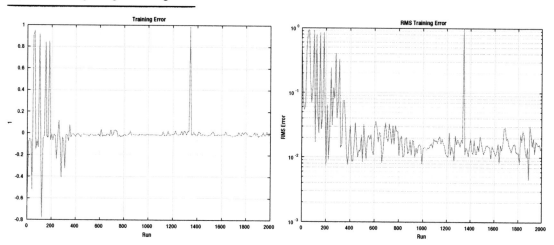

reserved the remainder for testing, using `randperm` to extract a random set of images. The training records the weights and biases for each run and generates plots on completion. We can easily plot these for the output node, which has just 30 nodes and 1 bias. See Figure 9.5.

The training function also outputs the training error as the net evolves and the root-mean-square (RMS) of the error.

Since we have a large number of input neurons, a line plot is not very useful for visualizing the evolution of the weights for the hidden later. However, we can view the weights at any given iteration as an image. Figure 9.7 shows the weights for the network with 30 nodes after training visualized using `imagesc`. We may wonder if we really need all 30 nodes in the hidden layer, or if we could extract the necessary number of features identifying our chosen digit with fewer. In the image on the right, the weights are shown sorted along the dimension of the input pixels for each node; we can clearly see that only a few nodes seem to have much variation from the random values they are initialized with. That is, many of our nodes seem to be having no impact.

159

Figure 9.7: Single-digit network, 30-node hidden layer weights. The image on the left shows the weight value. The image on the rights shows the weights sorted by pixel for each node.

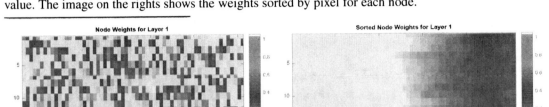

Since this visualization seems helpful, we add the code to the training GUI after the generation of the weights line plots. We create two images in one figure, the initial value of the weights on the left and the training values on the right. The HSV colormap looks more striking here than the default Parula map. The code that generates the images in `NeuralNetTrainer` looks like this:

```
% New figure: weights as image
newH = figure('name',['Node_Weights_for_Layer_' num2str(j)]);
endWeights = [h.train.network(j,1).w(:);h.train.network(j,end).w(:)];
minW = min(endWeights);
maxW = max(endWeights);
subplot(1,2,1)
imagesc(h.train.network(j,1).w,[minW maxW])
colorbar
ylabel('Output_Node')
xlabel('Input_Node')
title('Weights_Before_Training')
subplot(1,2,2)
imagesc(h.train.network(j,end).w,[minW maxW])
colorbar
xlabel('Input_Node')
title('Weights_After_Training')
        colormap hsv
h.resultsFig = [newH; h.resultsFig];
```

Note that we compute the minimum and maximum weight values among both the initial and final iterations, for scaling the two colormaps the same. Now, since many of our 30 initial nodes seemed unneeded, we reduce the number of nodes in that layer to 10, reinitialize the weights (randomly), and train again. Now we get our new figure with the weights displayed as an image bot before and after the training, Figure 9.8.

Now we can see more patches of colors that have diverged from the initial random weights in the images for the 256 pixel weights, and we see clear variation in the weights for the second layer as well.

Figure 9.8: Single-digit network, 10-node hidden layer weights before and after training. The first figure shows the images for the first layer, and the second for the second layer, which has just one output.

Node weights for Layer 1:

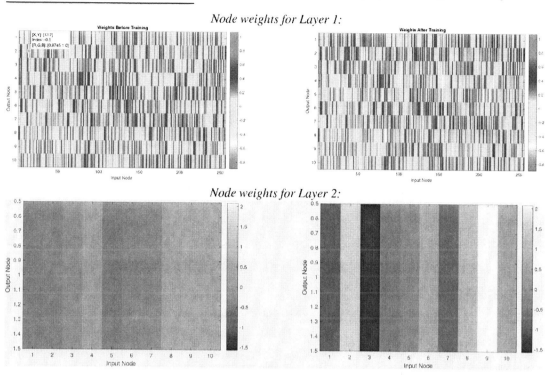

Node weights for Layer 2:

9.4 Testing the Neural Network

9.4.1 Problem

We want to test the neural net.

9.4.2 Solution

We can test the network with inputs that were not used in training. This is explicitly allowed in the GUI as it has separate indices for the training data and testing data. We selected 150 of our sample images for training and saved the remaining 50 for testing in our `DigitTrainingData` script.

9.4.3 How It Works

In the case of our GUI, simply click the test button to run the neural network with each of the cases selected for training.

Figure 9.9 shows the results for a network with the output node using the sigmoid magnitude function and another case with the output node using a step function; that is, the output is limited to 0 or 1.

The GUI allows you to save the trained net for future use.

Figure 9.9: Neural net results with sigmoid (left) and step (right) activation functions.

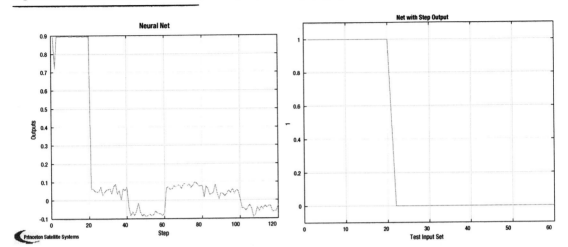

9.5   Train a Network with Multiple Output Nodes

9.5.1 Problem

We want to build a neural net that can detect all 10 digits separately.

9.5.2 Solution

Add nodes so that the output layer has 10 nodes, each of which will be 0 or 1 when the representative digit (0–9) is input. Try the output nodes with different functions, like logistic and step. Now that we have more digits, we will go back to having 30 nodes in the hidden layer.

9.5.3 How It Works

Our training data now consist of all 10 digits, with a binary output of zeros with a 1 in the correct slot. For example, a 1 will be represented as

$$[0\ 1\ 0\ 0\ 0\ 0\ 0\ 0\ 0]$$

We follow the same procedure for training. We initialize the net, load the training set into the GUI, and specify the number of training runs for the backpropagation.

The training data, in Figure 9.11, shows that much of the learning is achieved in the first 3000 runs.

The test data, in Figure 9.12, show that each set of digits (in sets of 20 in this case, for 200 total tests) is correctly identified.

Once you have saved a net that is working well to a MAT-file, you can call it with new data using the function `NeuralNetMLFF`.

162

```
>> data = load('NeuralNetMat');
>> network = data.DigitsStepNet;
>> y = NeuralNetMLFF( DigitTrainingTS.inputs(:,1), data.DigitsStepNet )
y =
     1
     0
     0
     0
     0
     0
     0
     0
     0
     0
```

Figure 9.10: Net with multiple outputs.

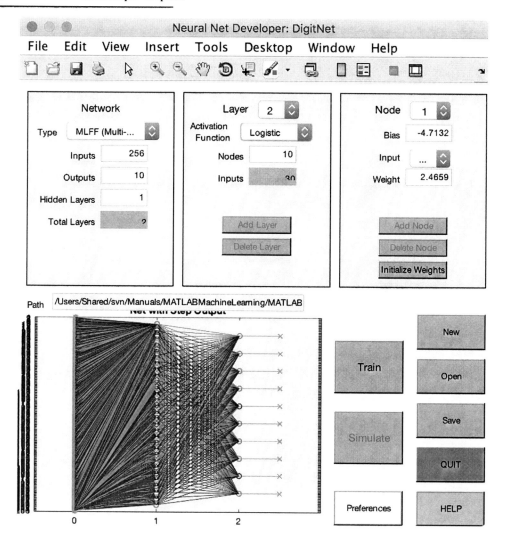

Figure 9.11: Training RMS for multiple-digit neural net.

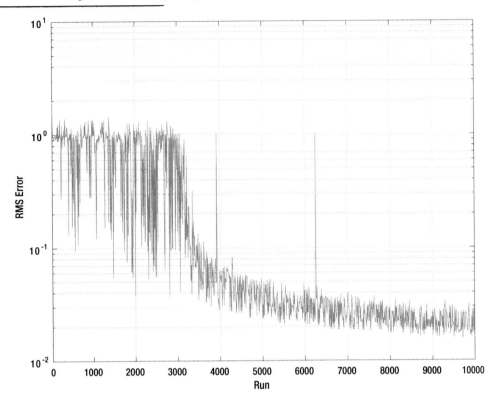

Figure 9.12: Test results for multiple-digit neural net.

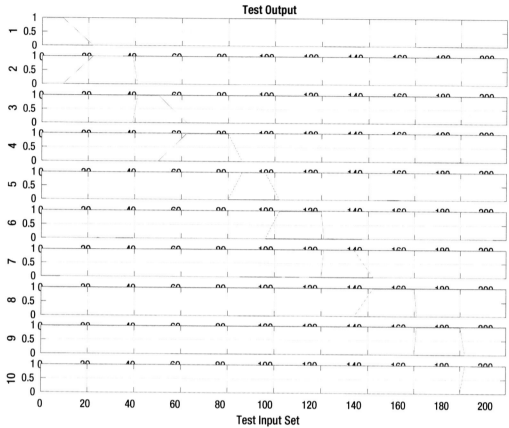

Again, it is fun to play with visualization of the neural net weights, to gain insight into the problem, and our problem is small enough that we can do so with images. We can view a single set of 256 weights for one hidden neuron as a 16 x 16 image, and view the whole set with each neuron its own row as before (Figure 9.13), to see the patterns emerging.

Figure 9.13: Multiple-digit neural net weights.

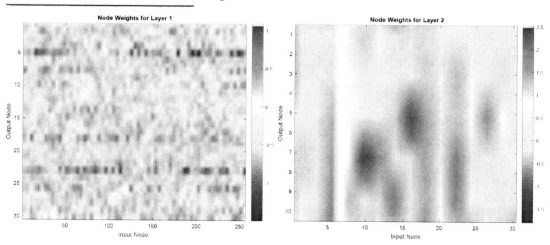

You can see parts of digits as mini-patterns in the individual node weights. Simply use `imagesc` with `reshape` like this:

```
>> figure;
>> imagesc(reshape(net.DigitsStepNet.layer(1).w(23,:),16,16));
>> title('Weights_to_Hidden_Node_23')
```

and see images as in Figure 9.14.

Figure 9.14: Multiple-digit neural net weights.

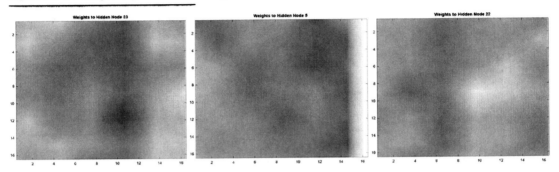

Summary

This chapter has demonstrated neural learning to classify digits. An interesting extension to our tool would be the use of image datastores, rather than a matrix representation of the input data. The tool as created can be used for any numeric input data, but once the data become "big," a more specific implementation will be called for. Table 9.1 gives the code introduced in the chapter.

Table 9.1: Chapter Code Listing

File	Description
DigitTrainingData	Create a training set of digit images
CreateDigitImage	Create a noisy image of a single digit
Neuron	Model an individual neuron with multiple activation functions
NeuralNetMLFF	Compute the output of a multilayer feedforward neural net
NeuralNetTraining	Training with backpropagation
DrawNeuralNet	Display a neural net with multiple layers
SaveTS	Save a training set MAT-file with index data

References

[1] Nils J. Nilsson. *Artificial Intelligence: A New Synthesis*. Morgan Kaufmann Publishers, 1998.

[2] S. Russell and P. Norvig. *Artificial Intelligence: A Modern Approach, Third Edition*. Prentice-Hall, 2010.

CHAPTER 10

■ ■ ■

Kalman Filters

Understanding or controlling a physical system often requires a model of the system, that is, knowledge of the characteristics and structure of the system. A model can be a predefined structure or can be determined solely through data. In the case of Kalman filtering, we create a model and use the model as a framework for learning about the system.

What is important about Kalman filters is that they rigorously account for uncertainty in a system that you want to know more about. There is uncertainty in the model of the system, if you have a model, and uncertainty (i.e., noise) in measurements of a system.

A system can be defined by its dynamical states and its parameters, which are nominally constant. For example, if you are studying an object sliding on a table, the states would be the position and velocity. The parameters would be the mass of the object and the friction coefficient. There might also be an external force on the object that we might want to estimate. The parameters and states compose the model. You need to know both to properly understand the system. Sometimes it is hard to decide if something should be a state of a parameter. Mass is usually a parameter, but in a plane, car, or rocket where the mass changes as fuel is consumed, it is often modeled as a state.

Kalman filters, invented by R. E. Kalman and others, are a mathematical framework for estimating or learning the states of a system. An estimator gives you statistically best estimates of the position and velocity. Kalman filters can also be written to identify the parameters of a system. Thus, the Kalman filter provides a framework for both state and parameter identification.

This field is also known as system identification. System identification is the process of identifying the structure and parameters of any system. For example, with a simple mass on a spring it would be the identification or determination of the mass and spring constant values along with determining the differential equation for modeling the system. It is a form of machine learning that has its origins in control theory. There are many methods of system identification. In this chapter we will study only the Kalman filter. The term "learning" is not usually associated with estimation, but it is really the same thing.

An important aspect of the system identification problem is determining what parameters and states can actually be estimated given the measurements that are available. This applies to all learning systems. The question is can we learn what we need to know about something through our observations? For this we want to know if a parameter or state is observable and can be independently distinguished. For example, suppose we are using Newton's law

$$F = ma \tag{10.1}$$

M. Paluszek and S. Thomas, *MATLAB Machine Learning*, DOI 10.1007/978-1-4842-2250-8_10

where F is force, m is mass, and a is acceleration as our model, and our measurement is acceleration. Can we estimate both force and mass? The answer is no because we are measuring the *ratio* of force to mass

$$a = \frac{F}{m} \qquad (10.2)$$

We can't separate the two. If we had a force sensor or a mass sensor we could determine each separately. You need to be aware of this issue in all learning systems including Kalman filters.

10.1 A State Estimator

10.1.1 Problem

You want to estimate the velocity and position of a mass attached through a spring and damper to a structure. The system is shown in Figure 10.1. m is the mass, k is the spring constant, c is the damping constant, and F is an external force. x is the position. The mass moves in only one direction.

Figure 10.1: Spring-mass-damper system. The mass is on the right. The spring is on the top to the left of the mass. The damper is below.

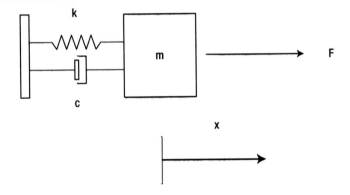

The continuous-time differential equations modeling the system are

$$\frac{dr}{dt} = v \qquad (10.3)$$

$$m\frac{dv}{dt} = f - cv - kx \qquad (10.4)$$

This says the change in position r with respect to time t is the velocity v. The change in velocity with respect to time is an external force, minus the damping constant times velocity, minus the spring constant times the position. The second equation is just Newton's law where

$$F = f - cv - kx \qquad (10.5)$$

$$\frac{dv}{dt} = a \qquad (10.6)$$

To simplify the problem we divide both sides of the second equation by mass and get

$$\frac{dr}{dt} = v \qquad (10.7)$$

$$\frac{dv}{dt} = a - 2\zeta\omega v - \omega^2 x \qquad (10.8)$$

where

$$\frac{c}{m} = 2\zeta\omega \tag{10.9}$$

$$\frac{k}{m} = \omega^2 \tag{10.10}$$

a is the acceleration, $\frac{f}{m}$, ζ is the damping ratio, and ω is the undamped natural frequency. The undamped natural frequency is the frequency at which the mass would oscillate if there was no damping. The damping ratio indicates how fast the system damps and what level of oscillations we observe. With a damping ratio of 0, the system never damps and the mass oscillates forever. With a damping ratio of 1, you don't see any oscillation. This form makes it easier to understand what damping and oscillation to expect. c and k don't make this clear.

The following simulation generates damped waveforms.

```
%% Damping ratio Demo
% Demonstrate an oscillator with different damping ratios.
%% See also
% RungeKutta, RHSOscillator, TimeLabel

%% Initialize
nSim          = 1000;         % Number of simulation steps
dT            = 0.1;          % Time step (sec)
d             = RHSOscillator;% Get the default data structure
d.a           = 0.0;          % Disturbance acceleration
d.omega       = 0.2;          % Oscillator frequency
zeta          = [0 0.2 0.7071 1];

%% Simulation
xPlot = zeros(length(zeta),nSim);
s     = cell(1,4);

for j = 1:length(zeta)
  d.zeta      = zeta(j);
  x           = [0;1];              % Initial state [position;velocity]
  s{j}    = sprintf('\\zeta_=_%6.4f',zeta(j));
  for k = 1:nSim
    % Plot storage
    xPlot(j,k)  = x(1);

    % Propagate (numerically integrate) the state equations
    x           = RungeKutta( @RHSOscillator, 0, x, dT, d );
  end
end

%% Plot the results
[t,tL]  = TimeLabel(dT*(0:(nSim-1)));
PlotSet(t,xPlot,'x_label',tL,'y_label','r','figure_title','Damping_Ratios','
    legend',s,'plot_set',{1:4})
```

The results of the simulation are shown in Figure 10.2. The initial conditions are a zero position and a velocity of 1. The responses to different levels of damping ratios are seen.

Figure 10.2: Spring-mass-damper system simulation with different damping ratios.

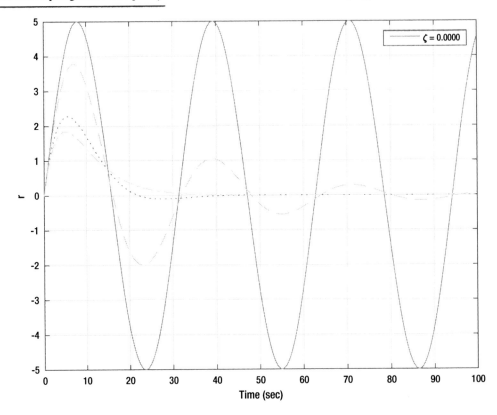

This is in true state-space form because the derivative of the state vector

$$x = \begin{bmatrix} r \\ v \end{bmatrix} \qquad (10.11)$$

has nothing multiplying it.

The right-hand side for the state equations (first-order differential equations) is shown in the following listing. Notice that if no inputs are requested, it returns the default data structure. The `if  (nargin < 1)` code tells the function to return the data structure if no inputs are given. This is a convenient way of helping people to use your functions.

```
%% RHSOSCILLATOR Right hand side of an oscillator.
%% Form
%   xDot = RHSOscillator( ~, x, a )
%
%% Description
% An oscillator models linear or rotational motion plus many other
% systems. It has two states, position and velocity. The equations of
% motion are:
%
%   rDot = v
%   vDot = a - 2*zeta*omega*v - omega^2*r
%
% This can be called by the MATLAB Recipes RungeKutta function or any MATLAB
```

```
% integrator. Time is not used.
%
% If no inputs are specified it will return the default data structure.
%
%% Inputs
%   t        (1,1) Time (unused)
%   x        (2,1) State vector [r;v]
%   d        (.)   Data structure
%                  .a     (1,1) Disturbance acceleration (m/s^2)
%                  .zeta  (1,1) Damping ratio
%                  .omega (1,1) Natural frequency (rad/s)
%
%% Outputs
%   x        (2,1) State vector derivative d[r;v]/dt
%

function xDot = RHSOscillator( ~, x, d )

if( nargin < 1 )
  xDot = struct('a',0,'omega',0.1,'zeta',0);
  return
end

xDot = [x(2);d.a-2*d.zeta*d.omega*x(2)-d.omega^2*x(1)];
```

The following listing is the simulation script. It causes the right-hand side to be numerically integrated. We start by getting the default data structure from the right-hand side. We fill it in with our desired parameters.

```
%% Initialize
nSim           = 1000;                 % Simulation end time (sec)
dT             = 0.1;                   % Time step (sec)
dRHS           = RHSOscillator;         % Get the default data structure
dRHS.a         = 0.1;                   % Disturbance acceleration
dRHS.omega     = 0.2;                   % Oscillator frequency
dRHS.zeta      = 0.1;                   % Damping ratio
x              = [0;0];                 % Initial state [position;velocity]
baseline       = 10;                    % Distance of sensor from start point
yR1Sigma       = 1;                     % 1 sigma position measurement noise
yTheta1Sigma   = asin(yR1Sigma/baseline);   % 1 sigma angle measurement
    noise

%% Simulation
xPlot = zeros(4,nSim);

for k = 1:nSim

  % Measurements
  yTheta       = asin(x(1)/baseline) + yTheta1Sigma*randn(1,1);
  yR           = x(1) + yR1Sigma*randn(1,1);

  % Plot storage
  xPlot(:,k)   = [x;yTheta;yR];
```

```
    % Propagate (numerically integrate) the state equations
    x             = RungeKutta( @RHSOscillator, 0, x, dT, dRHS );

end

%% Plot the results
yL      = {'r_ (m)' 'v_ (m/s)' 'y_\theta_ (rad)' 'y_r_ (m)'};
[t,tL]  = TimeLabel(dT*(0:(nSim-1)));

PlotSet( t, xPlot, 'x_label', tL, 'y_label', yL,...
  'plot_title', 'Oscillator', 'figure_title', 'Oscillator' );
```

The results of the simulation are shown in Figure 10.3. The input is a disturbance acceleration that goes from zero to its value at time $t = 0$. It is constant for the duration of the simulation. This is known as a step disturbance. This causes the system to oscillate. The magnitude of the oscillation slowly goes to zero because of the damping. If the damping ratio were 1, we would not see any oscillation.

Figure 10.3: Spring-mass-damper system simulation. The input is a step acceleration. The oscillation slowly damps out; that is, it goes to zero over time. The position develops an offset because of the constant acceleration.

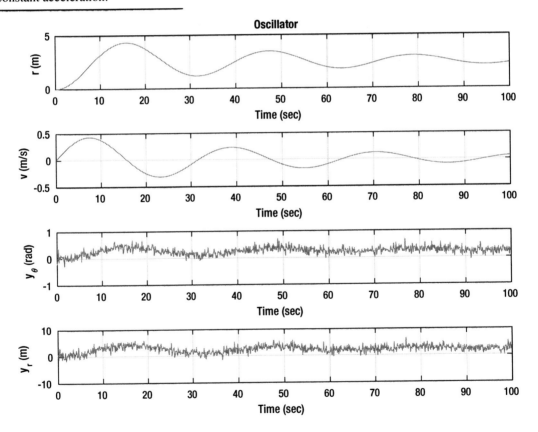

The offset is found analytically by setting $v = 0$. Essentially, the spring force is balancing the external force.

$$0 = \frac{dv}{dt} = a - \omega^2 x \tag{10.12}$$

$$x = \frac{a}{\omega^2} \tag{10.13}$$

We have now completed the derivation of our model and can move on to building the Kalman filters.

10.1.2 Solution

Kalman filters can be derived from Bayes' theorem. What is Bayes' theorem? Bayes' theorem is

$$P(A_i|B) = \frac{P(B|A_i)P(A_i)}{\sum P(B|A_i)} \tag{10.14}$$

$$P(A_i|B) = \frac{P(B|A_i)P(A_i)}{P(B)} \tag{10.15}$$

which is just the probability of A_i given B. P means "probability." The vertical bar $|$ means "given." This assumes that the probability of B is not zero; that is, $P(B) \neq 0$. In the Bayesian interpretation, the theorem introduces the effect of evidence on belief. This provides a rigorous framework for incorporating any data for which there is a degree of uncertainty. Put simply, given all evidence (or data) to date, Bayes' theorem allows you to determine how new evidence affects the belief. In the case of state estimation, this is the belief in the accuracy of the state estimate.

Figure 10.4 shows the Kalman filter family and how it relates to the Bayesian filter. In this book we are covering only the ones in the colored boxes. The complete derivation is given below; this provides a

Figure 10.4: The Kalman filter family tree.

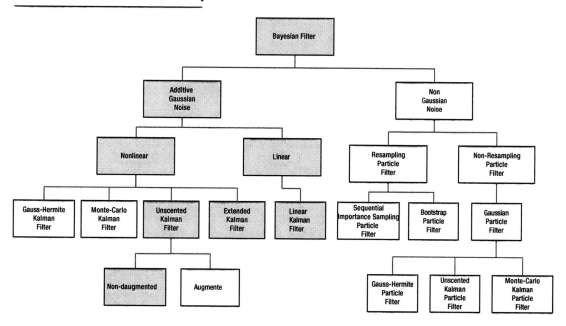

coherent framework for all Kalman filtering implementations. The different filters fall out of the Bayesian models based on assumptions about the model and sensor noise and the linearity or nonlinearity of the measurement and dynamics models. All of the filters are Markov; that is, the current dynamical state is entirely predictable from the previous state. Particle filters are not addressed in this book. They are a class of Monte Carlo methods. Monte Carlo (named after the famous casino) methods are computational algorithms that rely on random sampling to obtain results. For example, a Monte Carlo approach to our oscillator simulation would be to use the MATLAB function `nrandn` to generate the accelerations. We'd run many tests to verify that our mass moves as expected.

10.1.3 How It Works

Our derivation will use the notation $N(\mu, \sigma^2)$ to represent a normal, which is another word for Gaussian, variable, which means it is distributed as the normal distribution with mean μ (average) and variance σ^2. The following code computes a Gaussian or Normal distribution around a mean of 2 for a range of standard deviations. Figure 10.5 shows a plot. The height of the plot indicates how likely a given measurement of the variable is to have that value.

```
%% Initialize
mu          = 2;           % Mean
sigma       = [1 2 3 4];   % Standard deviation
n           = length(sigma);
x           = linspace(-7,10);

%% Simulation
xPlot = zeros(n,length(x));
s     = cell(1,n);

for k = 1:length(sigma)
  s{k}        = sprintf('Sigma_=_%3.1f',sigma(k));
  f           = -(x-mu).^2/(2*sigma(k)^2);
  xPlot(k,:) = exp(f)/sqrt(2*pi*sigma(k)^2);
end

%% Plot the results
h = figure;
set(h,'Name','Gaussian');
plot(x,xPlot)
grid
xlabel('x');
ylabel('Gaussian');
grid on
legend(s)
```

Figure 10.5: Normal or Gaussian random variable about a mean of 2.

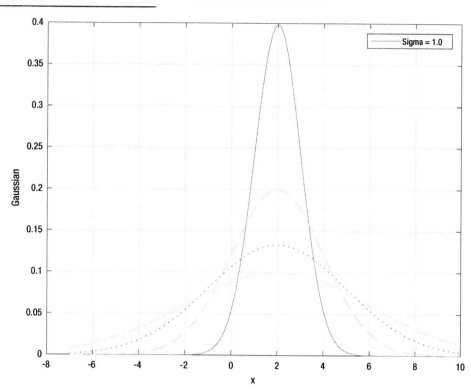

Given the probabilistic state-space model in discrete time [1]

$$x_k = f_k(x_{k-1}, w_{k-1}) \tag{10.16}$$

where x is the state vector and w is the noise vector, the measurement equation is

$$y_k = h_k(x_k, v_n) \tag{10.17}$$

where v_n is the measurement noise. This has the form of a hidden Markov model (HMM) because the state is hidden.

If the process is Markovian, that is, the future x_k is dependent only on the current state and is not dependent on the past states (the present is x_{k-1}), then

$$p(x_k|x_{1:k-1}, y_{1:k-1}) = p(x_k|x_{k-1}) \tag{10.18}$$

The | means given. In this case, the first term is read as "the probability of x_k given $x_{1:k-1}$ and $y_{1:k-1}$." This is the probability of the current state given all past states and all measurements up to the $k-1$ measurement. The past, x_{k-1}, is independent of the future given the present (which is x_k):

$$p(x_{k-1}|x_{k:T}, y_{k:T}) = p(x_{k-1}|x_k) \tag{10.19}$$

where T is the last sample and the measurements y_k are conditionally independent given x_k:

$$p(y_k|x_{1:k}, y_{1:k-1}) = p(y_k|x_k) \tag{10.20}$$

We can define the recursive Bayesian optimal filter that computes the distribution:

$$p(x_k|y_{1:k}) \tag{10.21}$$

given

- the prior distribution $p(x_0)$, where x_0 is the state prior to the first measurement,
- the state-space model

$$
\begin{aligned}
x_k &\sim p(x_k|x_{k-1}) &\tag{10.22}\\
y_k &\sim p(y_k|x_k) &\tag{10.23}
\end{aligned}
$$

- the measurement sequence $y_{1:k} = y_1, \ldots, y_k$.

Computation is based on the recursion rule

$$p(x_{k-1}|y_{1:k-1}) \to p(x_k|y_{1:k}) \tag{10.24}$$

This means we get the current state from the prior state and all the past measurements. Assume we know the posterior distribution of the previous time step

$$p(x_{k-1}|y_{1:k-1}) \tag{10.25}$$

The joint distribution of x_k, x_{k-1} given $y_{1:k-1}$ can be computed as

$$
\begin{aligned}
p(x_k, x_{k-1}|y_{1:k-1}) &= p(x_k|x_{k-1}, y_{1:k-1})p(x_{k-1}|y_{1:k-1}) &\tag{10.26}\\
&= p(x_k|x_{k-1})p(x_{k-1}|y_{1:k-1}) &\tag{10.27}
\end{aligned}
$$

because this is a Markov process. Integrating over x_{k-1} gives the prediction step of the optimal filter, which is the Chapman–Kolmogorov equation

$$p(x_k|y_{1:k-1}) = \int p(x_k|x_{k-1}, y_{1:k-1})p(x_{k-1}|y_{1:k-1})dx_{k-1} \tag{10.28}$$

The Chapman–Kolmogorov equation is an identity relating the joint probability distributions of different sets of coordinates on a stochastic process. The measurement update state is found from Bayes' rule

$$P(x_k|y_{1:k}) = \frac{1}{C_k}p(y_k|x_k)p(x_k|y_{k-1}) \tag{10.29}$$

$$C_k = p(y_k|y_{1:k-1}) = \int p(y_k|x_k)p(x_k|y_{1:k-1})dx_k \tag{10.30}$$

C_k is the probability of the current measurement, given all past measurements.

If the noise is additive and Gaussian with the state covariance Q_n and the measurement covariance R_n, the model and measurement noise have zero mean, we can write the state equation as

$$x_k = f_k(x_{k-1}) + w_{k-1} \tag{10.31}$$

where x is the state vector and w is the noise vector. The measurement equation becomes

$$y_k = h_k(x_k) + v_n \tag{10.32}$$

Given that Q is not time dependent, we can write

$$p(x_k|x_{k-1},y_{1:k-1}) = N(x_k; f(x_{k-1}),Q) \tag{10.33}$$

We can now write the prediction step, Eq. 10.28, as

$$p(x_k|y_{1:k-1}) = \int N(x_k; f(x_{k-1}),Q) p(x_{k-1}|y_{1:k-1}) dx_{k-1} \tag{10.34}$$

We need to find the first two moments of x_k. A moment is the expected value (or mean) of the variable. The first moment is of the variable, the second is of the variable squared, and so forth. They are

$$E[x_k] = \int x_k p(x_k|y_{1:k-1}) dx_k \tag{10.35}$$

$$E[x_k x_k^T] = \int x_k x_k^T p(x_k|y_{1:k-1}) dx_k \tag{10.36}$$

E means expected value. $E[x_k]$ is the mean and $E[x_k x_k^T]$ is the covariance. Expanding the first moment and using the identity $E[x] = \int x N(x; f(s),\Sigma) dx = f(s)$ where s is any argument gives

$$E[x_k] = \int x_k \left[\int N(x_k; f(x_{k-1}),Q) p(x_{k-1}|y_{1:k-1}) dx_{k-1} \right] dx_k \tag{10.37}$$

$$= \int x_k \left[\int N(x_k; f(x_{k-1}),Q) dx_k \right] p(x_{k-1}|y_{1:k-1}) dx_{k-1} \tag{10.38}$$

$$= \int f(x_{k-1}) p(x_{k-1}|y_{1:k-1}) dx_{k-1} \tag{10.39}$$

Assuming that $p(x_{k-1}|y_{1:k-1}) = N(x_{k-1}; \hat{x}_{k-1|k-1}, P_{k-1|k-1}^{xx})$ where P^{xx} is the covariance of x and noting that $x_k = f_k(x_{k-1}) + w_{k-1}$, we get

$$\hat{x}_{k|k-1} = \int f(x_{k-1}) N(x_{k-1}; \hat{x}_{k-1|k-1}, P_{k-1|k-1}^{xx}) dx_{k-1} \tag{10.40}$$

For the second moment we have

$$E[x_k x_k^T] = \int x_k x_k^T p(x_k|y_{1:k-1}) dx_k \tag{10.41}$$

$$= \int \left[\int (x_k; f(x_{k-1}),Q) x_k x_k^T dx_k \right] p(x_{k-1}|y_{1:k-1}) dx_{k-1} \tag{10.42}$$

which results in

$$P_{k|k-1}^{xx} = Q + \int f(x_{k-1}) f^T(x_{k-1}) N(x_{k-1}; \hat{x}_{k-1|k-1}, P_{k-1|k-1}^{xx}) dx_{k-1} - \hat{x}_{k|k-1}^T \hat{x}_{k|k-1} \tag{10.43}$$

The covariance for the initial state is Gaussian and is P_0^{xx}. The Kalman filter can be written without further approximations as

$$\hat{x}_{k|k} = \hat{x}_{k|k-1} + K_n \left[y_k - \hat{y}_{k|k-1} \right] \tag{10.44}$$

$$P_{k|k}^{xx} = P_{k|k-1}^{xx} - K_n P_{k|k-1}^{yy} K_n^T \tag{10.45}$$

$$K_n = P_{k|k-1}^{xy} \left[P_{k|k-1}^{yy} \right]^{-1} \tag{10.46}$$

179

where K_n is the Kalman gain and P^{yy} is the measurement covariance. The solution of these equations requires the solution of five integrals of the form

$$I = \int g(x)\mathrm{N}(x;\hat{x},P^{xx})dx \tag{10.47}$$

The three integrals needed by the filter are

$$P^{yy}_{k|k-1} = R + \int h(x_n)h^T(x_n)\mathrm{N}(x_n;\hat{x}_{k|k-1},P^{xx}_{k|k-1})dx_k - \hat{x}^T_{k|k-1}\hat{y}_{k|k-1} \tag{10.48}$$

$$P^{xy}_{k|k-1} = \int x_n h^T(x_n)\mathrm{N}(x_n;\hat{x}_{k|k-1},P^{xx}_{k|k-1})dx \tag{10.49}$$

$$\hat{y}_{k|k-1} = \int h(x_k)\mathrm{N}(x_k;\hat{x}_{k|k-1},P^{xx}_{k|k-1})dx_k \tag{10.50}$$

10.1.4 Conventional Kalman Filter

Assume we have a model of the form

$$x_k = A_{k-1}x_{k-1} + B_{k-1}u_{k-1} + q_{k-1} \tag{10.51}$$

$$y_k = H_k x_k + r_k \tag{10.52}$$

where

- $x_k \in \Re^n$ is the state of system at time k.
- A_{k-1} is the state transition matrix at time $k-1$.
- B_{k-1} is the input matrix at time $k-1$.
- $q_{k-1}\mathrm{N}(0,Q_k)$ is the process noise at time $k-1$.
- $y_k \in \Re^m$ is the measurement at time k.
- H_k is the measurement matrix at time k. This is found from the Jacobian of $h(x)$.
- $r_k\mathrm{N}(0,R_k)$ is the measurement noise at time k.
- The prior distribution of the state is $x_0 = \mathrm{N}(m_0,P_0)$, where parameters m_0 and P_0 contain all prior knowledge about the system. m_0 is the mean at time zero and P_0 is the covariance. Since our state is Gaussian, this completely describes the state.

$\Re^n$ means real numbers in a vector of order n; that is, the state has n quantities. In probabilistic terms the model is

$$p(x_k|x_{k-1}) = \mathrm{N}(x_k;A_{k-1}x_{k-1},Q_k) \tag{10.53}$$

$$p(y_k|x_k) = \mathrm{N}(y_k;H_k x_k,R_k) \tag{10.54}$$

The integrals become simple matrix equations. In these equations P^-_k means the covariance prior to the measurement update.

$$P^{yy}_{k|k-1} = H_k P^-_k H^T_k + R_k \tag{10.55}$$

$$P^{xy}_{k|k-1} = P^-_k H^T_k \tag{10.56}$$

$$P^{xx}_{k|k-1} = A_{k-1}P_{k-1}A^T_{k-1} + Q_{k-1} \tag{10.57}$$

$$\hat{x}_{k|k-1} = m^-_k \tag{10.58}$$

$$\hat{y}_{k|k-1} = H_k m^-_k \tag{10.59}$$

The prediction step becomes

$$m_k^- = A_{k-1}m_{k-1} \tag{10.60}$$
$$P_k^- = A_{k-1}P_{k-1}A_{k-1}^T + Q_{k-1} \tag{10.61}$$

The first term in the above covariance equation propagates the covariance based on the state transition matrix, A. Q_{k+1} adds to this to form the next covariance. Process noise Q_{k+1} is a measure of the accuracy of the mathematical model, A, in representing the system. For example, suppose A was a mathematical model that damped all states to zero. Without Q, P would go to zero. But if we really weren't that certain about the model, the covariance would never be less than Q. Picking Q can be difficult. In a dynamical system with uncertain disturbances you can compute the standard deviation of the disturbances to compute Q. If the model A is uncertain, then you might do a statistical analysis of the range of models. Or you can try different Q in simulation and see which ones work the best!

The update step is

$$v_k = y_k - H_k m_k^- \tag{10.62}$$
$$S_k = H_k P_k^- H_k^T + R_k \tag{10.63}$$
$$K_k = P_k^- H_k^T S_k^{-1} \tag{10.64}$$
$$m_k = m_k^- + K_k v_k \tag{10.65}$$
$$P_k = P_k^- - K_k S_k K_k^T \tag{10.66}$$

S_k is an intermediate quantity. v_k is the residual. The residual is the difference between the measurement and your estimate of the measurement given the estimated states. R is just the covariance matrix of the measurements. If the noise is not white, a different filter should be used. White noise has equal energy at all frequencies. Many types of noise, such as the noise from an imager, is not really white noise but are band limited; that is, it has noise in a limited range of frequencies. You can sometimes add additional states to A to model the noise better, for example, adding a low-pass filter to band limit the noise. This makes A bigger but is generally not an issue.

We will investigate the application of the Kalman filter to the oscillator. First we need a method of converting the continuous-time problem to discrete time. We only need to know the states at discrete times or at fixed intervals, T. We use the continuous to discrete transform that uses the MATLAB expm function shown in the following function.

```
function [f, g] = CToDZOH( a, b, T )

if( nargin < 1 )
  Demo;
  return
end

[n,m]   = size(b);
q       = expm([a*T b*T;zeros(m,n+m)]);
f       = q(1:n,1:n);
g       = q(1:n,n+1:n+m);

%% Demo
function Demo

T       = 0.5;
```

```
fprintf(1,'Double_integrator_with_a_%4.1f_second_time_step.\n',T);
a        = [0 1;0 0]
b        = [0;1]
[f, g]   = CToDZOH( a, b, T );
f
g
```

If you run the demo, for a double integrator, you get the following results. A double integrator is

$$\frac{d^2x}{dt^2} = a \qquad (10.67)$$

Written in state-space form, it is

$$\frac{dr}{dt} = v \qquad (10.68)$$

$$\frac{dv}{dt} = a \qquad (10.69)$$

or in matrix form

$$\dot{x} = Ax + Bu \qquad (10.70)$$

where

$$x = \begin{bmatrix} r \\ v \end{bmatrix} \qquad (10.71)$$

$$u = \begin{bmatrix} 0 \\ a \end{bmatrix} \qquad (10.72)$$

$$A = \begin{bmatrix} 0 & 1 \\ 0 & 0 \end{bmatrix} \qquad (10.73)$$

$$B = \begin{bmatrix} 0 \\ 1 \end{bmatrix} \qquad (10.74)$$

```
>> CToDZOH
Double integrator with a 0.5-s time step.
a =
      0      1
      0      0
b =
      0
      1
f =
    1.0000    0.5000
         0    1.0000
g =
    0.1250
    0.5000
```

The discrete plant matrix f is easy to understand. The position state at step $k+1$ is the state at k plus the velocity at step k multiplied by the time step T of 0.5 s. The velocity at step $k+1$ is the velocity at

k plus the time step times the acceleration at step k. The acceleration at the time k multiplies $\frac{1}{2}T^2$ to get the contribution to position. This is just the standard solution to a particle under a constant acceleration.

$$r_{k+1} = r_k + Tv_k + \frac{1}{2}T^2 a_k \qquad (10.75)$$

$$v_{k+1} = v_k + Ta_k \qquad (10.76)$$

In matrix form this is

$$x_{k+1} = fx_k + bu_k \qquad (10.77)$$

With the discrete-time approximation we can change the acceleration every step k to get the time history. This assumes that the acceleration is constant over the period T. We need to pick T so that this is approximately true if we are to get good results.

The script for testing the Kalman filter, KFSim.m, is shown below. KFInitialize is used to initialize the filter (a Kalman filter, 'kf', in this case).

```
%% KFINITIALIZE Kalman Filter initialization

%%  Form:
%   d = KFInitialize( type, varargin )
%
%% Description

%   Initializes Kalman Filter data structures for the KF, UKF,  EKF and
%   UKFP, parameter update..
%
%   Enter parameter pairs after the type.
%
%   If you return with only one input it will return the default data
%   structure for the filter specified by type. Defaults are returned
%   for any parameter you do not enter.
%
%
%% Inputs
%   type                (1,1) Type of filter 'ukf', 'kf', 'ekf'
%   varargin            {:}   Parameter pairs
%
%% Outputs
%   d                   (1,1) Data structure
%

function d = KFInitialize( type, varargin )

% Default data structures
switch lower(type)
        case 'ukf'
    d = struct( 'm',[],'alpha',1, 'kappa',0,'beta',2, 'dT',0,...
                'p',[],'q',[],'f','','fData',[], 'hData',[],'hFun','','t',0)
                ;

        case 'kf'
    d = struct( 'm',[],'a',[],'b',[],'u',[],'h',[],'p',[],...
```

183

```
              'q',[],'r',[], 'y',[]);

        case 'ekf'
    d = struct( 'm',[],'x',[],'a',[],'b',[],'u',[],'h',[],'hX',[],'hData'
        ,[],'fX',[],'p',[],...
                'q',[],'r',[],'t',0, 'y',[],'v',[],'s',[],'k',[]);

        case 'ukfp'
    d = struct( 'm',[],'alpha',1, 'kappa',0,'beta',2, 'dT',0,...
                'p',[],'q',[],'f','','fData',[], 'hData',[],'hFun','','t',0,
                'eta',[]);

  otherwise
    error([type '_is_not_available']);
end

% Return the defaults
if( nargin == 1 )
    return
end

% Cycle through all the parameter pairs
for k = 1:2:length(varargin)
    switch lower(varargin{k})
        case 'a'
            d.a      = varargin{k+1};

        case {'m' 'x'}
            d.m      = varargin{k+1};
            d.x      = varargin{k+1};

        case 'b'
            d.b      = varargin{k+1};

        case 'u'
            d.u      = varargin{k+1};

        case 'hx'
            d.hX     = varargin{k+1};

        case 'fx'
            d.fX     = varargin{k+1};

        case 'h'
            d.h      = varargin{k+1};

        case 'hdata'
            d.hData    = varargin{k+1};

        case 'hfun'
            d.hFun      = varargin{k+1};
```

```
    case 'p'
        d.p     = varargin{k+1};

    case 'q'
        d.q     = varargin{k+1};

    case 'r'
        d.r     = varargin{k+1};

    case 'f'
        d.f     = varargin{k+1};

    case 'eta'
        d.eta   = varargin{k+1};

    case 'alpha'
        d.alpha = varargin{k+1};

    case 'kappa'
        d.kappa = varargin{k+1};

    case 'beta'
        d.beta      = varargin{k+1};

    case 'dt'
        d.dT        = varargin{k+1};

    case 't'
        d.t   = varargin{k+1};

    case 'fdata'
        d.fData = varargin{k+1};

    case 'nits'
        d.nIts  = varargin{k+1};

    case 'kmeas'
        d.kMeas = varargin{k+1};

    end
end
```

You set up the Kalman filter by first converting the continuous-time model into discrete time. You add KFPredict and KFUpdate to the simulation loop. Be careful to put the predict and update steps in the right places so that the estimator is synchronized with simulation time. The simulation starts by assigning values to all of the variables used in the simulation. We get the data structure from the function RHSOscillator and then modify its values. We write the continuous-time model in matrix form and then convert it to discrete time. randn is used to add Gaussian noise to the simulation. The rest is the simulation loop with plotting afterward.

```
%% KFSim
% Demonstrate a Kalman Filter.
%% See also
% RungeKutta, RHSOscillator, TimeLabel, KFInitialize, KFUpdate, KFPredict

%% Initialize
tEnd            = 100.0;        % Simulation end time (sec)
dT              = 0.1;          % Time step (sec)
d               = RHSOscillator;   % Get the default data structure
d.a             = 0.1;          % Disturbance acceleration
d.omega         = 0.2;          % Oscillator frequency
d.zeta          = 0.1;          % Damping ratio
x               = [0;0];        % Initial state [position;velocity]
y1Sigma         = 1;            % 1 sigma position measurement noise

% xdot = a*x + b*u
a               = [0 1;-2*d.zeta*d.omega -d.omega^2]; % Continuous time model
b               = [0;1];        % Continuous time input matrix

% x[k+1] = f*x[k] + g*u[k]
[f,g]           = CToDZOH(a,b,dT);   % Discrete time model
xE              = [0.3; 0.1];   % Estimated initial state
q               = [1e-6 1e-6];  % Model noise covariance ;
                                % [1e-4 1e-4] is for low model noise test
dKF             = KFInitialize('kf','m',xE,'a',f,'b',g,'h',[1 0],...
                       'r',y1Sigma^2,'q',diag(q),'p',diag(xE.^2));

%% Simulation
nSim  = floor(tEnd/dT) + 1;
xPlot = zeros(5,nSim);

for k = 1:nSim

  % Measurements
  y          = x(1) + y1Sigma*randn(1,1);

  % Update the Kalman Filter
  dKF.y      = y;
  dKF        = KFUpdate(dKF);

  % Plot storage
  xPlot(:,k)  = [x;y;dKF.m-x];

  % Propagate (numerically integrate) the state equations
  x          = RungeKutta( @RHSOscillator, 0, x, dT, d );

  % Propagate the Kalman Filter
  dKF.u      = d.a;
      dKF            = KFPredict(dKF);

end
```

```
%% Plot the results
yL      = {'r_(m)' 'v_(m/s)'  'y_(m)' '\Delta_r_E_(m)' '\Delta_v_E_(m/s)' };
[t,tL] = TimeLabel(dT*(0:(nSim-1)));

PlotSet( t, xPlot, 'x_label', tL, 'y_label', yL,...
   'plot_title', 'Oscillator', 'figure_title', 'KF_Demo' );
```

The prediction Kalman filter step is shown in the following listing. The prediction propagates the state one time step and propagates the covariance matrix with it. It is saying that when we propagate the state there is uncertainty so we must add that to the covariance matrix.

```
function d = KFPredict( d )

% The first path is if there is no input matrix b
if( isempty(d.b) )
  d.m = d.a*d.m;
else
  d.m = d.a*d.m + d.b*d.u;
end

d.p = d.a*d.p*d.a' + d.q;
```

The update Kalman filter step is shown in the following listing. This adds the measurements to the estimate and accounts for the uncertainty (noise) in the measurements.

```
function d = KFUpdate( d )

s   = d.h*d.p*d.h' + d.r;      % Intermediate value
k   = d.p*d.h'/s;           % Kalman gain
v   = d.y - d.h*d.m;        % Residual
d.m = d.m + k*v;            % Mean update
d.p = d.p - k*s*k';         % Covariance update
```

You will note that the "memory" of the filter is stored in the data structure. No persistent data storage is used. This makes it easier to use these functions in multiple places in your code. Note also that you don't have to call KFUpdate every time step. You need only call it when you have new data. However, the filter does assume uniform time steps.

The script gives two examples for the model noise covariance matrix. Figure 10.6 shows results when high numbers, [1e-4 1e-4], for the model covariance are used. Figure 10.7 when lower numbers, [1e-6 1e-6], are used. We don't change the measurement covariance because only the ratio between noise covariance and model covariance is important.

When the higher numbers are used, the errors are Gaussian but noisy. When the low numbers are used, the result is very smooth, with little noise seen. However, the errors are large in the low model covariance case. This is because the filter is essentially ignoring the measurements since it thinks the model is very accurate. You should try different options in the script and see how it performs. As you can see, the parameters make a huge difference in how well the filter learns about the states of the system.

Figure 10.6: The Kalman filter results with the higher-model-noise matrix, `[1e-4 1e-4]`.

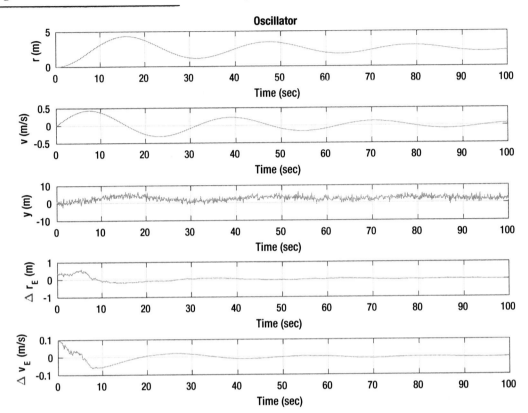

Figure 10.7: The Kalman filter results with the lower-model-noise matrix, [1e-6 1e-6]. Less noise is seen but the errors are large.

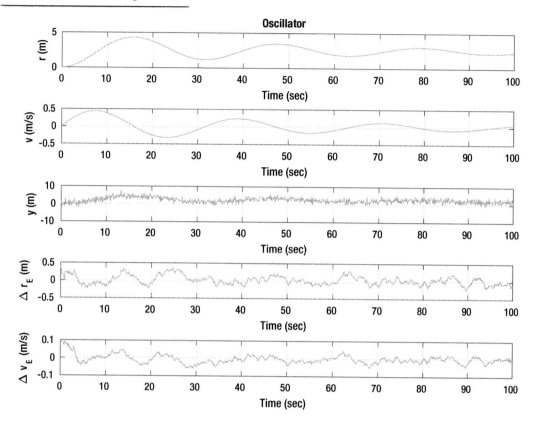

The extended Kalman filter was developed to handle models with nonlinear dynamical models and/or nonlinear measurement models. Given a nonlinear model of the form

$$x_k = f(x_{k-1}, k-1) + q_{k-1} \tag{10.78}$$

$$y_k = h(x_k, k) + r_k \tag{10.79}$$

the prediction step is

$$m_k^- = f(m_{k-1}, k-1) \tag{10.80}$$

$$P_k^- = F_x(m_{k-1}, k-1) P_{k-1} F_x(m_{k-1}, k-1)^T + Q_{k-1} \tag{10.81}$$

F is the Jacobian of f. The update step is

$$v_k = y_k - h(m_k^-, k) \tag{10.82}$$

$$S_k = H_x(m_k^-, k) P_k^- H_x(m_k^-, k)^T + R_k \tag{10.83}$$

$$K_k = P_k^- H_x(m_k^-, k)^T S_k^{-1} \tag{10.84}$$

$$m_k = m_k^- + K_k v_k \tag{10.85}$$

$$P_k = P_k^- - K_k S_k K_k^T \tag{10.86}$$

189

$F_x(m, k-1)$ and $H_x(m, k)$ are the Jacobians of the nonlinear functions f and h. The Jacobians are just a matrix of partial derivatives of F and H. This results in matrices from the vectors F and H. For example, assume we have $f(x, y)$, which is

$$f = \begin{bmatrix} f_x(x, y) \\ f_y(x, y) \end{bmatrix} \tag{10.87}$$

The Jacobian is

$$F_k = \begin{bmatrix} \frac{\partial f_x(x_k, y_k)}{\partial x} & \frac{\partial f_x(x_k, y_k)}{\partial y} \\ \frac{\partial f_y(x_k, y_k)}{\partial x} & \frac{\partial f_y(x_k, y_k)}{\partial y} \end{bmatrix} \tag{10.88}$$

The matrix is computed at x_k, y_k.

The Jacobians can be found analytically or numerically. If done numerically, the Jacobian needs to be computed about the current value of m_k. In the iterated extended Kalman filter, the update step is done in a loop using updated values of m_k after the first iteration. $H_x(m, k)$ needs to be updated on each step.

We don't give an example using the extended Kalman filter but include the code for you to explore.

10.2 Using the Unscented Kalman Filter for State Estimation

10.2.1 Problem

You want to learn the states of the spring-damper-mass system given a nonlinear angle measurement.

10.2.2 Solution

The solution is to create an unscented Kalman filter (UKF) as a state estimator. This will absorb measurements and determine the state. It will autonomously learn about the state of system based on a preexisting model.

10.2.3 How It Works

With the UKF we work with the nonlinear dynamical and measurement equations directly. We don't have to linearize them. The UKF is also known as a σ point filter because it simultaneously maintains models one sigma (standard deviation) from the mean.

In the following sections we develop the equations for the nonaugmented Kalman filter. This form only allows for additive Gaussian noise. This assumes additive Gaussian noise. Given a nonlinear model of the form

$$\begin{align} x_k &= f(x_{k-1}, k-1) + q_{k-1} \tag{10.89} \\ y_k &= h(x_k, k) + r_k \tag{10.90} \end{align}$$

define weights as

$$W_m^0 = \frac{\lambda}{n+\lambda} \tag{10.91}$$

$$W_c^0 = \frac{\lambda}{n+\lambda} + 1 - \alpha^2 + \beta \tag{10.92}$$

$$W_m^i = \frac{\lambda}{2(n+\lambda)}, i = 1, \dots, 2n \tag{10.93}$$

$$W_c^i = \frac{\lambda}{2(n+\lambda)}, i = 1, \dots, 2n \tag{10.94}$$

Note that $W_m^i = W_c^i$.

$$\lambda = \alpha^2(n + \kappa) - n \tag{10.95}$$
$$c = \lambda + n = \alpha^2(n + \kappa) \tag{10.96}$$

α, β, and κ are scaling constants. General rules for the scaling constants are

- α: 0 for state estimation, 3 minus the number of states for parameter estimation

- β: Determines spread of sigma points. Smaller means more closely spaced sigma points.

- κ: Constant for prior knowledge. Set to 2 for Gaussian processes.

n is the order of the system. The weights can be put into matrix form.

$$w_m = \begin{bmatrix} W_m^0 \cdots W_m^{2n} \end{bmatrix}^T \tag{10.97}$$

$$W = (I - [w_m \cdots w_m]) \begin{bmatrix} W_c^0 & \cdots & 0 \\ \vdots & \ddots & \vdots \\ 0 & \cdots & W_c^{2n} \end{bmatrix} (I - [w_m \cdots w_m])^T \tag{10.98}$$

I is the $2n + 1$ by $2n + 1$ identity matrix. In the equation vector w_m is replicated $2n + 1$ times. W is $2n + 1$ by $2n + 1$. The weights are computed in UKFWeight.

```
%% UKFWEIGHT Unscented Kalman Filter weight calculation
%% Form:
%   d = UKFWeight( d )
%
%% Description
%   Unscented Kalman Filter weights.
%
%   The weight matrix is used by the matrix form of the Unscented
%   Transform. Both UKSPredict and UKSUpdate use the data structure
%   generated by this function.
%
%   The constant alpha determines the spread of the sigma points around x
%   and is usually set to between 10e-4 and 1. beta incorporates prior
%   knowledge of the distribution of x and is 2 for a Gaussian
%   distribution. kappa is set to 0 for state estimation and 3 - number of
%   states for parameter estimation.
%   d = UKFWeight( d )
%% Inputs
%   d    (1,1)    Data structure with constants
%                 .kappa   (1,1)   0 for state estimation, 3-#states for
%                                  parameter estimation
%                 .m       (:,1)   Vector of mean states
%                 .alpha   (1,1)   Determines spread of sigma points
%                 .beta    (1,1)   Prior knowledge - 2 for Gaussian
%
%% Outputs
%   d    (1,1)    Data structure with constants
%                 .w       (2*n+1,2*n+1)   Weight matrix
```

```
%             .wM     (1,2*n+1)        Weight array
%             .wC     (2*n+1,1)        Weight array
%             .c      (1,1)            Scaling constant
%             .lambda (1,1)            Scaling constant
%

function d = UKFWeight( d )

% Compute the fundamental constants
n             = length(d.m);
a2            = d.alpha^2;
d.lambda      = a2*(n + d.kappa) - n;
nL            = n + d.lambda;
wMP           = 0.5*ones(1,2*n)/nL;
d.wM          = [d.lambda/nL              wMP]';
d.wC          = [d.lambda/nL+(1-a2+d.beta) wMP];

d.c           = sqrt(nL);

% Build the matrix
f             = eye(2*n+1) - repmat(d.wM,1,2*n+1);
d.w           = f*diag(d.wC)*f';
```

The prediction step is

$$X_{k-1} = \begin{bmatrix} m_{k-1} & \cdots & m_{k-1} \end{bmatrix} + \sqrt{c}\begin{bmatrix} 0 & \sqrt{P_{k-1}} & -\sqrt{P_{k-1}} \end{bmatrix} \tag{10.99}$$

$$\hat{X}_k = f(X_{k-1}, k-1) \tag{10.100}$$

$$m_k^- = \hat{X}_k w_m \tag{10.101}$$

$$P_k^- = \hat{X}_k W \hat{X}_k^T + Q_{k-1} \tag{10.102}$$

where X is a matrix where each column is the state vector possibly with an added sigma point vector. The update step is

$$X_k^- = \begin{bmatrix} m_k^- & \cdots & m_k^- \end{bmatrix} + \sqrt{c}\begin{bmatrix} 0 & \sqrt{P_k^-} & -\sqrt{P_k^-} \end{bmatrix} \tag{10.103}$$

$$Y_k^- = h(X_k^-, k) \tag{10.104}$$

$$\mu_k = Y_k^- w_m \tag{10.105}$$

$$S_k = Y_k^- W[Y_k^-]^T + R_k \tag{10.106}$$

$$C_k = X_k^- W[Y_k^-]^T \tag{10.107}$$

$$K_k = C_k S_k^{-1} \tag{10.108}$$

$$m_k = m_k^- + K_k(y_k - \mu_k) \tag{10.109}$$

$$P_k = P_k^- - K_k S_k K_k^T \tag{10.110}$$

μ_k is a matrix of the measurements in which each column is a copy modified by the sigma points. S_k and C_k are intermediate quantities. The brackets around Y_k^- are just for clarity.

The script for testing the UKF, UKFSim, is shown below. As noted earlier, we don't need to convert the continuous-time model into discrete time. Instead, we pass the filter the right-hand side of the differential equations. You must also pass it a measurement model which can be nonlinear. You add UKFPredict and UKFUpdate to the simulation loop. We start by initializing all parameters. KFInitialize takes parameter pairs, after 'ukf' to initialize the filter. The remainder is the simulation loop and plotting.

```
%% UKFSim
% Demonstrate an Unscented Kalman Filter.
%% See also
% RungeKutta, RHSOscillator, TimeLabel, KFInitialize, UKFUpdate, UKFPredict
% AngleMeasurement

%% Initialize
nSim             = 5000;                  % Simulation steps
dT               = 0.1;                   % Time step (sec)
d                = RHSOscillator;         % Get the default data structure
d.a              = 0.1;                   % Disturbance acceleration
d.zeta           = 0.1;                   % Damping ratio
x                = [0;0];                 % Initial state [position;velocity]
y1Sigma          = 0.01;                  % 1 sigma measurement noise
dMeas.baseline   = 10;                    % Distance of sensor from start
xE               = [0;0];                 % Estimated initial state
q                = diag([0.01 0.001]);
p                = diag([0.001 0.0001]);
dKF              = KFInitialize( 'ukf','m',xE,'f',@RHSOscillator,'fData',d
    ,...
                                  'r',y1Sigma^2,'q',q,'p',p,...
                                  'hFun',@AngleMeasurement,'hData',dMeas,'dT',
                                  dT);
dKF              = UKFWeight( dKF );

%% Simulation
xPlot = zeros(5,nSim);


for k = 1:nSim

  % Measurements
  y            = AngleMeasurement( x, dMeas ) + y1Sigma*randn;

  % Update the Kalman Filter
  dKF.y        = y;
  dKF          = UKFUpdate(dKF);

  % Plot storage
  xPlot(:,k)   = [x;y;dKF.m-x];

  % Propagate (numerically integrate) the state equations
  x            = RungeKutta( @RHSOscillator, 0, x, dT, d );

  % Propagate the Kalman Filter
      dKF          = UKFPredict(dKF);

end
```

```
%% Plot the results
yL      = {'r␣(m)' 'v␣(m/s)'  'y␣(rad)' '\Delta␣r_E␣(m)' '\Delta␣v_E␣(m/s)'
        };
[t,tL]  = TimeLabel(dT*(0:(nSim-1)));

PlotSet( t, xPlot, 'x␣label', tL, 'y␣label', yL,...
```

The prediction UKF step is shown in the following listing.

```
function d = UKFPredict( d )

pS      = chol(d.p)';
nS      = length(d.m);
nSig    = 2*nS + 1;
mM      = repmat(d.m,1,nSig);
x       = mM + d.c*[zeros(nS,1) pS -pS];

xH      = Propagate( x, d );
d.m     = xH*d.wM;
d.p     = xH*d.w*xH' + d.q;
d.p     = 0.5*(d.p + d.p'); % Force symmetry

%% Propagate each sigma point state vector
function x = Propagate( x, d )

for j = 1:size(x,2)
        x(:,j) = RungeKutta( d.f, d.t, x(:,j), d.dT, d.fData );
end
```

UKFPredict uses RungeKutta for prediction that is done by numerical integration. In effect, we are running a simulation of the model and just correcting the results with the next function, UKFUpdate. This gets to the core of the Kalman filter. It is just a simulation of your model with a measurement correction step. In the case of the conventional Kalman filter, we use a linear discrete-time model.

The update UKF step is shown in the following listing. The update propagates the state one time step.

```
function d = UKFUpdate( d )

% Get the sigma points
pS      = d.c*chol(d.p)';
nS      = length(d.m);
nSig    = 2*nS + 1;
mM      = repmat(d.m,1,nSig);
x       = mM + [zeros(nS,1) pS -pS];
[y, r]  = Measurement( x, d );
mu      = y*d.wM;
s       = y*d.w*y' + r;
c       = x*d.w*y';
k       = c/s;
d.v     = d.y - mu;
d.m     = d.m + k*d.v;
d.p     = d.p - k*s*k';

%%      Measurement estimates from the sigma points
function [y, r] = Measurement( x, d )
```

194

```
nSigma = size(x,2);

% Create the arrays
lR    = length(d.r);
y     = zeros(lR,nSigma);
r     = d.r;

for j = 1:nSigma
f           = feval(d.hFun, x(:,j), d.hData );
iR          = 1:lR;
y(iR,j)     = f;
end
```

The sigma points are generated using `chol`. `chol` is Cholesky factorization and generates an approximate square root of a matrix. A true matrix square root is more computationally expensive and the results don't really justify the penalty. The idea is to distribute the sigma points around the mean, and `chol` works well. Here is an example that compares the two approaches:

```
>> z = [1 0.2;0.2 2]
z =

    1.0000    0.2000
    0.2000    2.0000

>> b = chol(z)
b =

    1.0000    0.2000
         0    1.4000

>> b*b
ans =

    1.0000    0.4800
         0    1.9600

>> q = sqrtm(z)
q =

    0.9965    0.0830
    0.0830    1.4118

>> q*q
ans =

    1.0000    0.2000
    0.2000    2.0000
```

The square root actually produces a square root! The diagonal of `b*b` is close to `z`, which is all that is important. The measurement geometry in shown in Figure 10.8.

Figure 10.8: The measurement geometry. Our measurement is the angle.

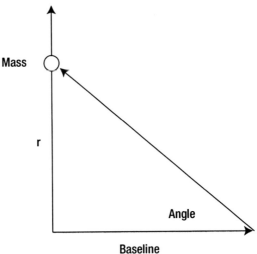

The results are shown in Figure 10.9. The errors Δr_E and Δv_E are just noise. The measurement goes over a large angle range, which would make a linear approximation problematic.

Figure 10.9: The unscented Kalman filter results for state estimation.

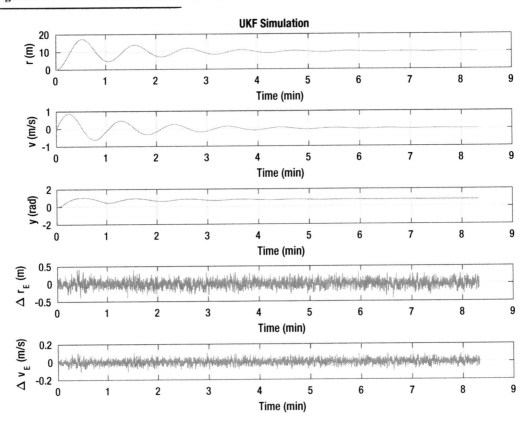

10.3   Using the UKF for Parameter Estimation

10.3.1 Problem

You want to learn the parameters of the spring-damper-mass system given a nonlinear angle measurement.

10.3.2 Solution

The solution is to create a UKF configured as a parameter estimator. This will absorb measurements and determine the mass, spring constant, and damping. It will autonomously learn about the system based on a preexisting model. We develop the version that requires an estimate of the state that could be generated with a UKF running in parallel, as in the previous recipe.

10.3.3 How It Works

Initialize the parameter filter with the expected value of the parameters, η [2]:

$$\hat{\eta}(t_0) = E\{\hat{\eta}_0\} \tag{10.111}$$

and the covariance for the parameters

$$P_{\eta_o} = E\{(\eta(t_0) - \hat{\eta}_0)(\eta(t_0) - \hat{\eta}_0)^T\} \tag{10.112}$$

The update sequence begins by adding the parameter model uncertainty, Q, to the covariance, P,

$$P = P + Q \tag{10.113}$$

Q is for the parameters, not the states. The sigma points are then calculated. These are points found by adding the square root of the covariance matrix to the current estimate of the parameters.

$$\eta_\sigma = \begin{bmatrix} \hat{\eta} & \hat{\eta} + \gamma\sqrt{P} & \hat{\eta} - \gamma\sqrt{P} \end{bmatrix} \tag{10.114}$$

γ is a factor that determines the spread of the sigma points. We use `chol` for the square root. If there are L parameters, the P matrix is $L \times L$, so this array will be $L \times (2L + 1)$.

The state equations are of the form

$$\dot{x} = f(x, u, t) \tag{10.115}$$

and the measurement equations are

$$y = h(x, u, t) \tag{10.116}$$

x is the previous state of the system, as identified by the state estimator or other process. u is a structure with all other inputs to the system that are not being estimated. η is a vector of parameters that are being estimated and t is time. y is the vector of measurements. This is the dual estimation approach in that we are not estimating x and η simultaneously.

The script, `UKFPSim`, for testing the UKF parameter estimation is shown below. We are not doing the UKF state estimation to simplify the script. Normally you would run the UKF in parallel. We start by initializing all parameters. `KFInitialize` takes parameter pairs to initialize the filters. The remainder is the simulation loop and plotting.

```
%% UKFPSim
% Demonstrate parameter learning using Unscented Kalman Filter.
%% See also
% RungeKutta, RHSOscillator, TimeLabel, KFInitialize, UKFPUpdate
% AngleMeasurement

%% Initialize
nSim            = 150;            % Simulation steps
dT              = 0.01;           % Time step (sec)
d               = RHSOscillator;  % Get the default data structure
d.a             = 0.0;            % Disturbance acceleration
d.zeta          = 0.0;            % Damping ratio
d.omega         = 2;             % Undamped natural frequency
x               = [1;0];          % Initial state [position;velocity]
y1Sigma         = 0.0001;         % 1 sigma measurement noise
q               = 0.001;          % Plant uncertainty
p               = 0.4;                % Initial covariance for the
     parameter
dRHSUKF         = struct('a',0.0,'zeta',0.0,'eta',0.1);
dKF             = KFInitialize( 'ukfp','x',x,'f',@RHSOscillatorUKF,...
                               'fData',dRHSUKF,'r',y1Sigma^2,'q',q,...
                               'p',p,'hFun',@LinearMeasurement,...
                               'dT',dT,'eta',d.omega/2,...
                               'alpha',1,'kappa',2,'beta',2);

dKF             = UKFPWeight( dKF );
y               = LinearMeasurement( x );

%% Simulation
xPlot = zeros(5,nSim);

for k = 1:nSim

  % Update the Kalman Filter parameter estimates
  dKF.x       = x;

  % Plot storage
  xPlot(:,k)  = [y;x;dKF.eta;dKF.p];

  % Propagate (numerically integrate) the state equations
  x           = RungeKutta( @RHSOscillator, 0, x, dT, d );

        % Measurements
  y           = LinearMeasurement( x ) + y1Sigma*randn;

  dKF.y       = y;
  dKF         = UKFPUpdate(dKF);

end

%% Plot the results
yL      = {'y_(rad)' 'r_(m)' 'v_(m/s)'  '\omega_(rad/s)' 'p' };
```

```
[t,tL] = TimeLabel(dT*(0:(nSim-1)));

PlotSet( t, xPlot, 'x_label', tL, 'y_label', yL,...
    'plot_title', 'UKF_Parameter_Estimation', 'figure_title', 'UKF_Parameter_
        Estimation' );
```

The UKF parameter update functional is shown in the following code. It uses the state estimate generated by the UKF. As noted, we are using the exact value of the state generated by the simulation. This function needs a specialized right-hand side that uses the parameter estimate, d.eta. We modified RHSOscillator for this purpose and wrote RHSOscillatorUKF.

```
%% UKFPUPDATE Unscented Kalman Filter parameter update step
%%  Form:
%   d = UKFPUpdate( d )
%
%% Description
%   Implement an Unscented Kalman Filter for parameter estimation.
%   The filter uses numerical integration to propagate the state.
%   The filter propagates sigma points, points computed from the
%   state plus a function of the covariance matrix. For each parameter
%   there are two sigma parameters. The current estimated state must be
%   input each step.
%
%% Inputs
%   d    (1,1)    UKF data structure
%            .x       (n,1)        State
%            .p          (n,n)     Covariance
%            .q       (n,n)     State noise covariance
%            .r       (m,m)     Measurement noise covariance
%            .wM         (1,2n+1)    Model weights
%            .wC         (1,2n+1)    Model weights
%            .f          (1,:)       Pointer for the right hand side function
%            .fData      (.)         Data structure with data for f
%               .hFun    (1,:)       Pointer for the measurement function
%               .hData   (.)         Data structure with data for hFun
%               .dT      (1,1)       Time step (s)
%               .t       (1,1)       Time (s)
%               .eta     (:,1)       Parameter vector
%               .c       (1,1)       Scaling constant
%            .lambda     (1,1)          Scaling constant
%
%% Outputs
%   d    (1,1)    UKF data structure
%               .p       (n,n)       Covariance
%               .eta     (:,1)       Parameter vector
%
%% References
%   References: Van der Merwe, R. and Wan, E., "Sigma-Point Kalman Filters
%       for
%               Probabilistic Inference in Dynamic State-Space Models".
%               Matthew C. VanDyke, Jana L. Schwartz, Christopher D. Hall,
```

```
%                       "UNSCENTED KALMAN FILTERING FOR SPACECRAFT ATTITUDE STATE
    AND
%                       PARAMETER ESTIMATION,"AAS-04-115.

function d = UKFPUpdate( d )

d.wA    = zeros(d.L,d.n);
D       = zeros(d.lY,d.n);
yD      = zeros(d.lY,1);

% Update the covariance
d.p     = d.p + d.q;

% Compute the sigma points
d       = SigmaPoints( d );

% We are computing the states, then the measurements
% for the parameters +/- 1 sigma
for k = 1:d.n
  d.fData.eta   = d.wA(:,k);
  x             = RungeKutta( d.f, d.t, d.x, d.dT, d.fData );
  D(:,k)        = feval( d.hFun, x, d.hData );
  yD            = yD + d.wM(k)*D(:,k);
end

pWD = zeros(d.L,d.lY);
pDD = d.r;
for k = 1:d.n
  wD    = D(:,k) - yD;
  pDD   = pDD + d.wC(k)*(wD*wD');
  pWD = pWD + d.wC(k)*(d.wA(:,k) - d.eta)*wD';
end

pDD = 0.5*(pDD + pDD');

% Incorporate the measurements
K       = pWD/pDD;
dY      = d.y - yD;
d.eta   = d.eta + K*dY;
d.p     = d.p - K*pDD*K';
d.p     = 0.5*(d.p + d.p'); % Force symmetry

%% Create the sigma points for the parameters
function d = SigmaPoints( d )

n           = 2:(d.L+1);
m           = (d.L+2):(2*d.L + 1);
etaM        = repmat(d.eta,length(d.eta));
sqrtP       = chol(d.p);
d.wA(:,1)   = d.eta;
d.wA(:,n)   = etaM + d.gamma*sqrtP;
d.wA(:,m)   = etaM - d.gamma*sqrtP;
```

It also has its own weight initialization function `UKFPWeight.m`.

```
%% UKFPWEIGHT Unscented Kalman Filter parameter estimation weights
%% Form:
%   d = UKFPWeight( d )
%
%% Description
%   Unscented Kalman Filter parameter estimation weights.
%
%   The weight matrix is used by the matrix form of the Unscented
%   Transform.
%
%   The constant alpha determines the spread of the sigma points around x
%   and is usually set to between 10e-4 and 1. beta incorporates prior
%   knowledge of the distribution of x and is 2 for a Gaussian
%   distribution. kappa is set to 0 for state estimation and 3 - number of
%   states for parameter estimation.
%
%%   Inputs
%   d    (.)      Data structure with constants
%         .kappa        (1,1)    0 for state estimation, 3-#states
%         .alpha        (1,1)    Determines spread of sigma points
%         .beta    (1,1) Prior knowledge - 2 for Gaussian
%
%% Outputs
%   d    (.)      Data structure with constants
%         .wM      (1,2*n+1)       Weight array
%         .wC      (1,2*n+1)       Weight array
%         .lambda        (1,1)           Scaling constant
%         .wA      (p,n)           Empty matrix
%         .L       (1,1)           Number of parameters to   estimate
%         .lY      (1,1)           Number of measurements
%         .D             (m,n)           Empty matrix
%         .n       (1,1)           Number of sigma i
%

function d = UKFPWeight( d )

d.L          = length(d.eta);
d.lambda     = d.alpha^2*(d.L + d.kappa) - d.L;
d.gamma      = sqrt(d.L + d.lambda);
d.wC(1)      = d.lambda/(d.L + d.lambda) + (1 - d.alpha^2 + d.beta);
d.wM(1)      = d.lambda/(d.L + d.lambda);
d.n          = 2*d.L + 1;
for k = 2:d.n
  d.wC(k) = 1/(2*(d.L + d.lambda));
  d.wM(k) = d.wC(k);
end

d.wA    = zeros(d.L,d.n);
y   = feval( d.hFun, d.x, d.hData );
d.lY    = length(y);
d.D     = zeros(d.lY,d.n);
```

RHSOscillatorUKF is the oscillator model used by the UKF. It has a different input format than RHSOscillatorUKF.

```
%% RHSOSCILLATORUKF Right hand side of a double integrator.
%% Form
%   xDot = RHSOscillatorUKF( t, x, a )
%
%% Description
% An oscillator models linear or rotational motion plus many other
% systems. It has two states, position and velocity. The equations of
% motion are:
%
%   rDot = v
%   vDot = a - omega^2*r
%
% This can be called by the MATLAB Recipes RungeKutta function or any MATLAB
% integrator. Time is not used. This function is compatible with the
% UKF parameter estimation. eta is the parameter to be estimated which is
% omega in this case.
%
% If no inputs are specified, it will return the default data structure.
%
%% Inputs
%   t          (1,1) Time (unused)
%   x          (2,1) State vector [r;v]
%   d          (.)   Data structure
%                    .a    (1,1) Disturbance acceleration (m/s^2)
%                    .zeta (1,1) Damping ratio
%                    .eta  (1,1) Natural frequency (rad/s)
%
%% Outputs
%   x          (2,1) State vector derivative d[r;v]/dt
%
%% References
% None.

function xDot = RHSOscillatorUKF( ~, x, d )

if( nargin < 1 )
  xDot = struct('a',0,'eta',0.1,'zeta',0);
  return
end

xDot = [x(2);d.a-2*d.zeta*d.eta*x(2)-d.eta^2*x(1)];
```

LinearMeasurement is a simple measurement function for demonstration purposes. The UKF can use arbitrarily complex measurement functions.

```
%% LINEARMEASUREMENT Function for an angle measurement
%% Form
%   y = LinearMeasurement( x, d )
%
%% Description
% A linear measurement
```

```
%
%% Inputs
%   x        (2,1)  State [r;v]
%   d        (.)    Data structure
%
%% Outputs
%   y        (1,1)  Distance
%
%% References
%  None.

function y = LinearMeasurement( x, ~ )

if( nargin < 1 )
  y = [];
  return
end

y = x(1);
```

The results of a simulation of an undamped oscillator are shown in Figure 10.10. The filter rapidly estimates the undamped natural frequency. The result is noisy, however. You can explore this script by varying the numbers in the script.

Figure 10.10: The UKF parameter estimation results.

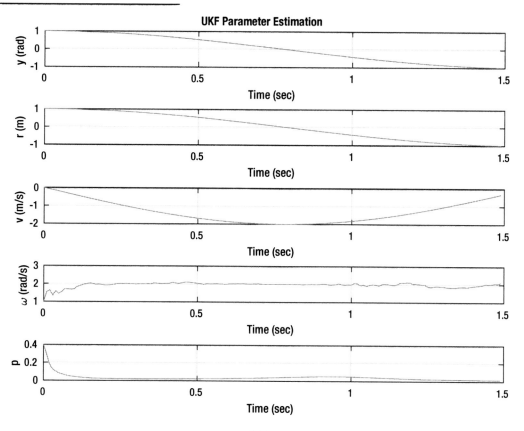

Summary

This chapter has demonstrated learning using Kalman filters. In this case learning is the estimation of states and parameters for a damped oscillator. We looked at conventional and unscented Kalman filters. We examined the parameter learning version of the latter. All examples were done using a damped oscillator. Table 10.1 lists the code used in this chapter.

Table 10.1: Chapter Code Listing

File	Description
AngleMeasurement	Angle measurement of the mass
LinearMeasurement	Position measurement of the mass
OscillatorSim	Simulation of the damped oscillator
OscillatorDampingRatioSim	Simulation of the damped oscillator with different damping ratios
RHSOscillator	Dynamical model for the damped oscillator
RungeKutta	Fourth-order Runge–Kutta integrator
PlotSet	Create two-dimensional plots from a data set
TimeLabel	Produce time labels and scaled time vectors
Gaussian	Plot a Gaussian distribution
KFInitialize	Initialize Kalman filters
KFSim	Demonstration of a conventional Kalman filter
KFPredict	Prediction step for a conventional Kalman filter
KFUpdate	Update step for a conventional Kalman filter
EKFPredict	Prediction step for an extended Kalman filter
EKFUpdate	Update step for an extended Kalman filter
UKFPredict	Prediction step for a UKF
UKFUpdate	Update step for a UKF
UKFPUpdate	Update step for a UKF parameter update
UKFSim	Demonstration of a UKF
UKFPSim	Demonstration of parameter estimation for a UKF
UKFWeights	Generates weights for the UKF
UKFPWeights	Generates weights for the UKF parameter estimator
RHSOscillatorUKF	Dynamical model for the damped oscillator for use in UKF parameter estimation

References

[1] S. Sarkka. Lecture 3: Bayesian Optimal Filtering Equations and the Kalman Filter. Technical report, Department of Biomedical Engineering and Computational Science, Aalto University School of Science, February 2011.

[2] M. C. VanDyke, J. L. Schwartz, and C. D. Hall. Unscented Kalman filtering for spacecraft attitude state and parameter estimation. *Advances in Astronautical Sciences*, 2005.

CHAPTER 11

■ ■ ■

Adaptive Control

Control systems need to react to the environment in a predicable and repeatable fashion. Control systems take measurements and use them to control the process. For example, a ship measures its heading and changes its rudder angle to attain that heading.

Typically, control systems are designed and implemented with all of the parameters hard coded into the software. This works very well in most circumstances, particularly when the system is well known during the design process. When the system is not well defined, or is expected to change significantly during operation, it may be necessary to implement learning control. For example, the batteries in an electric car degrade over time. This leads to less range. An autonomous driving system would need to learn that range was decreasing. This would be done by comparing the distance traveled with the battery state of charge. More drastic, and sudden, changes can alter a system. For example, in an aircraft the air data system might fail due to a sensor malfunction. If the Global Positioning System (GPS) were still operating, the plane would want to switch to a GPS-only system. In a multiinput–multioutput control system, a branch may fail, leaving other branches working fine. The system might have to modify to operating branches in that case.

Learning and adaptive control are often used interchangeably. In this chapter you will learn a variety of techniques for adaptive control for different systems. Each technique is applied to a different system, but all are generally applicable to any control system.

Figure 11.1 provides a taxonomy of adaptive and learning control. The paths depend on the nature of the dynamical system. The rightmost branch is tuning. This is something a designer would do during testing, but it could also be done automatically as will be described in the self-tuning recipe 11.1. The next path is for systems that will vary with time. Our first example is using model reference adaptive control for a spinning wheel. This is discussed in Section 11.2.

The aircraft section 11.3 is for the longitudinal control of an aircraft that needs to work as the altitude and speed change. You will learn how to implement a neural net to produce the critical parameters for nonlinear control. This is an example of online learning. You have seen examples of neural nets in the chapter on deep learning.

© Michael Paluszek, Stephanie Thomas 2017
M. Paluszek and S. Thomas, *MATLAB Machine Learning*, DOI 10.1007/978-1-4842-2250-8_11

Figure 11.1: Taxonomy of adaptive or learning control.

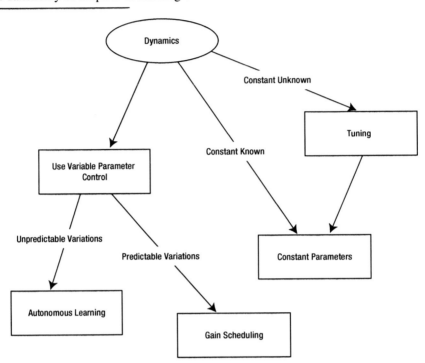

The final example in 11.4 is for ship control. You want to control the heading angle. The dynamics of the ship are a function of the forward speed. This is an example of gain scheduling. While it isn't really learning from experience, it is adapting based on information about its environment.

11.1 Self-Tuning: Finding the Frequency of an Oscillator

We want to tune a damper so that we critically damp a spring system for which the spring constant changes. Our system will work by perturbing the undamped spring with a step and measuring the frequency using a fast Fourier transform (FFT). We then compute the damping using the frequency and add a damper to the simulation. We then measure the undamped natural frequency again to see that it is the correct value. Finally, we set the damping ratio to 1 and observe the response. The system in shown in Figure 11.2.

Figure 11.2: Spring-mass-damper system. The mass is on the right. The spring is on the top to the left of the mass. The damper is below.

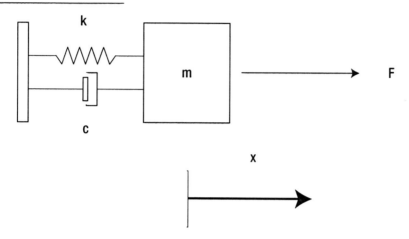

In Chapter 10 we introduced parameter identification, which is another way of finding the frequency. The approach here is to collect a large sample of data and process it in batch to find the natural frequency. The equations for the system are

$$\dot{r} = v \tag{11.1}$$
$$m\dot{v} = -cv - kr \tag{11.2}$$

A dot above the symbols means first derivative with respect to time. That is,

$$\dot{r} = \frac{dr}{dt} \tag{11.3}$$

The equations state that the change in position with respect to time is the velocity and the mass times the change in velocity with respect to time is equal to a force proportional to its velocity and position. The second equation is Newton's law,

$$F = ma \tag{11.4}$$

where

$$F = -cv - kr \tag{11.5}$$
$$a = \frac{dv}{dt} \tag{11.6}$$

Our control system generates the component of force $-cv$.

11.1.1 Problem

We want to identify the frequency of an oscillator.

11.1.2 Solution

The solution is to have the control system adapt to the frequency of the spring. We will use an FFT to identify the frequency of the oscillation.

11.1.3 How It Works

The following script shows how an FFT identifies the oscillation frequency for a damped oscillator.

The function is shown in the following code. We use the RHSOscillator dynamical model for the system. We start with a small initial position to get it to oscillate. We also have a small damping ratio so it will damp out. The resolution of the spectrum is dependent on the number of samples

$$r = \frac{2\pi}{nT} \tag{11.7}$$

where n is the number of samples and T is the sampling period. The maximum frequency is

$$\omega = \frac{nr}{2} \tag{11.8}$$

```
%% Initialize
nSim        = 2^16;             % Number of time steps
dT          = 0.1;              % Time step (sec)
dRHS        = RHSOscillator;    % Get the default data structure
dRHS.omega  = 0.1;             % Oscillator frequency
dRHS.zeta   = 0.1;             % Damping ratio
x           = [1;0];            % Initial state [position;velocity]
y1Sigma     = 0.000;            % 1 sigma position measurement noise

%% Simulation
xPlot = zeros(3,nSim);

for k = 1:nSim

  % Measurements
  y           = x(1) + y1Sigma*randn;

  % Plot storage
  xPlot(:,k)  = [x;y];

  % Propagate (numerically integrate) the state equations
  x           = RungeKutta( @RHSOscillator, 0, x, dT, dRHS );

end

%% Plot the results
yL      = {'r_(m)' 'v_(m/s)' 'y_r_(m)'};
[t,tL] = TimeLabel(dT*(0:(nSim-1)));

PlotSet( t, xPlot, 'x_label', tL, 'y_label', yL,...
   'plot_title', 'Oscillator', 'figure_title', 'Oscillator' );

FFTEnergy( xPlot(3,:), dT );
```

The FFTEnergy function is shown in the following listing. The FFT takes the sampled time sequence and computes the frequency spectrum. We compute the FFT using MATLAB's fft function. We take the result and multiply it by its conjugate to get the energy. The first half of the result has the frequency information.

```
function [e, w, wP] = FFTEnergy( y, tSamp, aPeak )

if( nargin < 3 )
  aPeak  = 0.95;
end

n = size( y, 2 );

% If the input vector is odd drop one sample
if( 2*floor(n/2) ~= n )
  n = n - 1;
  y = y(1:n,:);
end

x  = fft(y);
e  = real(x.*conj(x))/n;

hN = n/2;
e  = e(1,1:hN);
r  = 2*pi/(n*tSamp);
w  = r*(0:(hN-1));

if( nargin > 1 )
  k   = find( e > aPeak*max(e) );
  wP  = w(k);
end

if( nargout == 0 )
  tL = sprintf('FFT Energy Plot: Resolution = %10.2e rad/sec',r);
  PlotSet(w,log10(e),'x label','Frequency (rad/sec)','y label','Log
 (Energy)','figure title',tL,'plot title',tL,'plot type','xlog');
end
```

Figure 11.3 shows the damped oscillation. Figure 11.4 shows the spectrum. We find the peak by searching for the maximum value. The noise in the signal is seen at the higher frequencies. A noise-free simulation is shown in Figure 11.5.

Figure 11.3: Simulation of the damped oscillator.

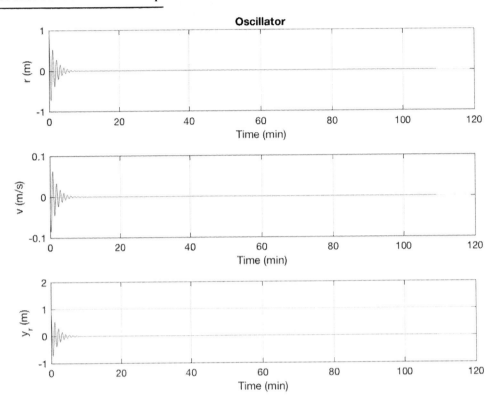

The tuning approach is to

1. Excite the oscillator with a pulse.

2. Run it for 2^n steps.

3. Do an FFT.

4. If there is only one peak, compute the damping gain.

The script is shown below. It calls `FFTEnergy.m` with `aPeak` set to 0.7. The disturbances are Gaussian-distributed accelerations and there is noise in the measurement.

```
n            = 4;                     % Number of measurement sequences
nSim         = 2^16;                  % Number of time steps
dT           = 0.1;                   % Time step (sec)
dRHS         = RHSOscillatorControl;  % Get the default data structure
dRHS.omega   = 0.1;                   % Oscillator frequency
zeta         = 0.5;                   % Damping ratio
x            = [0;0];                 % Initial state [position;velocity]
y1Sigma      = 0.001;                 % 1 sigma position measurement noise
a            = 1;                     % Perturbation
kPulseStop   = 10;
aPeak        = 0.7;
a1Sigma      = 0.01;
```

Figure 11.4: The frequency spectrum. The peak is at the oscillation frequency of 0.1 rad/s.

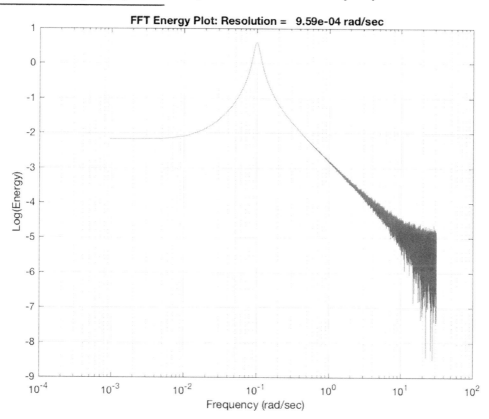

```
%% Simulation
xPlot = zeros(3,n*nSim);
yFFT  = zeros(1,nSim);
i     = 0;
tuned = false;
wOsc  = 0;

for j = 1:n
  aJ = a;
  for k = 1:nSim
    i = i + 1;
    % Measurements
    y           = x(1) + y1Sigma*randn;

    % Plot storage
    xPlot(:,i)  = [x;y];
    yFFT(k)     = y;
    dRHS.a      = aJ + a1Sigma*randn;
    if( k == kPulseStop )
```

Figure 11.5: The frequency spectrum without noise.

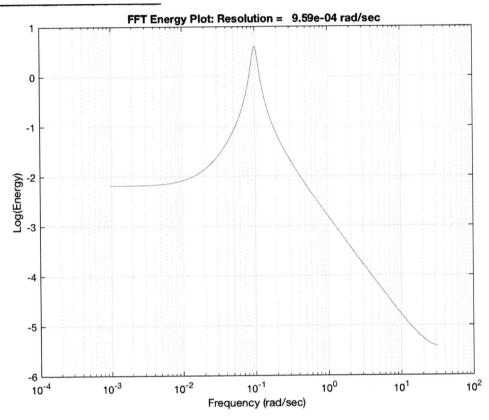

```
            aJ = 0;
      end

      % Propagate (numerically integrate) the state equations
      x             = RungeKutta( @RHSOscillatorControl, 0, x, dT, dRHS );
   end
   FFTEnergy( yFFT, dT );
   [~, ~, wP] = FFTEnergy( yFFT, dT, aPeak );
   if( length(wP) == 1 )
      wOsc       = wP;
      fprintf(1,'Estimated oscillator frequency %12.4f rad/s\n',wP);
      dRHS.c       = 2*zeta*wOsc;
   else
      fprintf(1,'Tuned\n');
   end
end

%% Plot the results
yL      = {'r (m)' 'v (m/s)' 'y_r (m)'};
[t,tL] = TimeLabel(dT*(0:(n*nSim-1)));
```

```
PlotSet( t, xPlot, 'x_label', tL, 'y_label', yL,...
   'plot_title', 'Oscillator', 'figure_title', 'Oscillator' );
```

The results in the command window are

```
TuningSim
Estimated oscillator frequency          0.0997 rad/s
Tuned
Tuned
Tuned
```

This is a crude approach. As you can see from the FFT plots, the spectra are "noisy" due to the sensor noise and Gaussian disturbance. The criterion for determining that it is underdamped is that it is a distinctive peak. If the noise is large enough, we have to set lower thresholds.

An important point is that we must stimulate the system to identify the peak. All system identification, parameter estimation, and tuning algorithms have this requirement. An alternative to a pulse (which has a broad frequency spectrum) would be to use a sinusoidal sweep. That would excite any resonances and make it easier to identify the peak.

Figure 11.6: Tuning simulation results. The first four plots are the frequency spectrums taken at the end of each sampling interval; the last shows the results over time.

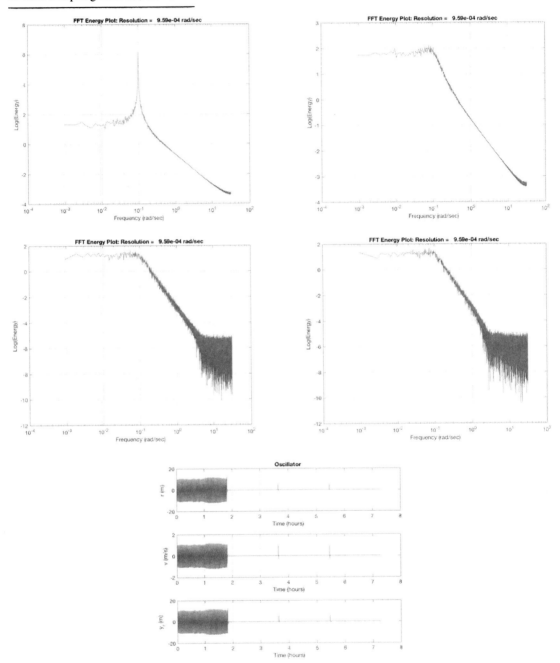

11.2   Model Reference Adaptive Control

We want to control a robot with an unknown load so that it behaves in a desired manner. The dynamical model of the robot joint is [1]

$$\frac{d\omega}{dt} = -a\omega + bu + u_d \tag{11.9}$$

where the damping a and/or input constants b are unknown. u is the input voltage and u_d is a disturbance angular acceleration. This is a first-order system. We would like the system to behave like the reference model

Figure 11.7: Speed control of a robot for the model reference adaptive control demo.

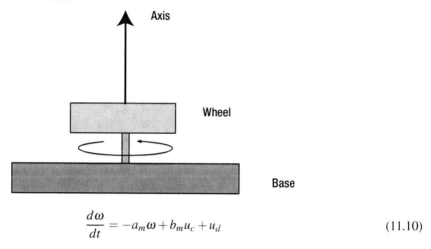

$$\frac{d\omega}{dt} = -a_m\omega + b_m u_c + u_d \tag{11.10}$$

11.2.1   Generating a Square Wave Input

11.2.1.1   Problem

We need to generate a square wave to stimulate the rotor.

11.2.1.2   Solution

For the purposes of simulation and testing our controller, we will generate a square wave with a MATLAB function.

11.2.1.3   How It Works

The following function generates a square wave `SquareWave`.

```
function [v,d] = SquareWave( t, d )

if( nargin < 1 )
  if( nargout == 0 )
    Demo;
  else
    v = DataStructure;
  end
        return
end

if( d.state == 0 )
```

```matlab
  if( t - d.tSwitch >= d.tLow )
    v            = 1;
    d.tSwitch = t;
    d.state   = 1;
  else
    v            = 0;
  end
else
  if( t - d.tSwitch >= d.tHigh )
    v            = 0;
    d.tSwitch = t;
    d.state   = 0;
  else
    v            = 1;
  end
end

function d = DataStructure
%% Default data structure

d                = struct();
d.tLow        = 10.0;
d.tHigh      = 10.0;
d.tSwitch    = 0;
d.state      = 0;

function Demo
%% Demo

d = SquareWave;
t = linspace(0,100,1000);
v = zeros(1,length(t));
for k = 1:length(t)
  [v(k),d] = SquareWave(t(k),d);
end

PlotSet(t,v,'x_label', 't_(sec)', 'y_label', 'v', 'plot_title','Square_Wave'
     ,... 'figure_title', 'Square_Wave');
```

A square wave is shown in Figure 11.8. There are many ways to specify a square wave. This function produces a square wave with a minimum of zero and maximum of 1. You specify the time at zero and the time at 1 to create the square wave.

Figure 11.8: Square wave.

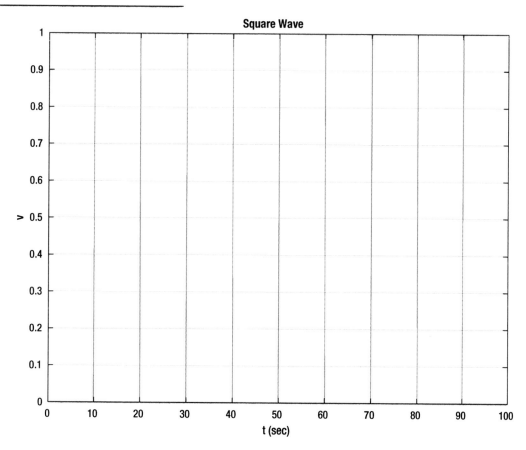

11.2.2 Implement Model Reference Adaptive Control

11.2.2.1 Problem

We want to control a system to behave like a particular model.

11.2.2.2 Solution

The solution is to implement model reference adaptive control (MRAC).

11.2.2.3 How It Works

Hence, the name model reference adaptive control. We will use the MIT rule to design the adaptation system. The MIT rule was first developed at the MIT Instrumentation Laboratory (now Draper Laboratory) that developed the Apollo and Shuttle guidance and control systems.

Consider a closed-loop system with one adjustable parameter, θ. The desired output is y_m. Let

$$e = y - y_m \tag{11.11}$$

Define a loss function (or cost) as

$$J(\theta) = \frac{1}{2}e^2 \tag{11.12}$$

The square removes the sign. If the error is zero, the cost is zero. We would like to minimize $J(\theta)$. To make J small we change the parameters in the direction of the negative gradient of J or

$$\frac{d\theta}{dt} = \gamma \frac{\partial J}{\partial \theta} = -\gamma e \frac{\partial e}{\partial \theta} \qquad (11.13)$$

This is the MIT rule. This can be applied when there is more than one parameter. If the system is changing slowly, then we can assume that θ is constant as the system adapts.

Let the controller be

$$u = \theta_1 u_c - \theta_2 \omega \qquad (11.14)$$

The second term provides the damping. The controller has two parameters. If they are

$$\theta_1 = \frac{b_m}{b} \qquad (11.15)$$

$$\theta_2 = \frac{a_m - a}{b} \qquad (11.16)$$

the error is

$$e = \omega - \omega_m \qquad (11.17)$$

With the parameters θ_1 and θ_2 the system is

$$\frac{d\omega}{dt} = -(a + b\theta_2)\omega + b\theta_1 u_c + u_d \qquad (11.18)$$

To continue with the implementation we introduce the operator $p = \frac{d}{dt}$. Set $u_d = 0$. We then write

$$p\omega = -(a + b\theta_2)\omega + b\theta_1 u_c \qquad (11.19)$$

or

$$\omega = \frac{b\theta_1}{p + a + b\theta_2} u_c \qquad (11.20)$$

We need to get the partial derivatives of the error with respect to θ_1 and θ_2. These are

$$\frac{\partial e}{\partial \theta_1} = \frac{b}{p + a + b\theta_2} u_c \qquad (11.21)$$

$$\frac{\partial e}{\partial \theta_2} = -\frac{b^2 \theta_1}{(p + a + b\theta_2)^2} u_c \qquad (11.22)$$

from the chain rule for differentiation. Noting that

$$u_c = \frac{p + a + b\theta_2}{b\theta_1} \omega \qquad (11.23)$$

the second equation becomes

$$\frac{\partial e}{\partial \theta_2} = \frac{b}{p + a + b\theta_2} y \qquad (11.24)$$

Since we don't know a, let's assume that we are pretty close to it. Then let

$$p + a \approx p + a + b\theta_2 \qquad (11.25)$$

Our adaptation laws are now

$$\frac{d\theta_1}{dt} = -\gamma\left(\frac{a_m}{p+a_m}u_c\right)e \tag{11.26}$$

$$\frac{d\theta_2}{dt} = \gamma\left(\frac{a_m}{p+a_m}\omega\right)e \tag{11.27}$$

where γ is the adaptation gain. The terms in the parentheses are two differential equations, so the complete set is

$$\frac{dx_1}{dt} = -a_m x_1 + a_m u_c \tag{11.28}$$

$$\frac{dx_2}{dt} = -a_m x_2 + a_m \omega \tag{11.29}$$

$$\frac{d\theta_1}{dt} = -\gamma x_1 e \tag{11.30}$$

$$\frac{d\theta_2}{dt} = \gamma x_2 e \tag{11.31}$$

$$\tag{11.32}$$

As noted before, the controller is

$$u = \theta_1 u_c - \theta_2 \omega \tag{11.33}$$

$$e = \omega - \omega_m \tag{11.34}$$

$$\frac{d\omega_m}{dt} = -a_m \omega_m + b_m u_c \tag{11.35}$$

The MRAC is implemented in the function MRAC. The controller has five differential equations that are propagated. RungeKutta is used for the propagation, but a less computationally intensive lower-order integrator, such as Euler, could be used instead.

```
function d = MRAC( omega, d )

if( nargin < 1 )
  d = DataStructure;
  return
end

d.x     = RungeKutta( @RHS, 0, d.x, d.dT, d, omega );
d.u = d.x(3)*d.uC - d.x(4)*omega;

function d = DataStructure
%% Default data structure

d        = struct();
d.aM     = 2.0;
d.bM     = 2.0;
d.x      = [0;0;0;0;0];
d.uC     = 0;
d.u      = 0;
d.gamma  = 1;
d.dT     = 0.1;
```

```
function xDot = RHS( ~, x, d, omega )
%% RHS for MRAC

e    = omega - x(5);
xDot = [-d.aM*x(1) + d.aM*d.uC;...
        -d.aM*x(2) + d.aM*omega;...
        -d.gamma*x(1)*e;...
         d.gamma*x(2)*e;...
        -d.aM*x(5) + d.bM*d.uC];
```

11.2.3 Demonstrate MRAC for a Rotor

11.2.3.1 Problem

We want to control our rotor using MRAC.

11.2.3.2 Solution

The solution is to implement MRAC in a MATLAB script.

11.2.3.3 How It Works

MRAC is implemented in the script RotorSim. It calls MRAC to control the rotor. As in our other scripts, we use PlotSet. Notice that we use two new options. One 'plot set' allows you to put more than one line on a subplot. The other 'legend' adds legends to each plot. The cell array argument to 'legend' has a cell array for each plot. In this case we have two plots each with two lines, so the cell array is

```
{{'true' 'estimated'} {'Control' 'Command'}}
```

Each plot legend is a cell entry within the overall cell array.

The rotor simulation script with MRAC is shown in the following listing. The square wave function generates the command to the system that ω should track. RHSRotor, SquareWave and MRAC all return default data structures.

```
%% Initialize
nSim    = 4000;      % Number of time steps
dT      = 0.1;       % Time step (sec)
dRHS    = RHSRotor;      % Get the default data structure
dC      = MRAC;
dS      = SquareWave;
x       = 0.1;       % Initial state vector

%% Simulation
xPlot = zeros(4,nSim);
theta = zeros(2,nSim);
t       = 0;
for k = 1:nSim

% Plot storage
  xPlot(:,k)    = [x;dC.x(5);dC.u;dC.uC];
  theta(:,k)    = dC.x(3:4);
  [uC, dS]      = SquareWave( t, dS );
  dC.uC         = 2*(uC - 0.5);
  dC            = MRAC( x, dC );
  dRHS.u        = dC.u;
```

```
% Propagate (numerically integrate) the state equations
x           = RungeKutta( @RHSRotor, t, x, dT, dRHS );
t           = t + dT;
end

%% Plot the results
yL          = {'\omega_(rad/s)' 'u'};
[t,tL]      = TimeLabel(dT*(0:(nSim-1)));

h = PlotSet( t, xPlot, 'x_label', tL, 'y_label', yL,'plot_title', {'Angular_
    Rate' 'Control'},... 'figure_title', 'Rotor', 'plot_set',{[1 2] [3 4]},'
    legend',{{'true' 'estimated'} {'Control' 'Command'}} );

PlotSet( theta(1,:), theta(2,:), 'x_label', '\theta_1',...
        'y_label','\theta_2', 'plot_title', 'Controller_Parameters',...
        'figure_title', 'Controller_Parameters' );
```

The results are shown in Figure 11.9. We set the adaptation gain γ to 1. a_m and b_m are set equal to 2. a is set equal to 1 and b to $\frac{1}{2}$.

Figure 11.9: MRAC control of a first-order system.

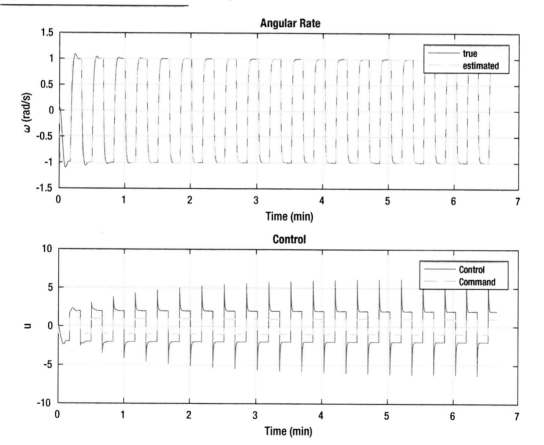

The first plot shows the angular rate of the rotor and the control demand and actual control sent to the wheel. The desired control is a square wave (generated by SquareWave). Notice the transient in the applied control at the transitions of the square wave. The control amplitude is greater than the commanded control. Notice also that the angular rate approaches the desired commanded square wave shape.

Figure 11.10 shows the convergence of the adaptive gains, θ_1 and θ_2. They have converged by the end of the simulation.

MRAC learns the gains of the system by observing the response to the control excitation. It requires excitation to converge. This is the nature of all learning systems. If there is no stimulation, it isn't possible to observe the behavior of the system so that the system can learn. It is easy to find an excitation for a first-order system. For higher-order systems, or nonlinear systems, this is more difficult.

Figure 11.10: Gain convergence in the MRAC controller.

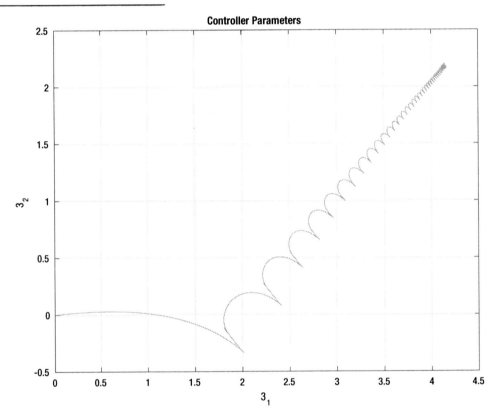

11.3   Longitudinal Control of an Aircraft

In this section we are going to control the longitudinal dynamics of an aircraft using learning control. We will derive a simple longitudinal dynamics model with a "small" number of parameters. Our control will use nonlinear dynamics inversion with a proportional–integral–derivative (PID) controller to control the pitch dynamics. Learning will be done using a sigma-pi neural network.

We will use the learning approach developed at NASA Dryden Research Center [4]. The baseline controller is a dynamic inversion-type controller with a PID control law. A neutral net [3] provides learning while the aircraft is operating. The neutral network is a sigma-pi–type network, meaning that the network sums the products of the inputs with their associated weights. The weights of the neural network are determined by a training algorithm that uses

1. Commanded aircraft rates from the reference model

2. PID errors and

3. Adaptive control rates fed back from the neural network

11.3.1   Write the Differential Equations for the Longitudinal Motion of an Aircraft

11.3.1.1   Problem

We want to model the longitudinal dynamics of an aircraft.

11.3.1.2   Solution

The solution is to write the right-hand-side function for the aircraft longitudinal dynamics differential equations.

11.3.1.3   How It Works

The longitudinal dynamics of an aircraft are also known as the pitch dynamics. The dynamics are entirely in the plane of symmetry of the aircraft. These dynamics include the forward and version motion of the aircraft and the pitching of the aircraft about the axis perpendicular to the plane of symmetry. Figure 11.11 shows an aircraft in flight. α is the angle of attack, the angle between the wing and the velocity vector. We assume that the wind direction is opposite that of the velocity vector; that is, the aircraft produces all of its wind. Drag is along the wind direction and lift is perpendicular to drag. The pitch moment is around the center of mass. The model we will derive uses a small set of parameters yet reproduces the longitudinal dynamics reasonably well. It is also easy for you to modify to simulate any aircraft of interest. We summarized the symbols for the dynamical model in Table 11.1. Our aerodynamic model is very simple. The lift and drag are

Figure 11.11: Diagram of an aircraft in flight showing all the important quantities for longitudinal dynamics simulation.

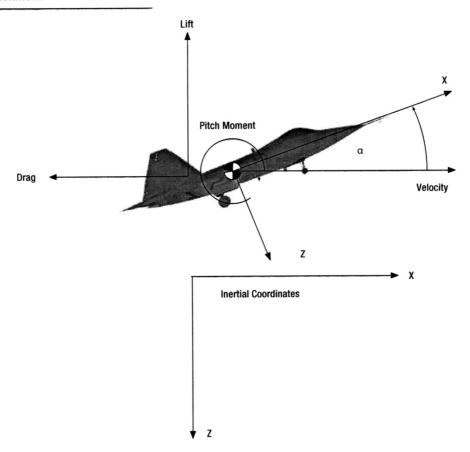

$$L = pSC_L \tag{11.36}$$
$$D = pSC_D \tag{11.37}$$

where S is the wetted area, or the area that is counted in computing the aerodynamic forces, and p is the dynamic pressure, the pressure on the aircraft caused by its velocity,

$$p = \frac{1}{2}\rho v^2 \tag{11.38}$$

where ρ is the atmospheric density and v is the magnitude of the velocity. Atmospheric density is a function of altitude. S is the wetted area, that is, the area of the aircraft that interacts with the airflow. For low-speed flight, this is mostly the wings. Most books use q for dynamic pressure. We use q for pitch angular rate (also a convention), so we use p here to avoid confusion.

The lift coefficient, C_L, is

$$C_L = C_{L_\alpha}\alpha \tag{11.39}$$

226

Table 11.1: Aircraft Dynamics Symbols

Symbol	Description	Units
g	Acceleration of gravity at sea level	9.806 m/s^2
h	Altitude	m
k	Coefficient of lift-induced drag	
m	Mass	kg
p	Dynamic pressure	N/m^2
q	Pitch angular rate	rad/s
u	x-velocity	m/s
w	z-velocity	m/s
C_L	Lift coefficient	
C_D	Drag coefficient	
D	Drag	N
I_y	Pitch moment of inertia	kg-m^2
L	Lift	N
M	Pitch moment (torque)	Nm
M_e	Pitch moment due to elevator	Nm
r_e	Elevator moment arm	m
S	Wetted area of wings	m^2
S_e	Wetted area of elevator	m^2
T	Thrust	N
X	X force in the aircraft frame	N
Z	Z force in the aircraft frame	N
α	Angle of attack	rad
γ	Flight path angle	rad
ρ	Air density	kg/m^3
θ	Pitch angle	rad

and the drag coefficient, C_D, is

$$C_D = C_{D_0} + kC_L^2 \tag{11.40}$$

The drag equation is called the drag polar. Increasing the angle of attack increases the aircraft lift but also increases the aircraft drag. The coefficient k is

$$k = \frac{1}{\pi \varepsilon_0 AR} \tag{11.41}$$

where ε_0 is the Oswald efficiency factor that is typically between 0.75 and 0.85. AR is the wing aspect ratio. The aspect ratio is the ratio of the span of the wing to its chord. For complex shapes it is approximately given by the formula

$$AR = \frac{b^2}{S} \tag{11.42}$$

where b is the span and S is the wing area. Span is measured from wingtip to wingtip. Gliders have very high aspect ratios and delta-wing aircraft have low aspect ratios.

The aerodynamic coefficients are nondimensional coefficients that when multiplied by the wetted area of the aircraft, and the dynamic pressure, produce the aerodynamic forces.

The dynamical equations, the differential equations of motion, are [2]

$$m(\dot{u} + qw) \;=\; X - mg\sin\theta + T\cos\varepsilon \tag{11.43}$$

$$m(\dot{w} - qu) \;=\; Z + mg\cos\theta - T\sin\varepsilon \tag{11.44}$$

$$I_y\dot{q} \;=\; M \tag{11.45}$$

$$\dot{\theta} \;=\; q \tag{11.46}$$

m is the mass, u is the x-velocity, w is the z-velocity, q is the pitch angular rate, θ is the pitch angle, T is the engine thrust, ε is the angle between the thrust vector and the x-axis, I_y is the pitch inertia, X is the x-force, Z is the z-force, and M is the torque about the pitch axis. The coupling between x- and z-velocities is caused by writing the force equations in the rotating frame. The pitch equation is about the center of mass. These are a function of u, w, q and altitude, h, which is found from

$$\dot{h} = u\sin\theta - w\cos\theta \tag{11.47}$$

The angle of attack, α, is the angle between the u- and w-velocities and is

$$\tan\alpha = \frac{w}{u} \tag{11.48}$$

The flight path angle γ is the angle between the vector velocity direction and the horizontal. It is related to θ and α by the relationship

$$\gamma = \theta - \alpha \tag{11.49}$$

This does not appear in the equations, but it is useful to compute when studying aircraft motion. The forces are

$$X \;=\; L\sin\alpha - D\cos\alpha \tag{11.50}$$

$$Z \;=\; -L\cos\alpha - D\sin\alpha \tag{11.51}$$

The moment, or torque, is assumed due to the offset of the center of pressure and center of mass, which is assumed to be along the x-axis.

$$M = (c_p - c)Z \tag{11.52}$$

where c_p is the location of the center of pressure. The moment from the elevator is

$$M_e = qr_eS_e\sin(\delta) \tag{11.53}$$

S_e is the wetted area of the elevator and r_E is the distance from the center of mass to the elevator. The dynamical model is in RHSAircraft. The atmospheric density model is an exponential model and is included as a subfunction in this function.

```
function [xDot, lift, drag, pD] = RHSAircraft( ~, x, d )

if( nargin < 1 )
  xDot = DataStructure;
  return
end
```

```
g        = 9.806;

u        = x(1);
w        = x(2);
q        = x(3);
theta    = x(4);
h        = x(5);

rho      = AtmDensity( h );

alpha    = atan(w/u);
cA       = cos(alpha);
sA       = sin(alpha);

v        = sqrt(u^2 + w^2);
pD       = 0.5*rho*v^2; % Dynamic pressure

cL       = d.cLAlpha*alpha;
cD       = d.cD0 + d.k*cL^2;

drag     = pD*d.s*cD;
lift     = pD*d.s*cL;

x        =  lift*sA - drag*cA;
z        = -lift*cA - drag*sA;
m        =  d.c*z + pD*d.sE*d.rE*sin(d.delta);

sT       = sin(theta);
cT       = cos(theta);

tEng     = d.thrust*d.throttle;
cE       = cos(d.epsilon);
sE       = sin(d.epsilon);

uDot     = (x + tEng*cE)/d.mass - q*w - g*sT + d.externalAccel(1);
wDot     = (z - tEng*sE)/d.mass + q*u + g*cT + d.externalAccel(2);
qDot     = m/d.inertia                      + d.externalAccel(3);
hDot     = u*sT - w*cT;

xDot     = [uDot;wDot;qDot;q;hDot];

function d = DataStructure
%% Data structure

% F-16
d               = struct();
d.cLAlpha       = 2*pi;                % Lift coefficient
d.cD0           = 0.0175;              % Zero lift drag coefficient
d.k             = 1/(pi*0.8*3.09);       % Lift coupling coefficient A/R
   3.09, Oswald Efficiency Factor 0.8
d.epsilon       = 0;                   % rad
d.thrust        = 76.3e3;              % N
```

229

```
d.throttle      = 1;
d.s             = 27.87;        % wing area m^2
d.mass          = 12000;       % kg
d.inertia       = 1.7295e5;    % kg-m^2
d.c             = 2;           % m
d.sE            = 25;          % m^2
```

We will use a model of the F-16 aircraft for our simulation. The F-16 is a single-engine supersonic multirole combat aircraft used by many countries. The F-16 is shown in Figure 11.12.

The inertia matrix is found by taking this model, distributing the mass among all the vertices, and computing the inertia from the formulas

$$m_k = \frac{m}{N} \tag{11.54}$$

$$c = \sum_k m_k r_k \tag{11.55}$$

$$I = \sum_k m_k (r_k - c)^2 \tag{11.56}$$

where N is the number of nodes and r_k is the vector from the origin (which is arbitrary) to node k.

```
inr =

   1.0e+05 *

    0.3672    0.0002   -0.0604
    0.0002    1.4778    0.0000
   -0.0604    0.0000    1.7295
```

Figure 11.12: F-16 model.

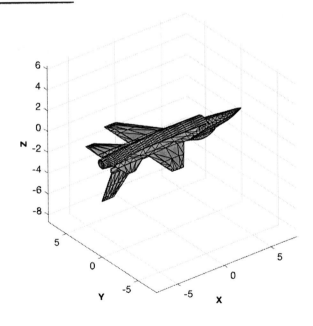

The F-16 data are given in Table 11.2.

Table 11.2: F-16 data.

Symbol	Field	Value	Description	Units
$C_{L\alpha}$	cLAlpha	6.28	Lift coefficient	
C_{D_0}	cD0	0.0175	Zero lift drag coefficient	
k	k	0.1288	Lift coupling coefficient	
ε	epsilon	0	Thrust angle from the x-axis	rad
T	thrust	76.3e3	Engine thrust	N
S	s	27.87	Wing area	m^2
m	mass	12000	Aircraft mass	kg
I_y	inertia	1.7295e5	z-axis inertia	kg-m^2
$c - c_p$	c	1	Offset of center of mass from the center of pressure	m
S_e	sE	3.5	Elevator area	m^2
r_e	(rE)	4.0	Elevator moment arm	m

There are many limitations to this model. First of all, the thrust is applied immediately with 100% accuracy. The thrust is also not a function of airspeed or altitude. Real engines take some time to achieve the commanded thrust and the thrust levels change with airspeed and altitude. The elevator also responds instantaneously. Elevators are driven by motors, usually hydraulic but sometimes pure electric, and they take time to reach a commanded angle. The aerodynamics are very simple. Lift and drag are complex functions of airspeed and angle of attack. Usually they are modeled with large tables of coefficients. We also model the pitching moment by a moment arm. Usually the torque is modeled by a table. No aerodynamic damping is modeled though this appears in most complete aerodynamic models for aircraft. You can easily add these features by creating functions

```
C_L = CL(v,h,alpha,delta)
C_D = CD(v,h,alpha,delta)
C_M = CL(v,h,vdot,alpha,delta)
```

11.3.2 Numerically Finding Equilibrium

11.3.2.1 Problem

We want to determine the equilibrium state for the aircraft.

11.3.2.2 Solution

The solution is to compute the Jacobian for the dynamics.

11.3.2.3 How It Works

We want to start every simulation from an equilibrium state. This is done using the function EquilibriumState. It uses fminsearch to minimize

$$\dot{u}^2 + \dot{w}^2 \tag{11.57}$$

given the flight speed, altitude, and flight path angle. It then computes the elevator angle needed to zero the pitch angular acceleration. It has a built-in demo for equilibrium-level flight at 10 km.

```
%% Code
if( nargin < 1 )
  Demo;
  return
end

x              = [v;0;0;0;h];
[~,~,drag]     = RHSAircraft( 0, x, d );
y0             = [0;drag];
cost(1)        = RHS( y0, d, gamma, v, h );
y              = fminsearch( @RHS, y0, [], d, gamma, v, h );
w              = y(1);
thrust         = y(2);
u              = sqrt(v^2-w^2);
alpha          = atan(w/u);
theta          = gamma + alpha;
cost(2)        = RHS( y, d, gamma, v, h );
x              = [u;w;0;theta;h];
d.thrust       = thrust;
d.delta        = 0;
[xDot,~,~,p]   = RHSAircraft( 0, x, d );
delta          = -asin(d.inertia*xDot(3)/(d.rE*d.sE*p));
d.delta        = delta;
radToDeg       = 180/pi;

fprintf(1,'Velocity_____%8.2f_m/s\n',v);
fprintf(1,'Altitude_____%8.2f_m\n',h);
fprintf(1,'Flight_path_angle_%8.2f_deg\n',gamma*radToDeg);
fprintf(1,'Z_speed_____%8.2f_m/s\n',w);
fprintf(1,'Thrust_____%8.2f_N\n',y(2));
fprintf(1,'Angle_of_attack___%8.2f_deg\n',alpha*radToDeg);
fprintf(1,'Elevator_____%8.2f_deg\n',delta*radToDeg);
fprintf(1,'Initial_cost_____%8.2e\n',cost(1));
fprintf(1,'Final_cost_____%8.2e\n',cost(2));

function cost = RHS( y, d, gamma, v, h )
%% Cost function for fminsearch

w          = y(1);
d.thrust       = y(2);
d.delta    = 0;
u          = sqrt(v^2-w^2);
alpha      = atan(w/u);
theta      = gamma + alpha;
x          = [u;w;0;theta;h];
xDot       = RHSAircraft( 0, x, d );
cost       = xDot(1:2)'*xDot(1:2);

function Demo
%% Demo
d    = RHSAircraft;
gamma = 0.0;
```

```
v     = 250;
```

The results of the demo are

```
>> EquilibriumState
Velocity             250.00 m/s
Altitude           10000.00 m
Flight path angle      0.00 deg
Z speed               13.84 m/s
Thrust             11148.95 N
Angle of attack        3.17 deg
Elevator             -11.22 deg
Initial cost        9.62e+01
Final cost          1.17e-17
```

The initial and final costs show how successful fminsearch was in achieving the objective of minimizing the *w* and *u* accelerations.

11.3.3 Numerical Simulation of the Aircraft

11.3.3.1 Problem

We want to simulate the aircraft.

11.3.3.2 Solution

The solution is to create a script that calls the right-hand side in a loop and plots the results.

11.3.3.3 How It Works

The simulation script is shown below. It computes the equilibrium state and then simulates the dynamics in a loop by calling RungeKutta. It then uses PlotSet to plot the results.

```
%% Initialize
nSim    = 2000;     % Number of time steps
dT      = 0.1;        % Time step (sec)
dRHS    = RHSAircraft;   % Get the default data structure has F-16 data
h       = 10000;
gamma   = 0.0;
v       = 250;
nPulse  = 10;
[x,   dRHS.thrust, dRHS.delta, cost] = EquilibriumState( gamma, v, h, dRHS );
fprintf(1,'Finding_Equilibrium:_Starting_Cost_%12.4e_Final_Cost_%12.4e\n',
   cost);

accel = [0.0;0.1;0.0];

%% Simulation
xPlot = zeros(length(x)+2,nSim);
for k = 1:nSim
  % Plot storage
  [~,L,D]     = RHSAircraft( 0, x, dRHS );
  xPlot(:,k)  = [x;L;D];
  % Propagate (numerically integrate) the state equations
  if( k > nPulse )
    dRHS.externalAccel = [0;0;0];
  else
```

```
      dRHS.externalAccel = accel;
  end
  x              = RungeKutta( @RHSAircraft, 0, x, dT, dRHS );
  if( x(5) <= 0 )
    break;
  end
end

xPlot = xPlot(:,1:k);

%% Plot the results
yL      = {'u_(m/s)' 'w_(m/s)' 'q_(rad/s)' '\theta_(rad)' 'h_(m)' 'L_(N)' 'D_
    (N)'};
[t,tL] = TimeLabel(dT*(0:(k-1)));

PlotSet( t, xPlot(1:5,:), 'x_label', tL, 'y_label', yL(1:5),...
```

This simulation puts the aircraft into a slight climb.

```
>> AircraftSimOpenLoop
Velocity              250.00 m/s
Altitude            10000.00 m
Flight path angle       0.57 deg
Z speed                13.83 m/s
Thrust              12321.13 N
Angle of attack         3.17 deg
Elevator               11.22 deg
Initial cost         9.62e+01
Final cost           5.66e-17
Finding Equilibrium: Starting Cost   9.6158e+01 Final Cost   5.6645e-17
```

The simulation results are shown in Figure 11.13. The aircraft climbs steadily. Two oscillations are seen: a high-frequency one primarily associated with pitch and a low-frequency one with the velocity of the aircraft.

Figure 11.13: Open-loop response to a pulse for the F-16 in a shallow climb.

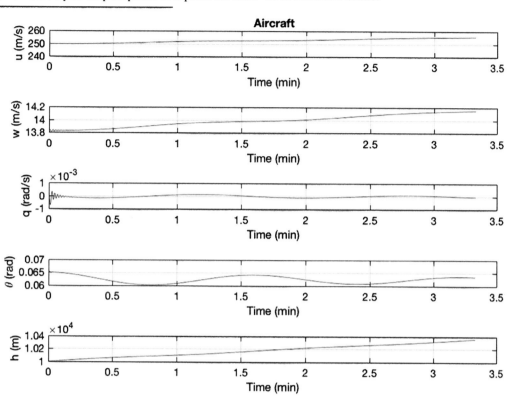

11.3.4   Find a Limiting and Scaling function for a Neural Net

11.3.4.1   Problem

You need a function to scale and limit measurements.

11.3.4.2   Solution

Use a sigmoid function.

11.3.4.3   How It Works

The neural net uses the following sigmoid function:

$$g(x) = \frac{1 - e^{-kx}}{1 + e^{-kx}} \tag{11.58}$$

The sigmoid function with $k = 1$ is plotted in the following script.

```
%% Initialize
x = linspace(-7,7);

%% Sigmoid
s = (1-exp(-x))./(1+exp(-x));

PlotSet( x, s, 'x_label', 'x', 'y_label', 's',...
  'plot_title', 'Sigmoid', 'figure_title', 'Sigmoid' );
```

Results are shown in Figure 11.14.

Figure 11.14: Sigmoid function. At large values of *x*, the sigmoid function returns ±1.

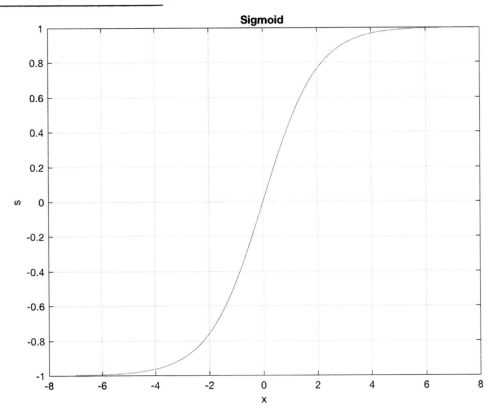

11.3.5 Find a Neural Net for the Learning Control

11.3.5.1 Problem

We need a neural net to add learning to the aircraft control system.

11.3.5.2 Solution

Use a sigma-pi function.

11.3.5.3 How It Works

The adaptive neural network for the pitch axis has seven inputs. The output of the neural network is a pitch angular acceleration that augments the control signal coming from dynamic inversion controller. The control system is shown in Figure 11.15.

Figure 11.15: Aircraft control.

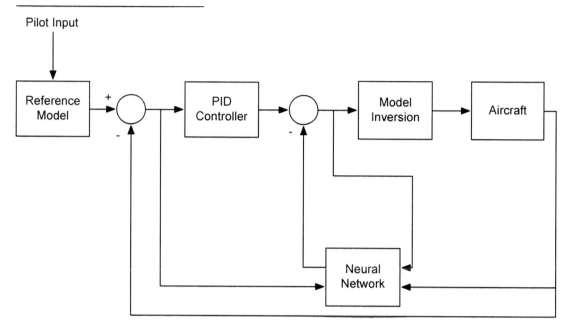

The sigma-pi neutral net is shown in Figure 11.16 for a two-input system.

Figure 11.16: Sigma-pi neural net. Π stands for product and Σ stands for sum.

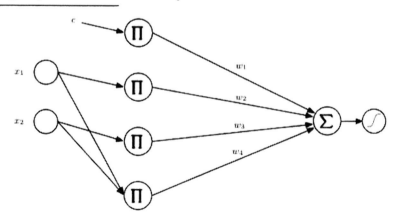

The output is

$$y = w_1 c + w_2 x_1 + w_3 x_2 + w_4 x_1 x_2 \tag{11.59}$$

The weights are selected to represent the nonlinear function. For example, suppose we want to represent the dynamic pressure

$$y = \frac{1}{2}\rho v^2 \tag{11.60}$$

We let $x_1 = \rho$ and $x_2 = v^2$. Set $w_4 = \frac{1}{2}$ and all other weights to zero. Suppose we didn't know the constant $\frac{1}{2}$. We would like our neural net to determine the weight through measurements.

Learning for a neural net means determining the weights so that our net replicates the function it is modeling. Define the vector z, which is the result of the product operations. In our two-input case this would be

$$z = \begin{bmatrix} 1 \\ x_1 \\ x_2 \\ x_1 x_2 \end{bmatrix} \qquad (11.61)$$

x_1 and x_2 are after the sigmoid operation. The output is

$$y = w^T z \qquad (11.62)$$

We could assemble multiple inputs and outputs

$$\begin{bmatrix} y_1 & y_2 & \cdots \end{bmatrix} = w^T \begin{bmatrix} z_1 & z_2 & \cdots \end{bmatrix} \qquad (11.63)$$

where z_k is a column array. We can solve for w using least squares. Define the vector of y to be Y and the matrix of z to be Z. The solution for w is

$$Y = Z^T w \qquad (11.64)$$

The least-squares solution is

$$w = (ZZ^T)^{-1} ZY^T \qquad (11.65)$$

This gives the best fit to w for the measurements Y and inputs Z. Suppose we take another measurement. We would then repeat this with bigger matrices. Clearly, this is impractical. As a side note you would really compute this using an inverse. There are better numerical methods for doing least squares. MATLAB has the pinv function. For example,

```
>> z = rand(4,4);
>> w = rand(4,1);
>> y = w'*z;
>> wL = inv(z*z')*z*y'

wL =

    0.8308
    0.5853
    0.5497
    0.9172

>> w

w =

    0.8308
    0.5853
    0.5497
    0.9172

>> pinv(z')*y'

ans =
```

```
0.8308
0.5853
0.5497
0.9172
```

As you can see, they all agree! This is a good way to initially train your neural net. Collect as many measurements as you have values of z and compute the weights. Your net is then ready to go.

The recursive approach is to initialize the recursive trainer with n values of z and y.

$$p = \left(ZZ^T\right)^{-1} \tag{11.66}$$

$$w = pZY \tag{11.67}$$

The recursive learning algorithm is

$$p = p - \frac{pzz^T p}{1+z^T pz} \tag{11.68}$$

$$k = pz \tag{11.69}$$

$$w = w + k\left(y - z^T w\right) \tag{11.70}$$

The following script demonstrates recursive learning or training. It starts with an initial estimate based on a four-element training set. It then recursively learns based on new data.

```
w    = rand(4,1); % Initial guess
Z    = randn(4,4);
Y    = Z'*w;

wN   = w + 0.1*randn(4,1); % True weights are a little different
n    = 300;
zA   = randn(4,n); % Random inputs
y    = wN'*zA; % 100 new measurements

% Batch training
p    = inv(Z*Z'); % Initial value
w    = p*Z*Y; % Initial value

%% Recursive learning
dW = zeros(4,n);
for j = 1:n
  z        = zA(:,j);
  p        = p - p*(z*z')*p/(1+z'*p*z);
  w        = w + p*z*(y(j) - z'*w);
  dW(:,j)  = w - wN; % Store for plotting
end

%% Plot the results
yL = cell(1,4);
for j = 1:4
  yL{j} = sprintf('\\Delta_W_%d',j);
end

PlotSet(1:n,dW,'x_label','Sample','y_label',yL,...
        'plot_title','Recursive_Training',...
        'figure_title','Recursive_Training');
```

Figure 11.17 shows the results. After an initial transient the learning converges. Every time you run this you will get different answers because we initialize with random values.

Figure 11.17: Recursive training or learning. After an initial transient the weights converge quickly.

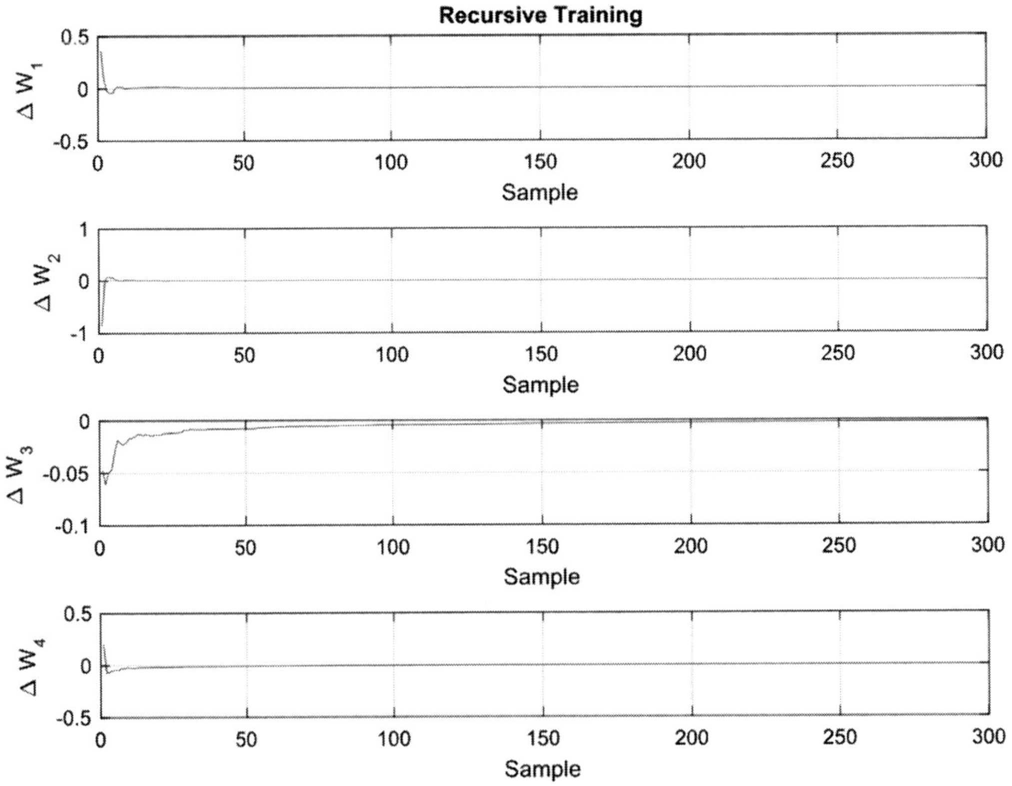

You will notice that the recursive learning algorithm is identical in form to the conventional Kalman filter given in Section 10.1.4. Our learning algorithm was derived from batch least squares, which is an alternative derivation for the Kalman filter.

11.3.6 Enumerate All Sets of Inputs

11.3.6.1 Problem

We need a function to enumerate all possible sets of combinations.

11.3.6.2 Solution

Write a combination function.

11.3.6.3 How It Works

We hand coded the products of the inputs. For more general code we want to enumerate all sets of inputs. If we have n inputs and want to take them k at a time, the number of sets is

$$\frac{n!}{(n-k)!k!} \tag{11.71}$$

The code to enumerate all sets is in the function Combinations.

```
%% Demo
if( nargin < 1 )
  Combinations(1:4,3)
  return
end

%% Special cases
if( k == 1 )
  c = r';
  return
elseif( k == length(r) )
  c = r;
  return
end

%% Recursion
rJ      = r(2:end);
c    = [];
if( length(rJ) > 1 )
  for j = 2:length(r)-k+1
    rJ            = r(j:end);
    nC            = NumberOfCombinations(length(rJ),k-1);
    cJ            = zeros(nC,k);
    cJ(:,2:end)   = Combinations(rJ,k-1);
    cJ(:,1)       = r(j-1);
    if( ~isempty(c) )
      c = [c;cJ];
    else
      c = cJ;
    end
  end
else
  c = rJ;
end
c = [c;r(end-k+1:end)];

function j = NumberOfCombinations(n,k)
%% Compute the number of combinations
j = factorial(n)/(factorial(n-k)*factorial(k));
```

This handles two special cases on input and then calls itself recursively for all other cases. Here are some examples:

```
>> Combinations(1:4,3)

ans =

        1       2       3
        1       2       4
        1       3       4
        2       3       4


>> Combinations(1:4,2)

ans =

        1       2
        1       3
        1       4
        2       3
        2       4
        3       4
```

You can see that if we have 4 inputs and want all possible combinations we end up with 14 total! This indicates a practical limit to a sigma-pi neural network as the number of weights will grow fast as the number of inputs increases.

11.3.7 Write a General Neural Net Function

11.3.7.1 Problem

We need a neural net function for general problems.

11.3.7.2 Solution

Use a sigma-pi function.

11.3.7.3 How It Works

The following code shows how we implement the sigma-pi neural net. SigmaPiNeuralNet has action as its first input. You use this to access the functionality of the function. Actions are

1. "initialize": initialize the function

2. "set constant": set the constant term

3. "batch learning": perform batch learning

4. "recursive learning": perform recursive learning

5. "output": generate outputs without training

You usually go in order when running the function. Setting the constant is not needed if the default of 1 is fine.

The functionality is distributed among subfunctions called from the switch statement.

```
% None.
```

```matlab
function [y, d] = SigmaPiNeuralNet( action, x, d )

% Demo or default data structure
if( nargin < 1 )
  if( nargout == 1 )
    y = DefaultDataStructure;
  else
    Demo;
  end
  return
end

switch lower(action)
      case 'initialize'
    d   = CreateZIndices( x, d );
    d.w = zeros(size(d.zI,1)+1,1);
    y   = [];

      case 'set_constant'
    d.c = x;
    y   = [];

  case 'batch_learning'
    [y, d] = BatchLearning( x, d );

  case 'recursive_learning'
    [y, d] = RecursiveLearning( x, d );

      case 'output'
    [y, d] = NNOutput( x, d );

  otherwise
    error('%s_is_not_an_available_action',action );
end

function d = CreateZIndices( x, d )
%% Create the indices

n    = length(x);
m    = 0;
nF   = factorial(n);
for k = 1:n
  m = m + nF/(factorial(n-k)*factorial(k));
end

d.z  = zeros(m,1);
d.zI = cell(m,1);

i    = 1;
for k = 1:n
      c = Combinations(1:n,k);
      for j = 1:size(c,1)
```

```
      d.zI{i} = c(j,:);
      i       = i + 1;
   end
end
d.nZ = m+1;

function d = CreateZArray( x, d )
%% Create array of products of x

n = length(x);

d.z(1) = d.c;
for k = 1:d.nZ-1
   d.z(k+1) = 1;
   for j = 1:length(d.zI(k))
      d.z(k+1) = d.z(k)*x(d.zI{k}(j));
   end
end

function [y, d] = RecursiveLearning( x, d )
%% Recursive Learning

d    = CreateZArray( x, d );
z    = d.z;
d.p     = d.p - d.p*(z*z')*d.p/(1+z'*d.p*z);
d.w     = d.w + d.p*z*(d.y - z'*d.w);
y    = z'*d.w;

function [y, d] = NNOutput( x, d )
%% Output without learning

x = SigmoidFun(x,d.kSigmoid);

d    = CreateZArray( x, d );
y    = d.z'*d.w;

function [y, d] = BatchLearning( x, d )
%% Batch Learning

z = zeros(d.nZ,size(x,2));

x = SigmoidFun(x,d.kSigmoid);

for k = 1:size(x,2)
   d        = CreateZArray( x(:,k), d );
   z(:,k)   = d.z;
end
d.p = inv(z*z');
d.w = (z*z')\z*d.y;
y    = z'*d.w;

function d = DefaultDataStructure
```

```
%% Default data structure

d             = struct();
d.w           = [];
d.c           = 1;  % Constant term
d.zI          = {};
d.z           = [];
d.kSigmoid    = 0.0001;
d.y           = [];
```

The demo shows an example of using the function to model dynamic pressure. Our inputs are the altitude and the square of the velocity. The neutral net will try to fit

$$y = w_1 c + w_2 h + w_3 v^2 + w_4 h v^2 \qquad (11.72)$$

to

$$y = 0.6125 e^{-0.0817 h^{1.15}} v^2 \qquad (11.73)$$

We get the default data structure. Then we initialize the filter with an empty x. We then get the initial weights by using batch learning. The number of columns of f x should be at least twice the number of inputs. This gives a starting p matrix and initial estimate of weights. We then perform recursive learning. It is important that the field kSigmoid is small enough so that valid inputs are in the linear region of the sigmoid function. Note that this can be an array so that you can use different scalings on different inputs.

```
%% Sigmoid function

kX   = k.*x;
s    = (1-exp(-kX))./(1+exp(-kX));


function Demo
%% Demo

x          = zeros(2,1);

d          = SigmaPiNeuralNet;
[~, d]     = SigmaPiNeuralNet( 'initialize', x, d );

h          = linspace(10,10000);
v          = linspace(10,400);
v2         = v.^2;
q          = 0.5*AtmDensity(h).*v2;

n          = 5;
x          = [h(1:n);v2(1:n)];
d.y        = q(1:n)';
[y, d]     = SigmaPiNeuralNet( 'batch learning', x, d );

fprintf(1,'Batch Results\n#          Truth   Neural Net\n');
for k = 1:length(y)
  fprintf(1,'%d: %12.2f %12.2f\n',k,q(k),y(k));
end
```

```
n = length(h);
y = zeros(1,n);
x = [h;v2];
for k = 1:n
  d.y = q(k);
  [y(k), d]  = SigmaPiNeuralNet( 'recursive_learning', x(:,k), d );
end
```

```
yL = { 'q_(N/m^2)' 'v_(m/s)' 'h_(m)' };
```

The batch results are as follows. This is at low altitude.

```
>> SigmaPiNeuralNet
Batch Results
#          Truth      Neural Net
1:          61.22          61.17
2:         118.24         118.42
3:         193.12         192.88
4:         285.38         285.52
5:         394.51         394.48
```

The recursive learning results are shown in Figure 11.18. The results are pretty good over a wide range of altitudes. You could then just use the "update" action during aircraft operation.

Figure 11.18: Recursive training for the dynamic pressure example.

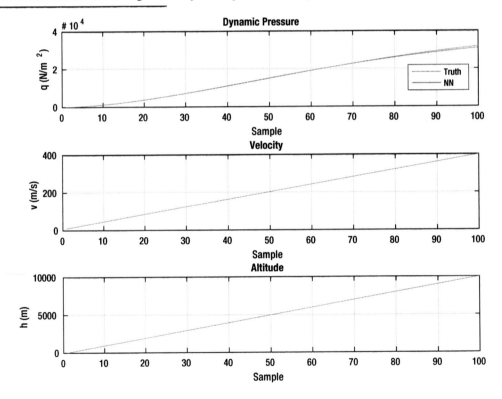

11.3.8 Implement PID Control

11.3.8.1 Problem

We want a PID controller.

11.3.8.2 Solution

Write a function to implement PID control.

11.3.8.3 How It Works

Assume with we have a double integrator driven by a constant input

$$\ddot{x} = u \tag{11.74}$$

where

$$\dot{x} = \frac{dx}{dt} \tag{11.75}$$

The result is

$$x = \frac{1}{2}ut^2 + x(0) + \dot{x}(0)t \tag{11.76}$$

The simplest control is to add a feedback controller

$$u_c = -K\left(\tau_d \dot{x} + x\right) \tag{11.77}$$

where K is the forward gain and τ is the damping time constant. Our dynamical equation is now

$$\ddot{x} + K\left(\tau_d \dot{x} + x\right) = u \tag{11.78}$$

The damping term will cause the transients to die out. When that happens the second derivative and first derivatives of x are zero and we end up with an offset

$$x = \frac{u}{K} \tag{11.79}$$

This is generally not desirable. You could increase K until the offset were small, but that would mean your actuator would need to produce higher forces or torques. What we have at the moment is a PD controller, or proportional derivative. Let's add another term to the controller

$$u_c = -K\left(\tau_d \dot{x} + x + \frac{1}{\tau_i}\int x\right) \tag{11.80}$$

This is now a PID controller, or proportional–integral–derivative controller. There is now a gain proportional to the integral of x. We add the new controller and then take another derivative to get

$$\dddot{x} + K\left(\tau_d \ddot{x} + \dot{x} + \frac{1}{\tau_i}x\right) = \dot{u} \tag{11.81}$$

Now in steady state

$$x = \frac{\tau_i}{K}\dot{u} \tag{11.82}$$

If u is constant, the offset is zero. Let

$$s = \frac{d}{dt} \tag{11.83}$$

Then

$$s^3 x(s) + K\left(\tau_d s^2 x(s) + sx(s) + \frac{1}{\tau_i} x(s)\right) = su(s) \tag{11.84}$$

$$\frac{u_c(s)}{w(s)} = K_p\left(1 + \tau_d s + \frac{1}{\tau_i s}\right) \tag{11.85}$$

where τ_d is the rate time constant, which is how long the system will take to damp, and τ_i is how fast the system will integrate out a steady disturbance.

The open-loop transfer function is

$$\frac{w(s)}{u(s)} = \frac{K_p}{s^2}\left(1 + \tau_d s + \frac{1}{\tau_i s}\right) \tag{11.86}$$

where $s = j\omega$ and $j = \sqrt{-1}$. The closed-loop transfer function is

$$\frac{w(s)}{u(s)} = \frac{s}{s^3 + K_p \tau_d s^2 + K_p s + K_p/\tau_i} \tag{11.87}$$

The desired closed-loop transfer function is

$$\frac{w(s)}{u_d(s)} = \frac{s}{(s+\gamma)(s^2 + 2\zeta\sigma s + \sigma^2)} \tag{11.88}$$

or

$$\frac{w(s)}{u(s)} = \frac{s}{s^3 + (\gamma + 2\zeta\sigma)s^2 + \sigma(\sigma + 2\zeta\gamma)s + \gamma\sigma^2} \tag{11.89}$$

The parameters are

$$K_p = \sigma(\sigma + 2\zeta\gamma) \tag{11.90}$$

$$\tau_i = \frac{\sigma + 2\zeta\gamma}{\gamma\sigma} \tag{11.91}$$

$$\tau_d = \frac{\gamma + 2\zeta\sigma}{\sigma(\sigma + 2\zeta\gamma)} \tag{11.92}$$

This is a design for a PID. However, it is not possible to write this in the desired state-space form

$$\dot{x} = Ax + Au \tag{11.93}$$

$$y = Cx + Du \tag{11.94}$$

because it has a pure differentiator. We need to add a filter to the rate term so that it looks like

$$\frac{s}{\tau_r s + 1} \tag{11.95}$$

instead of s. We aren't going to derive the constants and will leave it as an exercise for the reader. The code for the PID is in PID.

```
function [a, b, c, d] = PID(  zeta, omega, tauInt, omegaR, tSamp )

% Demo
if( nargin < 1 )
  Demo;
  return
end

% Input processing
if( nargin < 4 )
  omegaR = [];
end

% Default roll-off
if( isempty(omegaR) )
  omegaR = 5*omega;
end

% Compute the PID gains
omegaI  = 2*pi/tauInt;

c2   = omegaI*omegaR;
c1   = omegaI+omegaR;
b1   = 2*zeta*omega;
b2   = omega^2;
g    = c1 + b1;
kI   = c2*b2/g;
kP   = (c1*b2 + b1.*c2  - kI)/g;
kR   = (c1*b1 + c2 + b2 - kP)/g;

% Compute the state space model
a    = [0 0;0 -g];
b    = [1;g];
c    = [kI -kR*g];
```

It is interesting to evaluate the effect of the integrator. This is shown in Figure 11.19. The code is the demo in PID. Instead of numerically integrating the differential equations, we convert them into sampled time and propagate them. This is handy for linear equations. The double-integrator equations are in the form

$$x_{k+1} = ax_k + bu_k \qquad (11.96)$$
$$y = cx_k + du_k \qquad (11.97)$$

This is the same form as the PID controller.

```
% Convert to discrete time
if( nargin > 4 )
  [a,b] = CToDZOH(a,b,tSamp);
end

function Demo
%% Demo

% The double integrator plant
dT             = 0.1; % s
aP             = [0 1;0 0];
bP             = [0;1];
[aP, bP]       = CToDZOH( aP, bP, dT );

% Design the controller
[a, b, c, d]   = PID( 1, 0.1, 100, 0.5, dT );

% Run the simulation
n    = 2000;
p    = zeros(2,n);
x    = [0;0];
xC   = [0;0];

for k = 1:n
  % PID Controller
  y        = x(1);
  xC       = a*xC + b*y;
  uC       = c*xC + d*y;
  p(:,k)   = [y;uC];
  x        = aP*x + bP*(1-uC); % Unit step response
end
```

It takes about 2 minutes to drive *x* to zero, which is close to the 100 seconds specified for the integrator.

Figure 11.19: PID control given a unit input.

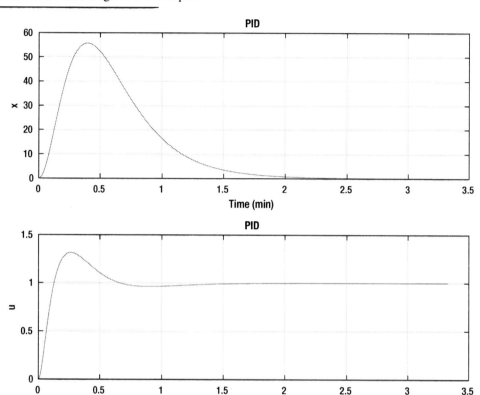

11.3.9 Demonstrate PID control of Pitch for the Aircraft

11.3.9.1 Problem

We want to control pitch with a PID control.

11.3.9.2 Solution

Write a script to implement the controller with the PID controller and pitch dynamic inversion compensation.

11.3.9.3 How It Works

The PID controller changes the elevator angle to produce a pitch acceleration to rotate the aircraft. In addition, additional elevator movement is needed to compensate for changes in the accelerations due to lift and drag as the aircraft changes its pitch orientation. This is done using the pitch dynamic inversion function. This returns the pitch acceleration that must be compensated for when applying the pitch control.

```
function qDot = PitchDynamicInversion( x, d )

if( nargin < 1 )
  qDot = DataStructure;
  return
end
```

```
u       = x(1);
w       = x(2);
h       = x(5);

rho     = AtmDensity( h );

alpha   = atan(w/u);
cA      = cos(alpha);
sA      = sin(alpha);

v       = sqrt(u^2 + w^2);
pD      = 0.5*rho*v^2;  % Dynamic pressure

cL      = d.cLAlpha*alpha;
cD      = d.cD0 + d.k*cL^2;

drag    = pD*d.s*cD;
lift    = pD*d.s*cL;

z       = -lift*cA - drag*sA;
m       = d.c*z;
qDot    = m/d.inertia;

function d = DataStructure
%% Data structure

% F-16
d                 = struct();
d.cLAlpha         = 2*pi;              % Lift coefficient
d.cD0             = 0.0175;           % Zero lift drag coefficient
d.k               = 1/(pi*0.8*3.09);     % Lift coupling coefficient A/R
    3.09, Oswald Efficiency Factor 0.8
d.s               = 27.87;            % wing area m^2
d.inertia         = 1.7295e5;         % kg-m^2
d.c               = 2;                % m
d.sE              = 25;               % m^2
d.delta           = 0;                % rad
d.rE              = 4;                % m
d.externalAccel   = [0;0;0];          % [m/s^2;m/s^2;rad/s^2[
```

The simulation incorporating the controls is shown below. There is a flag to turn on control and another to turn on the learning control.

```
% Options for control
addLearning    = true;
addControl     = true;

%% Initialize the simulation
nSim           = 1000;    % Number of time steps
dT             = 0.1;     % Time step (sec)
dRHS           = RHSAircraft;    % Get the default data structure has F-16
    data
```

```
h             = 10000;
gamma         = 0.0;
v             = 250;
nPulse        = 10;
pitchDesired  = 0.2;
dL            = load('PitchNNWeights');
[x,  dRHS.thrust, deltaEq, cost] = EquilibriumState( gamma, v, h, dRHS );
fprintf(1,'Finding_Equilibrium:_Starting_Cost_%12.4e_Final_Cost_%12.4e\n',
    cost);

if( addLearning )
  temp  = load('DRHSL');
  dRHSL = temp.dRHSL;
  temp  = load('DNN');
  dNN   = temp.d;
else
  temp  = load('DRHSL');
  dRHSL = temp.dRHSL;
end

accel = [0.0;0.0;0.0];

% Design the PID Controller
[aC, bC, cC, dC]  = PID( 1, 0.1, 100, 0.5, dT );
dRHS.delta        = deltaEq;
xDotEq            = RHSAircraft( 0, x, dRHS );
aEq               = xDotEq(3);
xC                = [0;0];

%% Simulation
xPlot = zeros(length(x)+8,nSim);
for k = 1:nSim

  % Control
        [~,L,D,pD]        = RHSAircraft( 0, x, dRHS );

  % Measurement
  pitch       = x(4);

  % PID control
  if( addControl )
    pitchError = pitch - pitchDesired;
    xC         = aC*xC + bC*pitchError;
    aDI        = PitchDynamicInversion( x, dRHSL );
    aPID       = -(cC*xC + dC*pitchError);
  else
    pitchError = 0;
    aPID       = 0;
  end
  % Learning
  if( addLearning )
    xNN       = [x(4);x(1)^2 + x(2)^2];
```

253

```
      aLearning = SigmaPiNeuralNet( 'output', xNN, dNN );
   else
      aLearning = 0;
   end

   if( addControl )
      aTotal       = aPID - (aDI + aLearning);

      % Convert acceleration to elevator angle
      gain         = dRHS.inertia/(dRHS.rE*dRHS.sE*pD);
      dRHS.delta   = asin(gain*aTotal);
   else
      dRHS.delta   = deltaEq;
   end

   % Plot storage
   xPlot(:,k)  = [x;L;D;aPID;pitchError;dRHS.delta;aPID;aDI;aLearning];

   % Propagate (numerically integrate) the state equations
   if( k > nPulse )
      dRHS.externalAccel = [0;0;0];
   else
      dRHS.externalAccel = accel;
   end
   x       = RungeKutta( @RHSAircraft, 0, x, dT, dRHS );

   % A crash
   if( x(5) <= 0 )
      break;
   end
end

%% Plot the results
xPlot   = xPlot(:,1:k);
yL      = {'u_(m/s)' 'w_(m/s)' 'q_(rad/s)' '\theta_(rad)' 'h_(m)' 'L_(N)' 'D
    _(N)' 'a_{PID}_(rad/s^2)' '\delta\theta_(rad)' '\delta_(rad)' ...
   'a_{PID}' 'a_{DI}' 'a_{L}'};
[t,tL]  = TimeLabel(dT*(0:(k-1)));

PlotSet( t, xPlot(1:5,:), 'x_label', tL, 'y_label', yL(1:5),...
   'plot_title', 'Aircraft', 'figure_title', 'Aircraft_State' );
PlotSet( t, xPlot(6:7,:), 'x_label', tL, 'y_label', yL(6:7),...
   'plot_title', 'Aircraft', 'figure_title', 'Aircraft_L_and_D' );
PlotSet( t, xPlot(8:10,:), 'x_label', tL, 'y_label', yL(8:10),...
   'plot_title', 'Aircraft', 'figure_title', 'Aircraft_Control' );
PlotSet( t, xPlot(11:13,:), 'x_label', tL, 'y_label', yL(11:13),...
   'plot_title', 'Aircraft', 'figure_title', 'Control_Acceleratins' );
```

We command a 0.2-radian pitch angle using the PID control. The results are shown in Figure 11.20, Figure 11.21, and Figure 11.22.

Figure 11.20: Aircraft pitch angle change. The aircraft oscillates due to the pitch dynamics.

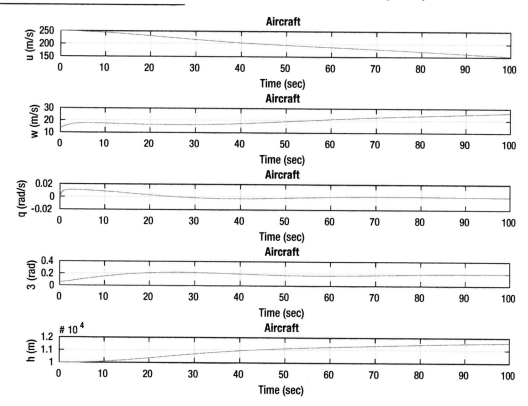

The maneuver increases the drag and we don't adjust the throttle to compensate. This will cause the airspeed to drop. In implementing the controller we neglected to consider coupling between states, but this can be added easily.

Figure 11.21: Aircraft pitch angle change. Notice the changes in lift and drag with angle.

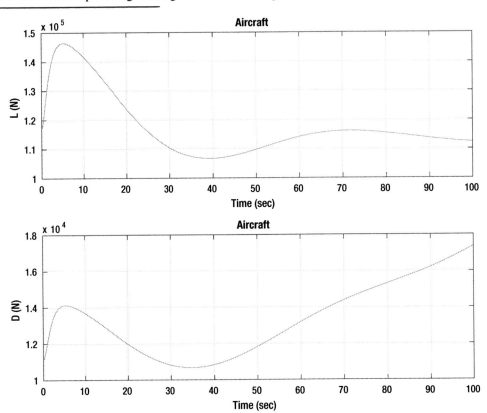

11.3.10 Create the Neural Net for the Pitch Dynamics

11.3.10.1 Problem

We want a nonlinear inversion controller with a PID controller and the neural net learning system.

11.3.10.2 Solution

Train the neural net with a script that takes the angle and velocity squared input and computes the pitch acceleration error.

11.3.10.3 How It Works

The following script computes the pitch acceleration for a slightly different set of parameters. It then processes the delta-acceleration. The script passes a range of pitch angles to the function and learns the acceleration. We use the velocity squared as an input because the dynamic pressure is proportional to the dynamic pressure. Thus, a base acceleration (in dRHSL) is for our "a priori" model. dRHS is the measured values. We assume that these are obtained during flight testing.

```
dRHS          = RHSAircraft;    % Get the default data structure has F-16
                                % data
h             = 10000;
gamma         = 0.0;
v             = 250;
```

Figure 11.22: Aircraft pitch angle change. The PID acceleration is much lower than the pitch inversion acceleration.

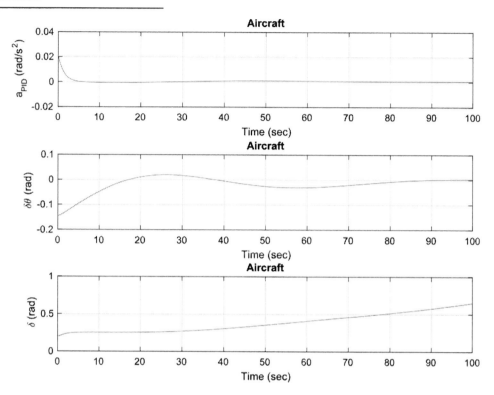

```
% Get the equilibrium state
[x,  dRHS.thrust, deltaEq, cost] = EquilibriumState( gamma, v, h, dRHS );

% Angle of attack
    alpha       = atan(x(2)/x(1));
    cA          = cos(alpha);
    sA          = sin(alpha);

% Create the assumed properties
dRHSL           = dRHS;
dRHSL.cD0       = 2.2*dRHS.cD0;
dRHSL.k         = 1.0*dRHSL.k;

% 2 inputs
xNN     = zeros(2,1);
d       = SigmaPiNeuralNet;
[~, d]  = SigmaPiNeuralNet( 'initialize', xNN, d );

theta   = linspace(0,pi/8);
v       = linspace(300,200);
n       = length(theta);
```

```
aT        = zeros(1,n);
aM        = zeros(1,n);

for k = 1:n
  x(4)   = theta(k);
  x(1)   = cA*v(k);
  x(2)   = sA*v(k);
  aT(k) = PitchDynamicInversion( x, dRHSL );
  aM(k) = PitchDynamicInversion( x, dRHS  );
end

% The delta pitch acceleration
dA        = aM - aT;

% Inputs to the neural net
v2        = v.^2;
xNN       = [theta;v2];

% Outputs for training
d.y       = dA';
[aNN, d]  = SigmaPiNeuralNet( 'batch_learning', xNN, d );

% Save the data for the aircraft simulation
save( 'DRHSL','dRHSL' );
save( 'DNN', 'd'  );
```

The resulting weights are saved in a MAT-file for use in AircraftSim. The simulation uses dRHS, but our pitch acceleration model uses dRHSL. The latter is saved in another MAT-file.

```
>> PitchNeuralNetTraining
Velocity              250.00 m/s
Altitude            10000.00 m
Flight path angle       0.00 deg
Z speed                13.84 m/s
Thrust              11148.95 N
Angle of attack         3.17 deg
Elevator               11.22 deg
Initial cost         9.62e+01
Final cost           1.17e-17
```

258

Figure 11.23: Neural net fit to the delta-acceleration

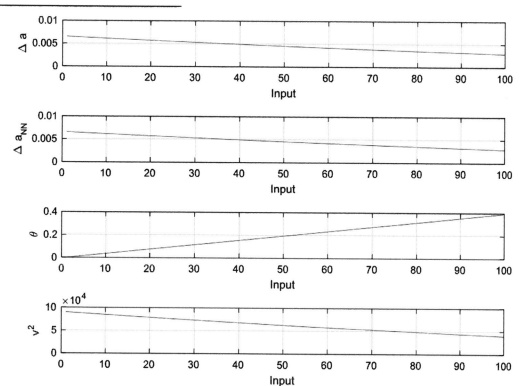

As can be seen, the neural net reproduces the model very well. The script also outputs DNN.mat, which contains the trained neural net data.

11.3.11 Demonstrate the Controller in a Nonlinear Simulation

11.3.11.1 Problem

We want to demonstrate our learning control system.

11.3.11.2 Solution

Enable the control functions to the simulation script described in this chapter.

11.3.11.3 How It Works

After training the neural net in the previous recipe we set addLearning to true. The weights are read in. When learning control is on, it uses the right-hand side. PitchDynamicInversion uses modified parameters that were used in the learning script to compute the weight. This simulates the uncertainty in the models.

We command a 0.2-radian pitch angle using the PID learning control. The results are shown in Figure 11.24, Figure 11.25, and Figure 11.26. The figures show without learning control on the left and with learning control on the right.

Figure 11.24: Aircraft pitch angle change. Lift and drag variations are shown.

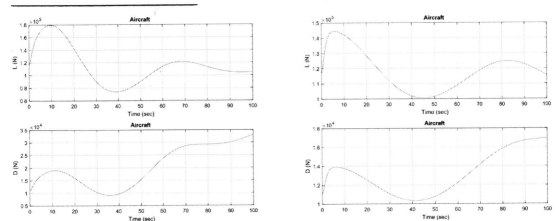

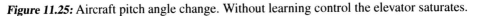

Figure 11.25: Aircraft pitch angle change. Without learning control the elevator saturates.

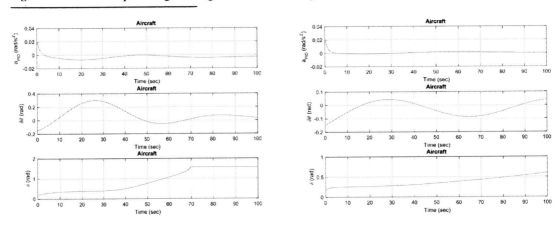

Learning control helps the performance of the controller. However, the weights are fixed throughout the simulation. Learning occurs prior to the controller becoming active. The control system is still sensitive to parameter changes since the learning part of the control was computed for a predetermined trajectory. Our weights were determined only as a function of pitch angle and velocity squared. Additional inputs would improve the performance. There are many opportunities for you to try to expand and improve the learning system.

Figure 11.26: Aircraft pitch angle change. The PID acceleration is much lower than the pitch inversion acceleration.

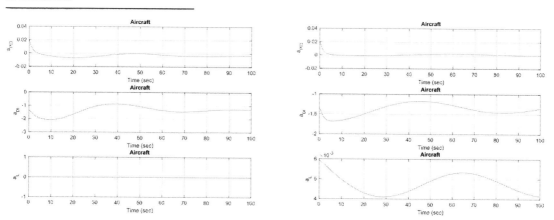

11.4 Ship Steering: Implement Gain Scheduling for Steering Control of a Ship

11.4.1 Problem

We want to steer a ship at all speeds.

11.4.2 Solution

The solution is to use gain scheduling to set the gains based on speeds. The gain scheduled is learned by automatically computing gains from the dynamical equations of the ship. This is similar to the self-tuning example except that we are seeking a set of gains for all speeds, not just one. In addition, we assume that we know the model of the system.

Figure 11.27: Ship heading control for gain scheduling control.

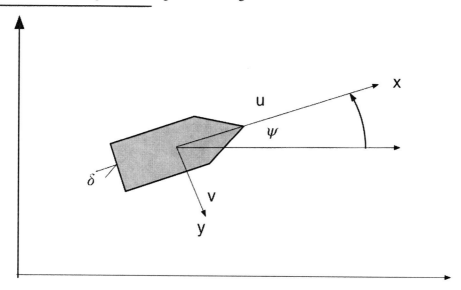

11.4.3 How It Works

The dynamical equations for the heading of a ship are in state-space form [1].

$$
\begin{bmatrix} \dot{v} \\ \dot{r} \\ \dot{\psi} \end{bmatrix} = \begin{bmatrix} \left(\frac{u}{l}\right)a_{11} & ua_{12} & 0 \\ \left(\frac{u}{l^2}\right)a_{21} & \left(\frac{u}{l}\right)a_{22} & 0 \\ 0 & 1 & 0 \end{bmatrix} \begin{bmatrix} v \\ r \\ \psi \end{bmatrix} + \begin{bmatrix} \left(\frac{u^2}{l}\right)b_1 \\ \left(\frac{u^2}{l^2}\right)b_2 \\ 0 \end{bmatrix} \delta + \begin{bmatrix} \alpha_v \\ \alpha_r \\ 0 \end{bmatrix}
\tag{11.98}
$$

v is the transverse speed, u is the ship's speed, l is the ship length, r is the turning rate, and ψ is the heading angle. α_v and α_r are disturbances. The ship is assumed to be moving at speed u. This is achieved by the propeller that is not modeled. You'll note we leave out the equation for forward motion. The control is the rudder angle δ. Notice that if $u = 0$, the ship cannot be steered. All of the coefficients in the state matrix are functions of u, except for the heading angle. Our goal is to control the heading given the disturbance acceleration in the first equation and the disturbance angular rate in the second.

The disturbances only affect the dynamics states, r and v. The last state, ψ, is a kinematic state and does not have a disturbance. Table 11.3 lists the files used in this chapter.

Table 11.3: Ship parameters [1].

Parameter	Minesweeper	Cargo	Tanker
l	55	161	350
a_{11}	-0.86	-0.77	-0.45
a_{12}	-0.48	-0.34	-0.44
a_{21}	-5.20	-3.39	-4.10
a_{22}	-2.40	-1.63	-0.81
b_1	0.18	0.17	0.10
b_2	1.40	-1.63	-0.81

The ship model is shown in the following code. The second and third outputs are for use in the controller. Notice that the differential equations are linear in the state and the control. Both matrices are a function of the forward velocity. The default parameters are for the minesweeper in the table.

```
function [xDot, a, b] = RHSShip( ~, x, d )

if( nargin < 1 )
  xDot = struct('l',100,'u',10,'a',[-0.86 -0.48;-5.2 -2.4],'b',[0.18;-1.4],'...
      alpha',[0;0;0],'delta',0);
  return
end

uOL   = d.u/d.l;
uOLSq = d.u/d.l^2;
uSqOl = d.u^2/d.l;
a     = [  uOL*d.a(1,1) d.u*d.a(1,2) 0;...
          uOLSq*d.a(2,1) uOL*d.a(2,2) 0;...
                      0              1 0];
b     = [uSqOl*d.b(1);...
        uOL^2*d.b(2);...
        0];

xDot = a*x + b*d.delta + d.alpha;
```

In the ship simulation we linearly increase the forward speed while commanding a series of heading psi changes. The controller takes the state-space model at each time step and computes new gains, which are used to steer the ship. The controller is a linear quadratic regulator. We can use full state feedback because the states are easily modeled. Such controllers will work perfectly in this case but are a bit harder to implement when you need to estimate some of the states or have unmodeled dynamics.

```
%% Initialize
nSim    = 10000;                 % Number of time steps
dT      = 1;                     % Time step (sec)
dRHS    = RHSShip;               % Get the default data structure
x       = [0;0.001;0.0];         % [lateral velocity;angular velocity;
    heading]
u       = linspace(10,20,nSim)*0.514;  % m/s
qC      = eye(3);                % State cost in the controller
rC      = 0.1;                   % Control cost in the controller

% Desired heading angle
psi     = [zeros(1,nSim/4) ones(1,nSim/4) 2*ones(1,nSim/4) zeros(1,nSim/4)];

%% Simulation
xPlot = zeros(3,nSim);
gain  = zeros(nSim,3);
delta = zeros(1,nSim);
for k = 1:nSim
    % Plot storage
    xPlot(:,k)   = x;
    dRHS.u       = u(k);

    % Control
    % Get the state space matrices
    [~,a,b]      = RHSShip( 0, x, dRHS );
    gain(k,:)    = QCR( a, b, qC, rC );
    dRHS.delta   = -gain(k,:)*[x(1);x(2);x(3) - psi(k)];  % Rudder angle
    delta(k)     = dRHS.delta;

    % Propagate (numerically integrate) the state equations
    x            = RungeKutta( @RHSShip, 0, x, dT, dRHS );
end

%% Plot the results
yL      = {'v_(m/s)' 'r_(rad/s)' '\psi_(rad)' 'u_(m/s)' 'Gain_v' 'Gain_r' '
    Gain_\psi' '\delta_(rad)' };
[t,tL] = TimeLabel(dT*(0:(nSim-1)));

PlotSet( t, [xPlot;u], 'x_label', tL, 'y_label', yL(1:4),...
    'plot_title', 'Ship', 'figure_title', 'Ship' );
```

The quadratic regulator generator code is shown in the following lists. It generates the gain from the matrix Riccati equation. A Riccati equation is an ordinary differential equation that is quadratic in the unknown function. In steady state this reduces to the algebraic Riccati equation that is solved in this function.

```
function k = QCR( a, b, q, r )

[sinf,rr] = Riccati( [a,-(b/r)*b';-q',-a'] );

if( rr == 1 )
  disp('Repeated_roots._Adjust_q,_r_or_n');
end

k = r\(b'*sinf);

function [sinf, rr] = Riccati( g )
%% Ricatti
%   Solves the matrix Riccati equation.
%
%   Solves the matrix Riccati equation in the form
%
%   g = [a    r ]
%       [q   -a']

rg = size(g);

[w, e] = eig(g);

es = sort(diag(e));

% Look for repeated roots
j = 1:length(es)-1;

if ( any(abs(es(j)-es(j+1))<eps*abs(es(j)+es(j+1))) ),
  rr = 1;
else
  rr = 0;
end

% Sort the columns of w
ws    = w(:,real(diag(e)) < 0);

sinf = real(ws(rg/2+1:rg,:)/ws(1:rg/2,:));
```

The results are given in Figure 11.28. Note how the gains evolve. The gain on the angular rate r is nearly constant. The other two gains increase with speed. This is an example of gain scheduling. The difference is that we autonomously compute the gains from measurements of the ship's forward speed.

Figure 11.28: Ship steering simulation. The states are shown on the left with the forward velocity. The gains and rudder angle are shown on the right. Notice the "pulses" in the rudder to make the maneuvers.

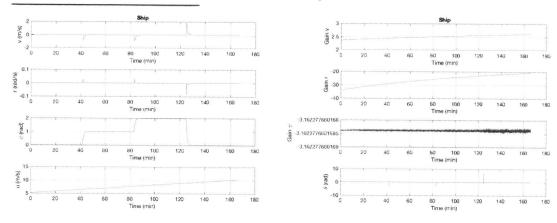

The next script is a modified version of ShipSim that is a shorter duration, with only one course change, and with disturbances in both angular rate and lateral velocity.

```
%% Initialize
nSim    = 300;                    % Number of time steps
dT      = 1;                      % Time step (sec)
dRHS    = RHSShip;                % Get the default data structure
x       = [0;0.001;0.0];          % [lateral velocity;angular velocity;
    heading]
u       = linspace(10,20,nSim)*0.514;  % m/s
qC      = eye(3);                 % State cost in the controller
rC      = 0.1;                    % Control cost in the controller
alpha   = [0.01;0.001];           % 1 sigma disturbances

% Desired heading angle
psi     = [zeros(1,nSim/6) ones(1,5*nSim/6)];

%% Simulation
xPlot = zeros(3,nSim);
gain  = zeros(nSim,3);
delta = zeros(1,nSim);
for k = 1:nSim
        % Plot storage
        xPlot(:,k)  = x;
        dRHS.u      = u(k);

        % Control
        % Get the state space matrices
        [~,a,b]     = RHSShip( 0, x, dRHS );
        gain(k,:)   = QCR( a, b, qC, rC );
        dRHS.alpha  = [alpha.*randn(2,1);0];
        dRHS.delta  = -gain(k,:)*[x(1);x(2);x(3) - psi(k)]; % Rudder angle
        delta(k)    = dRHS.delta;
```

265

```
            % Propagate (numerically integrate) the state equations
            x           = RungeKutta( @RHSShip, 0, x, dT, dRHS );
end


%% Plot the results
yL      = {'v␣(m/s)' 'r␣(rad/s)' '\psi␣(rad)' 'u␣(m/s)' 'Gain␣v' 'Gain␣r'
    'Gain␣\psi' '\delta␣(rad)' };
[t,tL] = TimeLabel(dT*(0:(nSim-1)));

PlotSet( t, [xPlot(1:3,:);delta], 'x␣label', tL, 'y␣label', yL([1:3 8]),...
```

The results are given in Figure 11.29.

Figure 11.29: Ship steering simulation. The states are shown on the left with the rudder angle. The disturbances are Gaussian white noise.

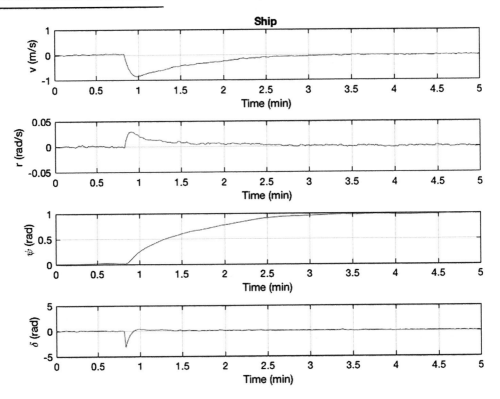

Summary

This chapter has demonstrated adaptive or learning control. You learned about model tuning, model reference adaptive control, adaptive control, and gain scheduling. Table 11.4 lists the files used in this chapter.

Table 11.4: Chapter Code Listing

File	Description
AircraftSim	Simulation of the longitudinal dynamics of an aircraft
AtmDensity	Atmospheric density using a modified exponential model
Combinations	Enumerates n integers for $1:n$ taken k at a time
EquilibriumState	Finds the equilibrium state for an aircraft
FFTEnergy	Generates FFT energy
FFTSim	Demonstration of the FFT
MRAC	Implement MRAC
PID	Implements a PID controller
PitchDynamicInversion	Pitch angular acceleration
PitchNeuralNetTraining	Train the pitch acceleration neural net
QCR	Generates a full state feedback controller
RecursiveLearning	Demonstrates recursive neural net training or learning
RHSAircraft	Right-hand side for aircraft longitudinal dynamics
RHSOscillatorControl	Right-hand side of a damped oscillator with a velocity gain
RHSRotor	Right-hand side for a rotor
RHSShip	Right-hand side for a ship steering model
RotorSim	Simulation of MRAC
ShipSim	Simulation of ship steering
ShipSimDisturbance	Simulation of ship steering with disturbances
SigmaPiNeuralNet	Implements a sigma-pi neural net
Sigmoid	Plot a sigmoid function
SquareWave	Generate a square wave
TuningSim	Controller tuning demonstration
WrapPhase	Keep angles between $-\pi$ and π

References

[1] K. J. Åström and B. Wittenmark. *Adaptive Control, Second Edition.* Addison-Wesley, 1995.

[2] A. E. Bryson Jr. *Control of Spacecraft and Aircraft.* Princeton, 1994.

[3] Byoung S. Kim and Anthony J. Calise. Nonlinear flight control using neural networks. *Journal of Guidance, Control, and Dynamics*, 20(1):26–33, 1997.

[4] Peggy S. Williams-Hayes. Flight Test Implementation of a Second Generation Intelligent Flight Control System. Technical Report NASA/TM-2005-213669, NASA Dryden Flight Research Center, November 2005.

CHAPTER 12

■ ■ ■

Autonomous Driving

Consider a primary car that is driving along a highway at variable speeds. It carries a radar that measures azimuth, range, and range rate. Many cars pass the primary car, some of which change lanes from behind the car and cut in front. The multiple-hypothesis system tracks all cars around the primary car. At the start of the simulation there are no cars in the radar field of view. One car passes and cuts in front of the radar car. The other two just pass in their lanes. You want to accurately track all cars that your radar can see.

There are two elements to this problem. One is to model the motion of the tracked automobiles using measurements to improve your estimate of each automobile's location and velocity. The second is to systematically assign measurements to different tracks. A track should represent a single car, but the radar is just returning measurements on echoes; it doesn't know anything about the source of the echoes.

You will solve the problem by first implementing a Kalman filter to track one automobile. We need to write measurement and dynamics functions that will be passed to the Kalman filter, and we need a simulation to create the measurements. You'll then combine the filter with the software to assign measurements to tracks, called multiple-hypothesis testing. You should master Chapter 10, on Kalman filters, before digging into this material.

12.1 Modeling the Automobile Radar

12.1.1 Problem

The sensor utilized for this example will be the automobile radar. The radar measures azimuth, range, and range rate. We need two functions: one for the simulation and the second for use by the unscented Kalman filter (UKF).

12.1.2 How It Works

The radar model is extremely simple. It assumes the radar measures line-of-sight range, range rate, and azimuth, the angle from the forward axis of the car. The model skips all the details of radar signal processing and outputs those three quantities. This type of simple model is always the best when you start a project. Later on you will need to add a very detailed model that has been verified against test data, to demonstrate that your system works as expected.

The position and velocity of the radar are entered through the data structure. This does not model the signal-to-noise ratio of a radar. The power received from a radar goes as $\frac{1}{r^4}$. In this model the signal goes

M. Paluszek and S. Thomas, *MATLAB Machine Learning*, DOI 10.1007/978-1-4842-2250-8_12

to zero at the maximum range. The range is found from the difference in position between the radar and the target.

$$\delta = \begin{bmatrix} x - x_r \\ y - y_r \\ z - z_r \end{bmatrix} \qquad (12.1)$$

The range is then

$$\rho = \sqrt{\delta_x^2 + \delta_y^2 + \delta_z^2} \qquad (12.2)$$

The delta velocity is

$$v = \begin{bmatrix} v_x - v_{x_r} \\ v_y - v_{y_r} \\ v_z - v_{z_r} \end{bmatrix} \qquad (12.3)$$

In both equations the subscript r denotes the radar. The range rate is

$$\dot{\rho} = \frac{v^T \delta}{\rho} \qquad (12.4)$$

12.1.3 Solution

The AutoRadar function handles multiple targets and can generate radar measurements for an entire trajectory. This is really convenient because you can give it your trajectory and see what it returns. This gives you a physical feel for the problem without running a simulation. It also allows you to be sure the sensor model is doing what you expect! This is important because all models have assumptions and limitations. It may be that the model really isn't suitable for your application. For example, this model is two dimensional. If you are concerned about your system getting confused about a car driving across a bridge above your automobile, this model will not be useful in testing that scenario.

Notice that the function has a built-in demo and, if there are no outputs, will plot the results. Adding demos to your code is a nice way to make your functions more user-friendly to other people using your code and even to you when you encounter the code again several months after writing the code! We put the demo in a subfunction because it is long. If the demo is one or two lines, a subfunction isn't necessary. Just before the demo function is the function defining the data structure.

```
%% AUTORADAR - Models automotive radar for simulation
%% Form:
%   [y, v] = AutoRadar( x, d )
%
%% Description
%   Automotive (2D) radar.
%
%   Returns azimuth, range and range rate. The state vector may be
%   any order. You pass the indices for the position and velocity states.
%   The angle of the car is passed in d even though it may be in the state

function [y, v] = AutoRadar( x, d )

% Demo
if( nargin < 1 )
  if(  nargout == 0 )
    Demo;
  else
    y = DataStructure;
```

```
  end
        return
end

m    = size(d.kR,2);
n    = size(x,2);
y    = zeros(3*m,n);
v    = ones(m,n);
cFOV = cos(d.fOV);

% Build an array of random numbers for speed
ran = randn(3*m,n);

% Loop through the time steps
for j = 1:n
  i     = 1;
  s     = sin(d.theta(j));
  c     = cos(d.theta(j));
  cIToC = [c s;-s c];

  % Loop through the targets
  for k = 1:m
    xT      = x(d.kR(:,k),j);
    vT      = x(d.kV(:,k),j);
    th      = x(d.kT(1,k),j);
    s       = sin(th);
    c       = cos(th);
    cTToIT  = [c -s;s c];
    dR      = cIToC*(xT - d.xR(:,j));
    dV      = cIToC*(cTToIT*vT - cIToC'*d.vR(:,j));
    rng     = sqrt(dR'*dR);
    uD      = dR/rng;

    % Apply limits
    if( d.noLimits || (uD(1) > cFOV && rng < d.maxRange) )
      y(i  ,j)  = rng                + d.noise(1)*ran(i  ,j);
      y(i+1,j)  = dR'*dV/y(i,j)      + d.noise(2)*ran(i+1,j);
      y(i+2,j)  = atan(dR(2)/dR(1))  + d.noise(3)*ran(i+2,j);
    else
      v(k,j)      = 0;
    end
    i   = i + 3;
  end
end

% Plot if no outputs are requested
if( nargout < 1 )
  [t, tL]      = TimeLabel( d.t );

  % Every 3rd y is azimuth
  i       = 3:3:3*m;
  y(i,:)  = y(i,:)*180/pi;
```

```
yL        = {'Range (m)' 'Range_Rate (m/s)', 'Azimuth (deg)' 'Valid Data'};
PlotSet(t,[y;v],'x label',tL','y label',yL,'figure title','Auto Radar',...
          'plot title','Auto Radar');

  clear y
end


function d = DataStructure
%% Default data structure
d.kR        = [1;2];
d.kV        = [3;4];
d.kT        = 5;
d.theta     = [];
d.xR        = [];
d.vR        = [];
d.noise     = [0.02;0.0002;0.01];
d.fOV       = 0.95*pi/16;
d.maxRange  = 60;
d.noLimits  = 1;
d.t         = [];


function Demo
%% Demo
omega       = 0.02;
d           = DataStructure;
n           = 1000;
d.xR        = [linspace( 0,1000,n);zeros(1,n)];
d.vR        = [ones(1,n);zeros(1,n)];
t           = linspace(0,1000,n);
a           = omega*t;
x           = [linspace(10,10+1.05*1000,n);2*sin(a);...
                1.05*ones(1,n); 2*omega*cos(a);zeros(1,n)];
d.theta     = zeros(1,n);
d.t         = t;

AutoRadar( x, d );
```

The second function, `AutoRadarUKF`, is the same core code but designed to be compatible with the UKF. We could have used `AutoRadar`, but this is more convenient.

```
%% AUTORADARUKF - radar model for the UKF
%% Form:
%   y = AutoRadarUKF( x, d )
%
%% Description
%   Automotive (2D) radar model for use with UKF.
%

function y = AutoRadarUKF( x, d )

s         = sin(d.theta);
c         = cos(d.theta);
```

```
cIToC   = [c s;-s c];
dR      = cIToC*x(1:2);
dV      = cIToC*x(3:4);

rng     = sqrt(dR'*dR);
```

Even though we are using radar as our sensor, there is no reason why you couldn't use a camera, laser rangefinder, or sonar instead. The limitation on the algorithms and software provided in this book is that it will only handle one sensor. You can get software from Princeton Satellite Systems that expands this to multiple sensors, for example, for a car with radar and cameras. Figure 12.1 shows the internal radar demo. The target car is weaving in front of the radar. It is receding at a steady velocity, but the weave introduces a time-varying range rate.

Figure 12.1: Built-in radar demo. The target is weaving in front of the radar.

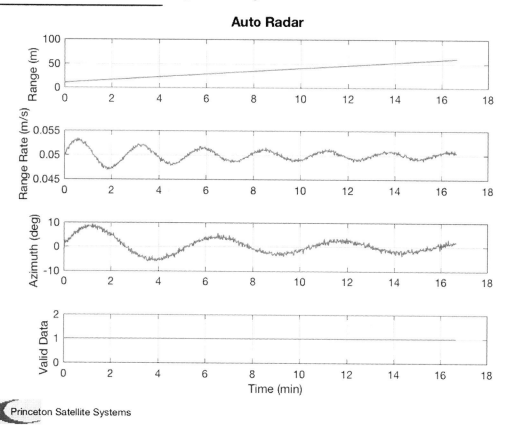

273

12.2   Automobile Autonomous Passing Control

12.2.1 Problem

In order to have something interesting for our radar to measure, we need our cars to perform some maneuvers. We will develop an algorithm for a car to change lanes.

12.2.2 Solution

The cars are driven by steering controllers that execute basic automobile maneuvers. The throttle (accelerator pedal) and steering angle can be controlled. Multiple maneuvers can be chained together. This provides a challenging test for the multiple-hypothesis testing (MHT) system. The first function is for autonomous passing and the second performs the lane change.

12.2.3 How It Works

The `AutomobilePassing` implements passing control by pointing the wheels at the target. It generates a steering angle demand and torque demand. Demand is what we want the steering to do. In a real automobile the hardware will try and meet the demand, but there will be a time lag before the wheel angle or motor torque meets the demand. In many cases, you are passing the demand to another control system that will try and meet the demand.

The state is defined by the `passState` variable. Prior to passing, the passState is 0. During the passing, it is 1. When it returns to its original lane, the state is set to 0.

```
%% AUTOMOBILEPASSING - Automobile passing control
%% Form:
%  passer = AutomobilePassing( passer, passee, dY, dV, dX, gain )
%
%% Description
% Implements passing control by pointing the wheels at the target.
% Generates a steering angle demand and torque demand.
%
% Prior to passing the passState is 0. During the passing it is 1.
% When it returns to its original lane the state is set to 0.
%
%% Inputs
%   passer        (1,1)  Car data structure
%                        .mass     (1,1) Mass (kg)
%                        .delta    (1,1) Steering angle (rad)
%                        .r        (2,4) Position of wheels (m)
%                        .cD       (1,1) Drag coefficient
%                        .cF       (1,1) Friction coefficient
%                        .torque      (1,1) Motor torque (Nm)
%                        .area     (1,1) Frontal area for drag (m^2)
%                        .x        (6,1) [x;y;vX;vZ;theta;omega]
%                        .errOld   (1,1) Old position error
%                        .passState (1,1) State of passing maneuver
%   passee (1,1)  Car data structure
%   dY     (1,1)  Relative position in y
%   dV     (1,1)  Relative velocity in x
%   dX     (1,1)  Relative position in x
%   gain   (1,3)  Gains [position velocity position derivative]
```

```
%
%% Outputs
%   passer        (1,1)   Car data structure with updated fields:
%                         .passState
%                         .delta
%                         .errOld
%                         .torque

function passer = AutomobilePassing( passer, passee, dY, dV, dX, gain )

% Default gains
if( nargin < 6 )
    gain = [0.05 80 120];
end

% Lead the target unless the passing car is in front
if( passee.x(1) + dX > passer.x(1) )
    xTarget = passee.x(1) + dX;
else
    xTarget = passer.x(1) + dX;
end

% This causes the passing car to cut in front of the car being passed
if( passer(1).passState == 0 )
    if( passer.x(1) > passee.x(1) + 2*dX )
        dY = 0;
        passer(1).passState = 1;
    end
else
    dY = 0;
end

% Control calculation
target          = [xTarget;passee.x(2) + dY];
theta           = passer.x(5);
dR              = target - passer.x(1:2);
angle           = atan2(dR(2),dR(1));
err             = angle - theta;
passer.delta    = gain(1)*(err + gain(3)*(err - passer.errOld));
passer.errOld   = err;
passer.torque   = gain(2)*(passee.x(3) + dV - passer.x(3));
```

The second function performs a lane change. It implements lane change control by pointing the wheels at the target. The function generates a steering angle demand and a torque demand.

```
function passer = AutomobileLaneChange( passer, dX, y, v, gain )

% Default gains
if( nargin < 5 )
        gain = [0.05 80 120];
end
```

```
% Lead the target unless the passing car is in front
xTarget          = passer.x(1) + dX;

% Control calculation
target           = [xTarget;y];
theta            = passer.x(5);
dR               = target - passer.x(1:2);
angle            = atan2(dR(2),dR(1));
err              = angle - theta;
passer.delta     = gain(1)*(err + gain(3)*(err - passer.errOld));
```

12.3   Automobile Dynamics

12.3.1   Problem

We need to model the car dynamics. We will limit this to a planar model in two dimensions. We are modeling the location of the car in x/y and the angle of the wheels which allows the car to change direction.

12.3.2   How It Works

Much like with the radar we will need two functions for the dynamics of the automobile. RHSAutomobile is used by the simulation and RHSAutomobileXY by the Kalman filter. RHSAutomobile has the full dynamic model including the engine and steering model. Aerodynamic drag, rolling resistance, and side force resistance (the car doesn't slide sideways without resistance) are modeled. RHSAutomobile handles multiple automobiles. An alternative would be to have a one-automobile function and call RungeKutta once for each automobile. The latter approach works in all cases, except when you want to model collisions. In many types of collisions two cars collide and then stick, effectively becoming a single car. A real tracking system would need to handle this situation.

Each vehicle has six states. They are

1. x-position

2. y-position

3. x-velocity

4. y-velocity

5. Angle about vertical

6. Angular rate about vertical

Figure 12.2: Planar automobile dynamical model.

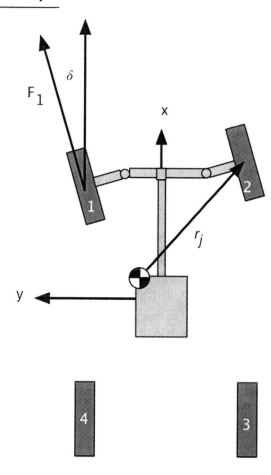

The velocity derivatives are driven by the forces and the angular rate derivative by the torques.

The planar dynamics model is illustrated in Figure 12.2 [7]. Unlike the reference we constrain the rear wheels to be fixed and the angles for the front wheels to be the same.

The dynamical equations are written in the rotating frame.

$$m(\dot{v}_x - \omega v_y) = \sum_{k=1}^{4} F_{k_x} - qC_{D_x}A_x u_x \tag{12.5}$$

$$m(\dot{v}_y + \omega v_x) = \sum_{k=1}^{4} F_{k_y} - qC_{D_y}A_y u_y \tag{12.6}$$

$$I\dot{\omega} = \sum_{k=1}^{4} r_k^{\times} F_k \tag{12.7}$$

where the dynamic pressure is

$$q = \frac{1}{2}\rho|v|^2 \tag{12.8}$$

and

$$v = \begin{bmatrix} v_x \\ v_y \end{bmatrix} \tag{12.9}$$

The unit vector is

$$u = \frac{\begin{bmatrix} v_x \\ v_y \end{bmatrix}}{|v|} \tag{12.10}$$

Figure 12.3 shows the wheel force and torque. The normal force is mg, where g is the acceleration of gravity. The force at the tire contact point (where the tire touches the road) is

Figure 12.3: Wheel force and torque.

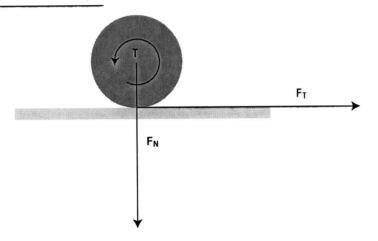

$$F_{t_k} = \begin{bmatrix} T/\rho - F_r \\ -F_c \end{bmatrix} \tag{12.11}$$

where F_f is the rolling friction and is

$$F_r = f_0 + K_1 v_{t_x}^2 \tag{12.12}$$

where v_{t_x} is the x-velocity in the tire frame. For front wheel drive cars the torque, T, is zero for the rear wheels. The contact friction is

$$F_c = \mu_c mg \frac{v_{t_y}}{|v_t|} \tag{12.13}$$

The velocity term ensures that the friction force does not cause limit cycling.

The transformation from tire to body frame is

$$c = \begin{bmatrix} \cos\delta & -\sin\delta \\ \sin\delta & \cos\delta \end{bmatrix} \tag{12.14}$$

so that

$$F_k = c F_{t_k} \tag{12.15}$$

$$v_t = c^T \begin{bmatrix} v_x \\ v_y \end{bmatrix} \tag{12.16}$$

The kinematic equations are

$$\dot{\theta} = \omega \tag{12.17}$$

and

$$V = \begin{bmatrix} \cos\theta & -\sin\theta \\ \sin\theta & \cos\theta \end{bmatrix} v \qquad\qquad (12.18)$$

12.3.3 Solution

The RHSAutomobile function is shown below.

```
function xDot = RHSAutomobile( ~, x, d )

% Constants
g          = 9.806; % Acceleration of gravity (m/s^2)
n          = length(x);
nS         = 6; % Number of states
xDot       = zeros(n,1);
nAuto      = n/nS;

j = 1;
% State  [j j+1 j+2 j+3   j+4     j+5]
%         x  y  vX  vY   theta  omega
for k = 1:nAuto
   vX          = x(j+2,1);
   vY          = x(j+3,1);
   theta       = x(j+4,1);
   omega       = x(j+5,1);

   % Car angle
   c           = cos(theta);
   s           = sin(theta);

   % Inertial frame
   v           = [c -s;s c]*[vX;vY];

   delta       = d.car(k).delta;
   c           = cos(delta);
   s           = sin(delta);
   mCToT       = [c s;-s c];

   % Find the rolling resistance of the tires
   vTire       = mCToT*[vX;vY];
   f0          = d.car(k).fRR(1);
   K1          = d.car(k).fRR(2);

   fRollingF   = f0 + K1*vTire(1)^2;
         fRollingR   = f0 + K1*vX^2;

   % This is the side force friction
   fFriction   = d.car(k).cF*d.car(k).mass*g;
   fT          = d.car(k).radiusTire*d.car(k).torque;

   fF          = [fT - fRollingF;-vTire(2)*fFriction];
   fR          = [   - fRollingR;-vY        *fFriction];
```

279

```
% Tire forces
f1              = mCToT'*fF;
f2              = f1;
f3              = fR;
f4              = f3;

% Aerodynamic drag
vSq             = vX^2 + vY^2;
vMag            = sqrt(vSq);
q               = 0.5*1.225*vSq;
fDrag           = q*[d.car(k).cDF*d.car(k).areaF*vX;...
                    d.car(k).cDS*d.car(k).areaS*vY]/vMag;

% Force summations
f               = f1 + f2 + f3 + f4 - fDrag;

% Torque
T               = Cross2D( d.car(k).r(:,1), f1 ) + Cross2D( d.car(k).r(:,2),
        f2 ) + ...
                    Cross2D( d.car(k).r(:,3), f3 ) + Cross2D( d.car(k).r(:,4),
                        f4 );

% Right hand side
xDot(j,  1) = v(1);
xDot(j+1,1) = v(2);
xDot(j+2,1) = f(1)/d.car(k).mass + omega*vY;
xDot(j+3,1) = f(2)/d.car(k).mass - omega*vX;
xDot(j+4,1) = omega;
xDot(j+5,1) = T/d.car(k).inr;

j               = j + nS;
end

function c = Cross2D( a, b )
%% Cross2D
c = a(1)*b(2) - a(2)*b(1);
```

The Kalman filter's right-hand side is just the differential equations

$$\dot{x} = v_x \qquad (12.19)$$

$$\dot{y} = v_y \qquad (12.20)$$

$$\dot{v}_x = 0 \qquad (12.21)$$

$$\dot{v}_y = 0 \qquad (12.22)$$

The dot means time derivative or rate of change with time. These are the state equations for the automobile. This model says that the position change with time is proportional to the velocity. It also says the velocity is constant. Information about velocity changes will come solely from the measurements. We also don't model the angle or angular rate. This is because we aren't getting information about it from the radar. However, you might try including it!

The RHSAutomobileXY function is shown below; it is only two lines of code!

```
function xDot = RHSAutomobileXY( ~, x, ~ )

xDot = [x(3:4);0;0];
```

12.4   Automobile Simulation and the Kalman Filter

12.4.1 Problem

You want to track a car using radar measurements to track an automobile maneuvering around your car. Cars may appear and disappear at any time. The radar measurement needs to be turned into the position and velocity of the tracked car. In between radar measurements you want to make your best estimate of where the automobile will be at a given time.

12.4.2 Solution

The solution is to implement a UKF to take radar measurements and update a dynamical model of the tracked automobile.

12.4.3 How It Works

The demonstration simulation is the same simulation used to demonstrate the multiple-hypothesis system tracking. This simulation just demonstrates the Kalman filter. Since the Kalman filter is the core of the package, it is important that it work well before adding the measurement assignment part.

MHTDistanceUKF finds the MHT distance for use in gating computations using the UKF. The measurement function is of the form $h(x,d)$, where d is the UKF data structure. MHTDistanceUKF uses sigma points. The code is similar to UKFUpdate. As the uncertainty gets smaller, the residual must be smaller to remain within the gate.

```
function [k, del] = MHTDistanceUKF( d )

% Get the sigma points
pS       = d.c*chol(d.p)';
nS       = length(d.m);
nSig     = 2*nS + 1;
mM       = repmat(d.m,1,nSig);
if( length(d.m) == 1 )
    mM = mM';
end

x        = mM + [zeros(nS,1) pS -pS];

[y, r]   = Measurement( x, d );
mu       = y*d.wM;
b        = y*d.w*y' + r;
del      = d.y - mu;
k        = del'*(b\del);

function [y, r] = Measurement( x, d )
%%       Measurement from the sigma points

nSigma   = size(x,2);
```

281

```
lR        = length(d.r);
y         = zeros(lR,nSigma);
r         = d.r;
iR        = 1:lR;

for j = 1:nSigma
        f                = feval( d.hFun, x(:,j), d.hData );
        y(iR,j)          = f;
        r(iR,iR)         = d.r;
```

The simulation UKFAutomobileDemo uses a car data structure to contain all of the car information. A MATLAB function AutomobileInitialize takes parameter pairs and builds the data structure. This is a lot cleaner than assigning the individual fields in your script. It will return a default data structure if nothing is entered as an argument.

The first part of the demo, shown in the following listing, is the automobile simulation. It generates the measurements of the automobile positions to be used by the Kalman filter.

```
%% Initialize

% Set the seed for the random number generators.
% If the seed is not set each run will be different.
seed = 45198;
rng(seed);

% Car control
laneChange = 1;

% Clear the data structure
d = struct;

% Car 1 has the radar
d.car(1) = AutomobileInitialize( ...
                'mass', 1513,...
                'position_tires', [1.17 1.17 -1.68 -1.68; -0.77 0.77 -0.77
                    0.77], ...
                'frontal_drag_coefficient', 0.25, ...
                'side_drag_coefficient', 0.5, ...
                'tire_friction_coefficient', 0.01, ...
                'tire_radius', 0.4572, ...
                'engine_torque', 0.4572*200, ...
                'rotational_inertia', 2443.26, ...
                'rolling_resistance_coefficients', [0.013 6.5e-6], ...
                'height_automobile', 2/0.77, ...
                'side_and_frontal_automobile_dimensions', [1.17+1.68 2*0.77]);
% Make the other car identical
d.car(2) = d.car(1);
nAuto     = length(d.car);
% Velocity set points for the cars
vSet   = [12 13];

% Time step setup
dT          = 0.1;
```

```
tEnd          = 20*60;
tLaneChange   = 10*60;
tEndPassing   =  6*60;
n             = ceil(tEnd/dT);

% Car initial states
x = [140; 0;12;0;0;0;...
        0; 0;11;0;0;0];

% Radar - the radar model has a field of view and maximum range
% Range drop off or S/N is not modeled
m                  = length(x)-1;
dRadar.kR          = [ 7:6:m; 8:6:m]; % State position indices
dRadar.kV          = [ 9:6:m;10:6:m]; % State velocity indices
dRadar.kT          = 11:6:m; % State yaw angle indices
dRadar.noise       = 0.1*[0.02;0.001;0.001]; % [range; range rate; azimuth]
dRadar.fOV         = pi/4; % Field of view
dRadar.maxRange    = inf;
dRadar.noLimits    = 0; % Limits are checked (fov and range)

% Plotting
yP = zeros(3*(nAuto-1),n);
vP = zeros(nAuto-1,n);

xP = zeros(length(x)+2*nAuto,n);
s  = 1:6*nAuto;

%% Simulate
t = (0:(n-1))*dT;
fprintf(1,'\nRunning_the_simulation...');
for k = 1:n

    % Plotting
    xP(s,k)      = x;
    j            = s(end)+1;

    for i = 1:nAuto
        p            = 6*i-5;
        d.car(i).x   = x(p:p+5);
        xP(j:j+1,k)  = [d.car(i).delta;d.car(i).torque];
        j            = j + 2;
    end

    % Get radar measurements
    dRadar.theta       = d.car(1).x(5);
    dRadar.t           = t(k);
    dRadar.xR          = x(1:2);
    dRadar.vR          = x(3:4);
    [yP(:,k), vP(:,k)] = AutoRadar( x, dRadar );

    % Implement Control
```

```
    % For all but the passing car control the velocity
        d.car(1).torque = -10*(d.car(1).x(3) - vSet(1));

    % The active car
    if( t(k) < tEndPassing )
        d.car(2)        = AutomobilePassing( d.car(2), d.car(1), 3, 1.3, 10
            );
    elseif ( t(k) > tLaneChange && laneChange )
        d.car(2)        = AutomobileLaneChange( d.car(2), 10, 3, 12 );
    else
        d.car(2).torque = -10*(d.car(2).x(3) - vSet(2));
    end


    % Integrate
    x               = RungeKutta(@RHSAutomobile, 0, x, dT, d );
end
fprintf(1,'DONE.\n');

% The state of the radar host car
xRadar = xP(1:6,:);

% Plot the simulation results
NewFigure( 'Auto' )
kX = 1:6:length(x);
kY = 2:6:length(x);
c  = 'bgrcmyk';
j  = floor(linspace(1,n,20));
for k = 1:nAuto
    plot(xP(kX(k),j),xP(kY(k),j),[c(k) '.']);
    hold on
end
legend('Auto_1','Auto_2');
for k = 1:nAuto
    plot(xP(kX(k),:),xP(kY(k),:),c(k));
end
xlabel('x_ (m)');
ylabel('y_ (m)');
set(gca,'ylim',[-5 5]);
grid
```

The second part of the demo, shown in this listing, processes the measurements in the UKF to generate the estimates of the automobile track.

```
%% Implement UKF

% Covariances
r0      = diag(dRadar.noise.^2);      % Measurement 1-sigma
q0      = [1e-7;1e-7;.1;.1];          % The baseline plant covariance diagonal
p0      = [5;0.4;1;0.01].^2;          % Initial state covariance matrix
    diagonal

% Each step is one scan
ukf = KFInitialize( 'ukf','f',@RHSAutomobileXY,'alpha',1,...
```

```matlab
                        'kappa',0,'beta',2,'dT',dT,'fData',struct('f',0),...
                        'p',diag(p0),'q',diag(q0),'x',[0;0;0;0],'hData',struct('
                            theta',0),...
                          'hfun',@AutoRadarUKF,'m',[0;0;0;0],'r',r0);
ukf = UKFWeight( ukf );

% Size arrays
k1 = find( vP > 0 );
k1 = k1(1);

% Limit to when the radar is tracking
n      = n - k1 + 1;
yP     = yP(:,k1:end);
xP     = xP(:,k1:end);
pUKF   = zeros(4,n);
xUKF   = zeros(4,n);
dMHTU  = zeros(1,n);
t      = (0:(n-1))*dT;

for k = 1:n
    % Prediction step
    ukf.t        = t(k);
    ukf          = UKFPredict( ukf );

    % Update step
    ukf.y        = yP(:,k);
    ukf          = UKFUpdate( ukf );

    % Compute the MHT distance
    dMHTU(1,k)   = MHTDistanceUKF( ukf );

    % Store for plotting
    pUKF(:,k)          = diag(ukf.p);
    xUKF(:,k)    = ukf.m;
end

% Transform the velocities into the inertial frame
for k = 1:n
    c            = cos(xP(5,k));
    s            = sin(xP(5,k));
    cCarToI      = [c -s;s c];
    xP(3:4,k)    = cCarToI*xP(3:4,k);

    c            = cos(xP(11,k));
    s            = sin(xP(11,k));
cCarToI      = [c -s;s c];
    xP(9:10,k)   = cCarToI*xP(9:10,k);
end

% Relative position
dX = xP(7:10,:) - xP(1:4,:);
```

```
%% Plotting
[t,tL] = TimeLabel(t);

% Plot just select states
k    = [1:4 7:10];
yL     = {'p_x' 'p_y' 'p_{v_x}' 'p_{v_y}'};
pS  = {[1 5] [2 6] [3 7] [4 8]};

PlotSet(t, pUKF,        'x_label',  tL,'y_label', yL,'figure_title', '
    Covariance', 'plot_title', 'Covariance');
PlotSet(t, [xUKF;dX], 'x_label',          tL,'y_label',{'x' 'y' 'v_x' 'v_y'
    },...
                          'plot_title','UKF_State:_Blue_is_UKF,_Green_is_Truth',
                              'figure_title','UKF_State','plot_set', pS );
PlotSet(t, dMHTU,      'x_label',  tL,'y_label','d_(m)', 'plot_title','MHT_
    Distance_UKF', 'figure_title','MHT_Distance_UKF','plot_type','ylog');
```

The results of the script are shown in Figure 12.4, Figure 12.5, and Figure 12.6.

Figure 12.4: Automobile trajectories.

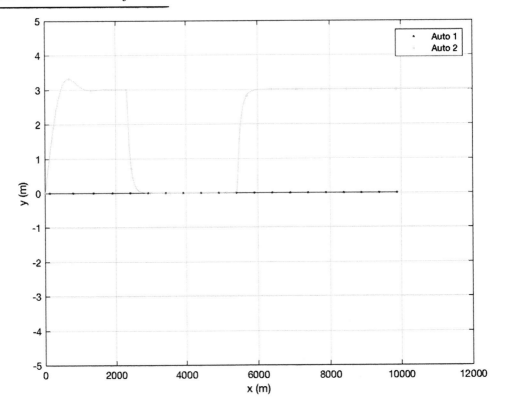

Figure 12.5: The true states and UKF estimated states.

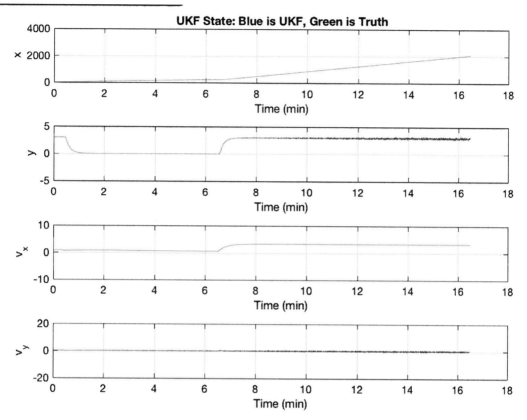

Figure 12.6: The MHT distance between the automobiles during the simulation. Notice the spike in distance when the automobile maneuver starts.

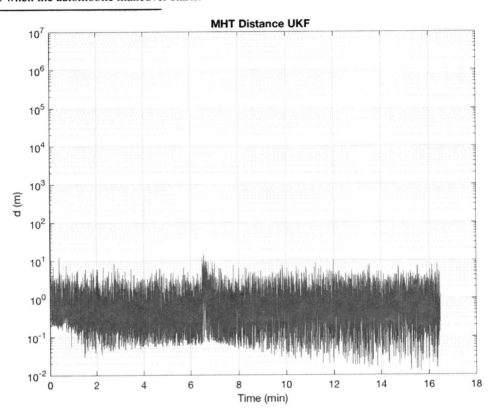

12.5 Perform MHT on the Radar Data

12.5.1 Problem

You want to use hypothesis testing to track multiple cars. You need to take measurements returned by the radar and assign them methodically to the state histories, that is, position and velocity histories, of the automobiles. The radar doesn't know one car from the other so you need a methodical and repeatable way to assign radar pings to tracks.

12.5.2 Solution

The solution is to implement track-oriented MHT. This system will learn the trajectories of all cars that are visible to the radar system.

Figure 12.7 shows the general tracking problem. Two scans of data are shown. When the first scan is done there are two tracks. The uncertainty ellipsoids are shown and they are based on all previous information. In the $k - 1$ scan three measurements are observed. 1 and 3 are within the ellipsoids of the two tracks but 2 is in both. It may be a measurement of either of the tracks or a spurious measurement. In scan k four measurements are taken. Only measurement 4 is in one of the uncertainty ellipsoids. 3 might be interpreted as spurious, but it is actually caused by a new track from a third vehicle that separates from the blue track. 1 is outside the red ellipsoid but is actually a good measurement of the red track and (if correctly interpreted) indicates that the model is erroneous. 4 is a good measurement of the blue

Figure 12.7: Tracking problem.

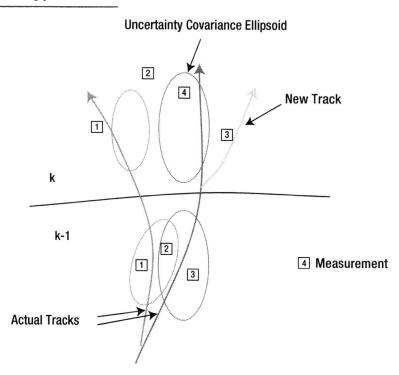

track and indicates that the model is valid. The illustration shows how the tracking system should behave but without the tracks it would be difficult to interpret the measurements. A measurement can be valid, spurious, or a new track.

We define a contact as an observation where the signal-to-noise ratio is above a certain threshold. The observation then constitutes a measurement. Low signal-to-noise ratio observations can happen in both optical and radar systems. Thresholding reduces the number of observations that need to be associated with tracks but may lose valid data. An alternative is to treat all observations as contact but adjust the measurement error accordingly.

Valid measurements must then be assigned to tracks. An ideal tracking system would be able to categorize each measurement accurately and then assign them to the correct track. The system must also be able to identify new tracks and remove tracks that no longer exist.

If we were confident that we were only tracking one vehicle, all of the data might be incorporated into the state estimate. An alternative is to incorporate only the data within the covariance ellipsoids and treat the remainders as outliers. If the latter strategy were taken, it would be sensible to remember that data in case future measurements also were "outliers," in which case the filter might go back and incorporate different sets of outliers into the solution. This could easily happen if the model were invalid, for example, if the vehicle, which had been coasting, suddenly began maneuvering and the filter model did not allow for maneuvers.

In classical multiple-target tracking [6], the problem is divided into two steps, association and estimation. Step 1 associates contacts with targets and step 2 estimates each target's state. Complications arise when there is more than one reasonable way to associate contacts with targets. The MHT approach is to form alternative hypotheses to explain the source of the observations. Each hypothesis assigns observations to targets or false alarms.

There are two approaches to MHT [3]. The first, following Reid [5], operates within a structure in which hypotheses are continually maintained and updated as observation data are received. In the second, the track-oriented approach to MHT, tracks are initiated, updated, and scored before being formed into hypotheses. The scoring process consists of comparing the likelihood that the track represents a true target versus the likelihood that it is a collation of false alarms. Thus, unlikely tracks can be deleted before the next stage in which tracks are formed into hypotheses.

The track-oriented approach recomputes the hypotheses using the newly updated tracks after each scan of data is received. Rather than maintaining, and expanding, hypotheses from scan to scan, the track-oriented approach discards the hypotheses formed on scan $k - 1$. The tracks that survive pruning are predicted to the next scan k where new tracks are formed, using the new observations, and reformed into hypotheses. Except for the necessity to delete some tracks based upon low probability or N-scan pruning, no information is lost because the track scores, which are maintained, contain all the relevant statistical data. MHT terms are defined in Table 12.1.

Table 12.1: MHT Terms

Term	Definition
Clutter	Transient objects of no interest to the tracking system
Cluster	A collection of tracks that are linked by common observations
Family	A set of tracks with a common root node. At most one track per family can be included in a hypothesis. A family can represent at most one target
Hypothesis	A set of tracks that do not share any common observations
N-Scan Pruning	Using the track scores from the last N scans of data to prune tracks. The count starts from a root node. When the tracks are pruned, a new root node is established
Observation	A measurement that indicates the presence of an object. The observation may be of a target or be spurious
Pruning	Removal of low-score tracks
Root Node	An established track to which observations can be attached and which may spawn additional tracks
Scan	A set of data taken simultaneously
Target	An object being tracked
Trajectory	The path of a target
Track	A trajectory that is propagated
Track Branch	A track in a family that represents a different data association hypothesis. Only one branch can be correct
Track Score	The log-likelihood ratio for a track

Track scoring is done using log-likelihood ratios:

$$L(K) = \log[\text{LR}(K)] = \sum_{k=1}^{K} [\text{LLR}_K(k) + \text{LLR}_S(k)] + \log[L_0] \tag{12.23}$$

where the subscript K denotes kinematic and the subscript S denotes signal. It is assumed that the two are statistically independent.

$$L_0 = \frac{P_0(H_1)}{P_0(H_0)} \tag{12.24}$$

where H_1 and H_0 are the true target and false alarm hypotheses. log is the natural logarithm. The likelihood ratio for the kinematic data is the probability that the data are a result of the true target divided by the probability that the data are from a false alarm:

$$LR_K = \frac{p(D_K|H_1)}{p(D_K|H_0)} = \frac{e^{-d^2/2}/((2\pi)^{M/2}\sqrt{|S|}}{1/V_C} \tag{12.25}$$

where M is the measurement dimension, V_C is the measurement volume, $S = HPT^T + R$ is the measurement residual covariance matrix, and $d^2 = y^T S^{-1} y$ is the normalized statistical distance for the measurement defined by the residual y and the covariance matrix S. The numerator is the multivariate Gaussian.

The following are the rules for each measurement:

- Each measurement creates a new track.

- Each measurement in each gate updates the existing track. If there is more than one measurement in a gate, the existing track is duplicated with the new measurement.

- All existing tracks are updated with a "missed" measurement, creating a new track.

Figure 12.8 gives an example. There are two tracks and three measurements. All three measurements are in the gate for track 1, but only one is in the gate for track 2. Each measurement produces a new track. The three measurements produce three tracks based on track 1 and the one measurement produces one track based on track 2. Each track also spawns a new track assuming that there was no measurement for the track. Thus, in this case three measurements and two tracks result in nine tracks. Tracks 7–9 are initiated based only on the measurement, which may not be enough information to initiate the full state vector. If this is the case, there would be an infinite number of tracks associated with each measurement, not just one new track. If we have a radar measurement we have azimuth, elevation, range, and range rate. This gives all position states and one velocity state.

Figure 12.8: Measurement and gates. M0 is an "absent" measurement.

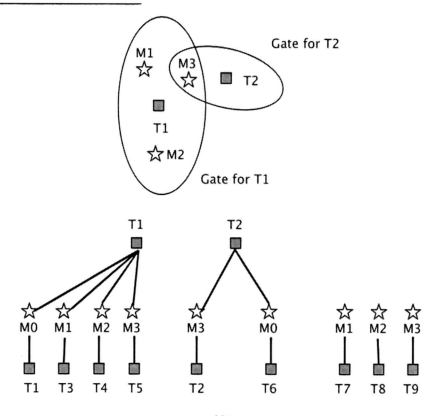

12.5.3 How It Works

Track management is done by MHTTrackMgmt. This implements track-oriented MHT. It creates new tracks each scan. A new track is created

1. For each measurement

2. For any track which has more than one measurement in its gate

3. For each existing track with a "null" measurement

Tracks are pruned to eliminate those of low probability and find the hypothesis which includes consistent tracks. Consistent tracks do not share any measurements.

This is typically used in a loop in which each step has new measurements, known as "scans." Scan is radar terminology for a rotating antenna beam. A scan is a set of sensor data taken at the same time.

The simulation can go in a loop to generate y or you can run the simulation separately and store the measurements in y. This can be helpful when you are debugging your MHT code.

For real-time systems y would be read in from your sensors. The MHT code would update every time you received new measurements. The code snippet below is from the header of MHTTrackMgmt, showing the overall approach to implementation.

```
zScan = [];

for k = 1:n

zScan = AddScan( y(:,k), [], [], [], zScan ) ;

[b, trk, sol, hyp] = MHTTrackMgmt( b, trk, zScan, trkData, k, t );

MHTGUI(trk,sol);

for j = 1:length(trk)
    trkData.fScanToTrackData.v =  myData
end

if( ~isempty(zScan) && makePlots )
    TOMHTTreeAnimation( 'update', trk );
end

t = t + dT;

end
```

Reference [1] provides good background reading, but the code in this function is not based on the reference. Other good references are books and papers by Blackman including [2] and [4].

```
%% MHTTrackMgmt - manages tracks
%
%% Form:
%    [b, trk, sol, hyp] = MHTTrackMgmt( b, trk, zScan, d, scan, t )
%
%% Description
% Manage Track Oriented Multiple Hypothesis Testing tracks.
```

```
%
% Performs track reduction and track pruning.
%
% It creates new tracks each scan. A new track is created
% - for each measurement
% - for any track which has more than one measurement in its gate
% - for each existing track with a "null" measurement.
%
% Tracks are pruned to eliminate those of low probability and find the
% hypothesis which includes consistent tracks. Consistent tracks do
% not share any measurements.
%
% This is typically used in a loop in which each step has new
% measurements, known as "scans". Scan is radar terminology for a
% rotating antenna beam. A scan is a set of sensor data taken at the
% ame time.
%
% The simulation can go in ths loop to generate y or you can run the
% simulation separately and store the measurements in y. This can be
% helpful when you are debugging your MHT code.
%
% For real time systems y would be read in from your sensors. The MHT
% code would update every time you received new measurements.
%
% zScan = [];
%
% for k = 1:n
%
%  zScan = AddScan( y(:,k), [], [], [], zScan ) ;
%
%  [b, trk, sol, hyp] = MHTTrackMgmt( b, trk, zScan, trkData, k, t );
%
%  MHTGUI(trk,sol);
%
%  for j = 1:length(trk)
%    trkData.fScanToTrackData.v =  myData
%  end
%
%  if( ~isempty(zScan) && makePlots )
%    TOMHTTreeAnimation( 'update', trk );
%  end
%
%  t = t + dT;
%
%      end
%
% The reference provides good background reading but the code in this
% function is not based on the reference. Other good references are
% books and papers by Blackman.
%
%% Inputs
%   b          (m,n)   [scans, tracks]
```

```
%    trk      (:)     Track data structure
%    zScan    (1,:)   Scan data structure
%    d        (1,1)   Track management parameters
%    scan     (1,1)   The scan id
%    t        (1,1)   Time
%
%% Outputs
%    b        (m,1)   [scans, tracks]
%    trk      (:)     Track data structure
%    sol      (.)     Solution data structure from TOMHTAssignment
%    hyp      (:)     Hypotheses
%
%% Reference
% A. Amditis1, G. Thomaidis1, P. Maroudis, P. Lytrivis1 and
% G. Karaseitanidis1, "Multiple Hypothesis Tracking
% Implementation," www.intechopen.com.

function [b, trk, sol, hyp] = MHTTrackMgmt( b, trk, zScan, d, scan, t )

% Warn the user that this function does not have a demo
if( nargin < 1 )
    disp('Error: 6 inputs are required');
    return;
end

MLog('add',sprintf('============= SCAN %d ==============',scan),scan);

% Add time to the filter data structure
for j = 1:length(trk)
        trk(j).filter.t = t;
end

% Remove tracks with an old scan history
earliestScanToKeep = scan-d.nScan;
keep = zeros(1,length(trk));
for j=1:length(trk);
  if( isempty(trk(j).scanHist) || max(trk(j).scanHist)>=earliestScanToKeep )
    keep(j) = 1;
  end
end
if any(~keep)
  txt = sprintf('DELETING %d tracks with old scan histories.\n',length(find
      (~keep)));
  MLog('add',txt,scan);
end
trk = trk( find(keep) );
nTrk = length(trk);

% Remove old scanHist and measHist entries
for j=1:nTrk
  k = find(trk(j).scanHist<earliestScanToKeep);
  if( ~isempty(k) )
```

```
      trk(j).measHist(k)   = [];
      trk(j).scanHist(k)   = [];
   end
end


% Above removal of old entries could result in duplicate tracks
%-------------------------------------------------------------
dup = CheckForDuplicateTracks( trk, d.removeDuplicateTracksAcrossAllTrees );
trk = RemoveDuplicateTracks( trk, dup, scan );
nTrk = length(trk);


% Perform the Kalman Filter prediction step
%------------------------------------------
for j = 1:nTrk
       trk(j).filter    = feval( d.predict, trk(j).filter );
       trk(j).mP        = trk(j).filter.m;
       trk(j).pP        = trk(j).filter.p;
   trk(j).m         = trk(j).filter.m;
       trk(j).p         = trk(j).filter.p;
end


% Track assignment
% 1. Each measurement creates a new track
% 2. One new track is created by adding a null measurement to each existing
%    track
% 3. Each measurement within a track's gate is added to a track. If there
%    are more than 1 measurement for a track create a new track.
%
% Assign to a track. If one measurement is within the gate we just assign
% it. If more than one we need to create a new track
nNew        = 0;
newTrack      = [];
newScan     = [];
newMeas     = [];
nS          = length(zScan);

maxID = 0;
maxTag = 0;
for j = 1:nTrk
       trk(j).d = zeros(1,nS);
   trk(j).new = [];
       for i = 1:nS
       trk(j).filter.x = trk(j).m;
       trk(j).filter.y = zScan(i);
       trk(j).d(i)      = feval( d.fDistance,  trk(j).filter );

       end
   trk(j).gate = trk(j).d < d.gate;
   hits        = find(trk(j).gate==1);
   trk(j).meas = [];
   lHits       = length(hits);
   if( lHits > 0 )
```

```
        if( lHits > 1)
            for k = 1:lHits-1
                newTrack(end+1) = j;
                newScan(end+1)  = trk(j).gate(hits(k+1));
                newMeas(end+1)  = hits(k+1);
            end
            nNew = nNew + lHits - 1;
        end
        trk(j).meas            = hits(1);
        trk(j).measHist(end+1) = hits(1);
        trk(j).scanHist(end+1) = scan;
        if( trk(j).scan0 == 0 )
            trk(j).scan0 = scan;
        end
    end
    maxID  = max(maxID,trk(j).treeID);
    maxTag = max(maxTag,trk(j).tag);
end
nextID  = maxID+1;
nextTag = maxTag+1;

% Create new tracks assuming that existing tracks had no measurements
%-----------------------------------------------------------------------
nTrk0 = nTrk;
for j = 1:nTrk0

  if( ~isempty(trk(j).scanHist) && trk(j).scanHist(end) == scan )

    % Add a copy of track "j" to the end with NULL measurement
    %-------------------------------------------------------
    nTrk                   = nTrk + 1;
    trk(nTrk)              = trk(j);
    trk(nTrk).meas         = [];
    trk(nTrk).treeID       = trk(nTrk).treeID; % Use the SAME track
        tree ID
    trk(nTrk).scan0        = scan;
    trk(nTrk).tag          = nextTag;

    nextTag = nextTag + 1;     % increment next tag number

    % The track we copied already had a measurement appended for this
    % scan, so replace these entries in the history
    %---------------------------------------------
    trk(nTrk).measHist(end)  = 0;
    trk(nTrk).scanHist(end)  = scan;

  end

end

% Do this to notify us if any duplicate tracks are created
%---------------------------------------------------------
```

```
dup    = CheckForDuplicateTracks( trk );
trk    = RemoveDuplicateTracks( trk, dup, scan );

% Add new tracks for existing tracks which had multiple measurements
%-------------------------------------------------------------------
if( nNew > 0 )
    nTrk = length(trk);
    for k = 1:nNew
        j                       = k + nTrk;
        trk(j)                  = trk(newTrack(k));
        trk(j).meas             = newMeas(k);
        trk(j).treeID           = trk(j).treeID;
        trk(j).measHist(end)    = newMeas(k);
        trk(j).scanHist(end)    = scan;
        trk(j).scan0            = scan;
        trk(j).tag              = nextTag;

        nextTag = nextTag + 1;

    end
end

% Do this to notify us if any duplicate tracks are created
dup    = CheckForDuplicateTracks( trk );
trk    = RemoveDuplicateTracks( trk, dup, scan );
nTrk   = length(trk);

% Create a new track for every measurement
for k = 1:nS
    nTrk                = nTrk + 1;

    % Use next track ID
    %------------------
    trkF                = feval(d.fScanToTrack, zScan(i), d.fScanToTrackData
    , scan, nextID, nextTag );
    if( isempty(trk) )
        trk = trkF;
    else
        trk(nTrk) = trkF;
    end
    trk(nTrk).meas      = k;
    trk(nTrk).measHist  = k;
    trk(nTrk).scanHist  = scan;
    nextID              = nextID + 1;   % increment next track-tree ID
    nextTag             = nextTag + 1;  % increment next tag number
end

% Exit now if there are no tracks
if( nTrk == 0 )
  b      = [];
  hyp    = [];
  sol    = [];
```

297

```
  return;
end

% Do this to notify us if any duplicate tracks are created
dup   = CheckForDuplicateTracks( trk );
trk   = RemoveDuplicateTracks( trk, dup, scan );
nTrk  = length(trk);

% Remove any tracks that have all NULL measurements
kDel = [];
if( nTrk > 1 ) % do this to prevent deletion of very first track
  for j=1:nTrk
    if( ~isempty(trk(j).measHist) && all(trk(j).measHist==0) )
      kDel = [kDel j];
    end
  end
  if( ~isempty(kDel) )
    keep = setdiff(1:nTrk,kDel);
    trk = trk( keep );
  end
  nTrk = length(trk);
end

% Compute track scores for each measurement
for j = 1:nTrk
  if( ~isempty(trk(j).meas ) )
      i = trk(j).meas;
      trk(j).score(scan)    = MHTTrackScore( zScan(i), trk(j).filter, d.
        pD, d.pFA, d.pH1, d.pH0 );
  else
      trk(j).score(scan)    = MHTTrackScore( [],        trk(j).filter, d.
        pD, d.pFA, d.pH1, d.pH0 );

  end
end

% Find the total score for each track
nTrk = length(trk);
for j = 1:nTrk
  if( ~isempty(trk(j).scanHist) )
    k1 = trk(j).scanHist(1);
    k2 = length(trk(j).score);
    kk = k1:k2;

    if( k1<length(trk(j).score)-d.nScan )
      error('The_scanHist_array_spans_back_too_far.')
    end

  else
    kk = 1;
  end
```

```
    trk(j).scoreTotal = MHTLLRUpdate( trk(j).score(kk) );

    % Add a weighted value of the average track score
    if( trk(j).scan0 > 0 )
      kk2 = trk(j).scan0 : length(trk(j).score);
      avgScore = min(0,MHTLLRUpdate( trk(j).score(kk2) ) / length(kk2));
      trk(j).scoreTotal = trk(j).scoreTotal + d.avgScoreHistoryWeight *
          avgScore;
    end

end

% Update the Kalman Filters
for j = 1:nTrk
      if( ~isempty(zScan) && ~isempty(trk(j).meas) )
      trk(j).filter.y       = zScan(trk(j).meas);
      trk(j).filter         = feval( d.update, trk(j).filter );
      trk(j).m              = trk(j).filter.m;
      trk(j).p              = trk(j).filter.p;
      trk(j).mHist(:,end+1) = trk(j).filter.m;
      end
end

% Examine the tracks for consistency
duplicateScans = zeros(1,nTrk);
for j=1:nTrk
  if( length(unique(trk(j).scanHist)) < length(trk(j).scanHist))
    duplicateScans(j)=1;
  end
end

% Update the b matrix and delete the oldest scan if necessary
b = MHTTrkToB( trk );

rr = rand(size(b,2),1);
br = b*rr;
if( length(unique(br))<length(br) )
  MLog('add',sprintf('DUPLICATE_TRACKS!!!\n'),scan);
end

% Solve for "M best" hypotheses
sol = TOMHTAssignment( trk, d.mBest );

% prune by keeping only those tracks whose treeID is present in the list of
% "M best" hypotheses
trk0 = trk;
if( d.pruneTracks )
  [trk,kept,pruned] = TOMHTPruneTracks( trk, sol, d.hypScanLast );
  b = MHTTrkToB( trk );

  % Do this to notify us if any duplicate tracks are created
  dup    = CheckForDuplicateTracks( trk );
```

299

```matlab
trk    = RemoveDuplicateTracks( trk, dup, scan );

% Make solution data compatible with pruned tracks
if( ~isempty(pruned) )
  for j=1:length(sol.hypothesis)
    for k = 1:length(sol.hypothesis(j).trackIndex)
      sol.hypothesis(j).trackIndex(k) = find( sol.hypothesis(j).trackIndex
          (k) == kept );
    end
  end
end

end

if( length(trk)<length(trk0) )
  txt = sprintf('Pruning: Reduce from %d to %d tracks.\n',length(trk0),
      length(trk));
  MLog('add',txt,scan);
else
  MLog('add',sprintf('Pruning: All tracks survived.\n'),scan);
end

% Form hypotheses
if( scan >= d.hypScanLast + d.hypScanWindow )
  hyp = sol.hypothesis(1);
else
  hyp = [];
end

function trk = RemoveDuplicateTracks( trk, dup, scan )
%% Remove duplicate tracks

if( ~isempty(dup) )
  MLog('update',sprintf('DUPLICATE TRACKS: %s\n',mat2str(dup)),scan);
  kDup = unique(dup(:,2));
  kUnq = setdiff(1:length(trk),kDup);
  trk(kDup) = [];
  dup2 = CheckForDuplicateTracks( trk );
  if( isempty(dup2) )
    txt = sprintf('Removed %d duplicates, kept tracks: %s\n',length(kDup),
        mat2str(kUnq));
    MLog('add',txt,scan);
  else
    error('Still have duplicates. Something is wrong with this pruning.')
  end
end
```

MHTTrackMgmt uses hypothesis forming and track pruning from the following two recipes.

12.5.4 Hypothesis Formation

12.5.4.1 Problem

Form hypotheses about tracks.

12.5.4.2 Solution

Formulate as a mixed integer-linear programming (MILP) and solve using GNU Linear Programming Kit (GLPK).

12.5.4.3 How It Works

Hypotheses are sets of tracks with consistent data, that is, where no measurements are assigned to more than one track. The track-oriented approach recomputes the hypotheses using the newly updated tracks after each scan of data is received. Rather than maintaining, and expanding, hypotheses from scan to scan, the track-oriented approach discards the hypotheses formed on scan $k - 1$. The tracks that survive pruning are propagated to the next scan k where new tracks are formed, using the new observations, and reformed into hypotheses. Except for the necessity to delete some tracks based upon low probability, no information is lost because the track scores, which are maintained, contain all the relevant statistical data.

In MHT, a valid hypothesis is any compatible set of tracks. In order for two or more tracks to be compatible, they cannot describe the same object, and they cannot share the same measurement at any of the scans. The task in hypothesis formation is to find one or more combinations of tracks that (1) are compatible and (2) maximize some performance function.

Before discussing the method of hypothesis formation, it is useful to first consider track formation and how tracks are associated with unique objects. New tracks may be formed in one of two ways:

1. The new track is based on some existing track, with the addition of a new measurement.

2. The new track is NOT based on any existing tracks; it is based solely on a single new measurement.

Recall that each track is formed as a sequence of measurements across multiple scans. In addition to the raw measurement history, every track also contains a history of state and covariance data that is computed from a Kalman filter. When a new measurement is appended to an existing track, we are spawning a new track that includes all of the original track's measurements, plus this new measurement. Therefore, the new track is describing the same object as the original track.

A new measurement can also be used to generate a completely new track that is independent of past measurements. When this is done, we are effectively saying that the measurement does not describe any of the objects that are already being tracked. It therefore must correspond to a new or different object.

In this way, each track is given an object ID to distinguish which object it describes. Within the context of track-tree diagrams, all of the tracks inside the same track-tree have the same object ID. For example, if at some point there are 10 separate track-trees, this means that 10 separate objects are being tracked in the MHT system. When a valid hypothesis is formed, it may turn out that only a few of these objects have compatible tracks.

The hypothesis formation step is formulated as an MILP and solved using GLPK. Each track is given an aggregate score that reflects the component scores attained from each measurement. The MILP formulation is constructed to select a set of tracks that add to give the highest score, such that

1. No two tracks have the same object ID.

2. No two tracks have the same measurement index for any scan.

In addition, we extended the formulation with an option to solve for multiple hypotheses, rather than just one. The algorithm will return the "M best" hypotheses, in descending order of score. This enables tracks to be preserved from alternate hypotheses that may be very close in score to the best.

The following code shows how hypothesis formation is done. GLPK is available for free. Its website includes installation instructions.

TOMHTAssignment generates hypotheses. The "*b*" matrix represents a stacked set of track-trees. Each row is a different path through a track-tree. Each column is a different scan. Values in the matrix are the index of the measurement for that scan. A valid hypothesis is a combination of rows of *b* (a combination of track-tree paths), such that the same measurement is not repeated. The solution vector "*x*" is an array with 0s and 1s that selects a set of track-tree paths. The objective is to find the hypothesis that maximizes the total score.

```
%% TOMHTASSIGNMENT - generates hypotheses
%
%% Form:
%   d = TOMHTAssignment( trk, M, glpkParams );
%
%% Description
% Track oriented MHT assignment. Generates hypotheses.
%
% The "b" matrix represents a stacked set of track-trees.
% Each row is a different path through a track-tree
% Each column is a different scan
% Values in matrix are index of measurement for that scan
%
% A valid hypothesis is a combination of rows of b (a combination of
% track-tree paths), such that the same measurement is not repeated.
%
% Solution vector "x" is 0|1 array that selects a set of track-tree-paths.
%
% Objective is to find the hypothesis that maximizes total score.
%
%
%% Inputs
%   trk          (.)       Data structure array of track information
%                          From this data we will obtain:
%   b            (nT,nS)    Matrix of measurement IDs across scans
%   trackScores  (1,nT)    Array of total track scores
%   treeIDs      (1,nT)    Array of track ID numbers. A common ID across
%                          multiple tracks means they are in the same
%                          track-tree.
%   M            (1,1)     Number of hypotheses to generate.
%   glpkParams   (.)       Data structure with glpk parameters.
%
%% Outputs
%   d            (.)       Data structure with fields:
%                          .nT     Number of tracks
%                          .nS     Number of scans
%                          .M      Number of hypotheses
%                          .pairs  Pairs of hypotheses for score constraints
%                          .nPairs Number of pairs
%                          .A      Constraint matrix for optimization
%                          .b      Constraint vector for optimization
%                          .c      Cost vector for optimization
%                          .lb     lower bounds on solution vector
```

```
%                          .ub     upper bounds on solution vector
%                          .conType  Constraint type array
%                          .varType  Variable type array
%                          .x        Solution vector for optimization
%                          .hypothesis(:)  Array of hypothesis data
%
%      d.hypothesis(:)   Data strcuture array with fields:
%                   .treeID      Vector of track-tree IDs in hypothesis
%                   .trackIndex  Vector of track indices in hypothesis.
%                                Maps to rows of "b" matrix.
%                   .tracks      Set of tracks in hypothesis. These are
%                                the selected rows of "b" matrix.
%                   .trackScores Vector of scores for selected tracks.
%                   .score       Total score for hypothesis.
%
%% References
%      Blackman, S. and R. Popoli, "Design and Analysis of  Modern
%      Tracking Systems," Artech House, 1999.

%% Copyright
%   Copyright (c) 2012-2013 Princeton Satellite Systems, Inc.
%   All rights reserved.

function d = TOMHTAssignment( trk, M, glpkParams )

%=====================================
%     --- OPTIONS ---
%
%   Prevent tracks with all zeros
%   from being selected?
%
preventAllZeroTracks = 0;
%
%
%
%   Choose a scoring method:
%     log-LR   sum of log of likelihood ratios
%     LR       sum of likelihood ratios
%     prob     sum of probabilities
%
scoringMethod = 'log-LR';
%
%=====================================

% how many solutions to generate?
if( nargin<2 )
  M = 2;
end

% GLPK parameters
if( nargin<5 )
  % Searching time limit, in seconds.
  %  If this value is positive, it is decreased each
```

303

```
%    time when one simplex iteration has been performed by the
%    amount of time spent for the iteration, and reaching zero
%    value signals the solver to stop the search. Negative
%    value means no time limit.
glpkParams.tmlim = 10;

% Level of messages output by solver routines:
%    0 - No output.
%    1 - Error messages only.
%    2 - Normal output.
%    3 - Full output (includes informational messages).
glpkParams.msglev = 0;

end

% extract "b" matrix
b = MHTTrkToB(trk);

% the track tree IDs
treeIDs = [trk.treeID];

scans = unique([trk.scanHist]);
scan = max(scans);

% the track scores
switch lower(scoringMethod)
  case 'log-lr'
    % the "scoreTotal" field is the sum of log likelihood ratios
    trackScores = [trk.scoreTotal];
  case 'lr'
    % Redefine scores this way rather than sum of log of each scan score
    trackScores = zeros(1,nT);
    for j=1:nT
      if( ~isempty(trk(j).scanHist) )
        trackScores(j) = sum(trk(j).score(trk(j).scanHist(1):end));
      else
        trackScores(j) = sum(trk(j).score);
      end
    end
  case 'prob'
    error('Probability_scoring_not_implemented_yet.')
end

% remove occurrence of "inf"
kinf = find(isinf(trackScores));
trackScores(kinf) = sign(trackScores(kinf))*1e8;

% remove treeIDs column from b
b = b(:,2:end);

[nT,nS] = size(b);
```

```
nCon = 0;    % number of constraints not known yet. compute below
nVar = nT;   % number of variables is equal to total # track-tree-paths

% compute number of constraints
for i=1:nS
  % number of measurements taken for this scan
  nMeasForThisScan = max(b(:,i));
  nCon = nCon + nMeasForThisScan;
end

% Initialize A, b, c
d.A = zeros(nCon,nVar*M);
d.b = zeros(nCon,1);
d.c = zeros(nVar*M,1);
d.conType = char(zeros(1,nCon));
d.varType = char(zeros(1,nVar));
for i=1:M
  col0 = (i-1)*nT;
  for j=1:nT
    d.varType(col0+j) = 'B'; % all binary variables
    %d.c(col0+j) = trackProb(j);
    d.c(col0+j) = trackScores(j);
    %d.c(col0+j) = trackScoresPos(j);
  end
end

% coefficients for unique tag generation
%coeff = 2.^[0 : 1 : nT-1];

conIndex = 0;

col0 = 0;

% find set of tracks that have all zeros, if any
bSumCols = sum(b,2);
kAllZeroTracks = find(bSumCols==0);

for mm = 1:M

  % for each track-tree ID
  treeIDsU = unique(treeIDs);
  for i=1:length(treeIDsU)
    rows = find(treeIDs==treeIDsU(i));

    % for each row of b with this track ID
    conIndex = conIndex+1;
    for j=rows
      d.A(conIndex,col0+j) = 1;
      d.b(conIndex)        = 1;
      d.conType(conIndex)  = 'U'; % upper bound: A(conIndex,:)*x <= 1
    end
  end

  % for each scan
```

305

```
for i=1:nS

   % number of measurements taken for this scan
   nMeasForThisScan = max(b(:,i));

   % for each measurement (not 0)
   for k=1:nMeasForThisScan

      % get rows of b matrix with this measurement index
      bRowsWithMeasK = find(b(:,i)==k);

      conIndex = conIndex+1;

      % for each row
      for j = bRowsWithMeasK

         d.A(conIndex,col0+j)  = 1;
         d.b(conIndex)         = 1;
         d.conType(conIndex)   = 'U'; % upper bound: A(conIndex,:)*x <= 1

      end
   end
end

% prevent tracks with all zero measurements from being selected
if( preventAllZeroTracks )
   for col = kAllZeroTracks
      conIndex = conIndex+1;
      d.A(conIndex,col) = 1;
      d.b(conIndex) = 0;
      d.conType(conIndex) = 'S';
   end
end

col0 = col0 + nT;

end

% variable bounds
d.lb = zeros(size(d.c));
d.ub = ones(size(d.c));

% add set of constraints / vars for each pair of solutions
if( M>1 )
   pairs = nchoosek(1:M,2);
   nPairs = size(pairs,1);

   for i=1:nPairs
      k1 = pairs(i,1);
      k2 = pairs(i,2);
      xCol1 = (k1-1)*nT+1 : k1*nT;
      xCol2 = (k2-1)*nT+1 : k2*nT;
```

```
    % enforce second score to be less than first score
    % c1*x1 - c2*x2 >= tol
    conIndex = conIndex + 1;
    d.A(conIndex,xCol1)  = d.c(xCol1);
    d.A(conIndex,xCol2)  = -d.c(xCol2);
    d.b(conIndex)        = 10;              % must be non-negative and small
    d.conType(conIndex)  = 'L';

  end
else
  pairs = [];
  nPairs = 0;
end


if( nT>1 )

  % call glpk to solve for optimal hypotheses
  %glpkParams.msglev = 3; % use this for detailed GLPK printout

  d.A( abs(d.A)<eps ) = 0;
  d.b( abs(d.b)<eps ) = 0;

  [d.x,~,status] = glpk(d.c,d.A,d.b,d.lb,d.ub,d.conType,d.varType,-1,
      glpkParams);
  switch status
    case 1
      MLog('add',sprintf('GLPK: 1: solution is undefined.\n'),scan);
    case 2
      MLog('add',sprintf('GLPK: 2: solution is feasible.\n'),scan);
    case 3
      MLog('add',sprintf('GLPK: 3: solution is infeasible.\n'),scan);
    case 4
      MLog('add',sprintf('GLPK: 4: no feasible solution exists.\n'),scan);
    case 5
      MLog('add',sprintf('GLPK: 5: solution is optimal.\n'),scan);
    case 6
      MLog('add',sprintf('GLPK: 6: solution is unbounded.\n'),scan);
    otherwise
      MLog('add',sprintf('GLPK: %d\n',status),scan);
  end

else

  d.x = ones(M,1);

end

d.nT = nT;
d.nS = nS;
d.M = M;
d.pairs = pairs;
d.nPairs = nPairs;
d.trackMat = b;
```

307

```
for mm=1:M
  rows = (mm-1)*nT+1 : mm*nT;
  sel = find(d.x(rows));
  d.hypothesis(mm).treeID      = treeIDs(sel);
  d.hypothesis(mm).tracks      = b(sel,:);
  for j=1:length(sel)
    d.hypothesis(mm).meas{j}   = trk(sel).measHist;
    d.hypothesis(mm).scans{j}  = trk(sel).scanHist;
  end
  d.hypothesis(mm).trackIndex  = sel;
  d.hypothesis(mm).trackScores = trackScores(sel);
  d.hypothesis(mm).score       = sum(trackScores(sel));
end
```

12.5.5 Track Pruning

12.5.5.1 Problem

We need to prune tracks to prevent an explosion of tracks.

12.5.5.2 Solution

Implement N-scan track pruning.

12.5.5.3 How It Works

The N-scan track pruning is carried out at every step using the last n scans of data. We use a pruning method in which the following tracks are preserved:

- Tracks with the "N" highest scores

- Tracks that are included in the "M best" hypotheses

- Tracks that have both (1) the object ID and (2) the first "P" measurements found in the "M best" hypotheses

We use the results of hypothesis formation to guide track pruning. The parameters N, M, P can be tuned to improve performance. The objective with pruning is to reduce the number of tracks as much as possible while not removing any tracks that should be part of the actual true hypothesis.

The second item listed above is to preserve all tracks included in the "M best" hypotheses. Each of these is a full path through a track-tree, which is clear. The third item listed above is similar, but less constrained. Consider one of the tracks in the "M best" hypotheses. We will preserve this full track. In addition, we will preserve all tracks that stem from scan "P" of this track.

Figure 12.9 provides an example of which tracks in a track-tree might be preserved. The diagram shows 17 different tracks over 5 scans. The green track represents one of the tracks found in the set of "M best" hypotheses, from the hypothesis formation step. This track would be preserved. The orange tracks all stem from the node in this track at scan 2. These would be preserved if we set $P = 2$ from the description above. The following code shows how track pruning is done.

Figure 12.9: Track pruning example

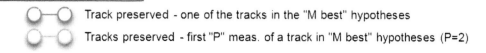

Track preserved - one of the tracks in the "M best" hypotheses

Tracks preserved - first "P" meas. of a track in "M best" hypotheses (P=2)

- Scan 1

- Scan 2

- Scan 3

- Scan 4

- Scan 5

```
function [tracksP,keep,prune,d] = TOMHTPruneTracks( tracks, soln, scan0,
    opts )

% default value for starting scan index
if( nargin<3 )
  scan0 = 0;
end

% default algorithm options
if( nargin<4 )
  opts.nHighScoresToKeep  = 5;
  opts.nFirstMeasMatch    = 3;
end

% increment the # scans to match
opts.nFirstMeasMatch = opts.nFirstMeasMatch + scan0;

% output structure to record which criteria resulted in preservation of
% which tracks
d.bestTrackScores       = [];
d.bestHypFullTracks     = [];
d.bestHypPartialTracks  = [];
```

```matlab
% number of hypotheses, tracks, scans
nHyp    = length(soln.hypothesis);
nTracks = length(tracks);
nScans  = size(soln.hypothesis(1).tracks,2);

% must limit # required matching measurements to # scans
if( opts.nFirstMeasMatch > nScans )
  opts.nFirstMeasMatch = nScans;
end

% if # high scores to keep equals or exceeds # tracks
% then just return original tracks
if( opts.nHighScoresToKeep > nTracks )
  tracksP = tracks;
  keep    = 1:length(tracks);
  prune   = [];
  d.bestTrackScores = keep;
  return
end

% get needed vectors out of trk array
scores  = [tracks.scoreTotal];
treeIDs = [tracks.treeID];

% get list of all treeIDs in hypotheses
treeIDsInHyp = [];
for j=1:nHyp
  treeIDsInHyp = [treeIDsInHyp, soln.hypothesis(j).treeID];
end
treeIDsInHyp = unique(treeIDsInHyp);

% create a matrix of hypothesis data with ID and tracks
hypMat = [soln.hypothesis(1).treeID', soln.hypothesis(1).tracks];
for j=2:nHyp
  for k=1:length(soln.hypothesis(j).treeID)
    % if this track ID is not already included,
    if( all(soln.hypothesis(j).treeID(k) ~= hypMat(:,1)) )
      % then append this row to bottom of matrix
      hypMat = [hypMat; ...
        soln.hypothesis(j).treeID(k), soln.hypothesis(j).tracks(k,:)];
    end
  end
end

% Initialize "keep" array to all zeros
keep    = zeros(1,nTracks);

% Keep tracks with the "N" highest scores
if( opts.nHighScoresToKeep>0 )

  [~,ks] = sort(scores,2,'descend');
  index = ks(1:opts.nHighScoresToKeep);
```

```
  keep( index ) = 1;

  d.bestTrackScores = index(:)';
end

% Keep tracks in the "M best" hypotheses
for j=1:nHyp
  index = soln.hypothesis(j).trackIndex;
  keep( index ) = 1;

  d.bestHypFullTracks = index(:)';
end

% If we do not require any measurements to match,
% then include ALL tracks with an ID contained in "M best hypotheses"
if( opts.nFirstMeasMatch == 0 )

  % This means we include the entire track-tree for those IDs in included
  % in the set of best hypotheses.
  for k = 1:length(trackIDsInHyp)
    index = find(treeIDs == trackIDsInHyp(k));
    keep( index ) = 1;

    d.bestHypPartialTracks = index(:)';
  end

  % If the # measurements we require to match is equal to # scans, then
  % this is equivalent to the set of tracks in the hypothesis solution.
elseif( opts.nFirstMeasMatch == nScans )
  % We have already included these tracks, so nothing more to do here.

else
  % Otherwise, we have some subset of measurements to match.
  % Find the set of tracks that have:
  %       1. track ID and
  %       2. first "P" measurements
  % included in "M best" hypotheses
  nTracksInHypSet = size(hypMat,1);
  tagMap = rand(opts.nFirstMeasMatch+1,1);
  b = MHTTrkToB2( tracks );
  trkMat = [ trackIDs', b ];
  trkTag = trkMat(:,1:opts.nFirstMeasMatch+1)*tagMap;
  for j=1:nTracksInHypSet
    hypTrkTag = hypMat(j,1:opts.nFirstMeasMatch+1)*tagMap;
    index = find( trkTag == hypTrkTag );
    keep( index ) = 1;

    d.bestHypPartialTracks = [d.bestHypPartialTracks, index(:)'];
  end
  d.bestHypPartialTracks = sort(unique(d.bestHypPartialTracks));

end
```

```
% prune index list is everything not kept
prune = ~keep;

% switch from logical array to index
keep  = find(keep);
prune = find(prune);
```

12.5.5.4 Simulation

The simulation is for a two-dimensional model of automobile dynamics. The primary car is driving along a highway at variable speeds. It carries a radar. Many cars pass the primary car, some of which change lanes from behind the car and cut in front. The MHT system tracks all cars. At the start of the simulation there are no cars in the radar field of view. One car passes and cuts in front of the radar car. The other two just pass in their lanes. This is a good test of track initiation.

The radar, covered in the first recipe of the chapter, measures range, range rate, and azimuth in the radar car frame. The model generates those values directly from the target and tracking cars' relative velocity and positions. The radar signal processing is not modeled, but the radar has field-of-view and range limitations. See `AutoRadar`.

The cars are driven by steering controllers that execute basic automobile maneuver. The throttle (accelerator pedal) and steering angle can be controlled. Multiple maneuvers can be chained together. This provides a challenging test for the MHT system. You can try different maneuvers and add additional maneuver functions of your own.

The UKFilter described in Chapter 10 is used in this demo since the radar is a highly nonlinear measurement. The UKF dynamical model, `RHSAutomobileXY`, is a pair of double integrators in the inertial frame relative to the radar car. The model accommodates steering and throttle changes by making the plant covariance, both position and velocity, larger than would be expected by analyzing the relative accelerations. An alternative would be to use interactive multiple models (IMMs) with a "steering" model and "acceleration" model. This added complication does not appear to be necessary. A considerable amount of uncertainty would be retained even with IMMs since a steering model would be limited to one or two steering angles.

The script implementing the simulation with MHT is `MHTAutomobileDemo`. There are four cars in the demo; car 4 will be passing. Figure 12.10 shows the maneuver.

```
% Set the seed for the random number generators.
% If the seed is not set each run will be different.
seed = 45198;
rng(seed);

% Control screen output
% This demo takes about 4 minutes with the graphics OFF.
% It takes about 10 minutes with the graphics on.
printTrackUpdates   = 0; % includes a pause at every MHT step
graphicsOn          = 0;
treeAnimationOn     = 0;

% Car 1 has the radar

% 'mass' (1,1)
% 'steering angle' (1,1) (rad)
% 'position tires' (2,4)
```

```
d.car(1) = AutomobileInitialize(   'mass', 1513,...
                                   'position_tires', [  1.17 1.17 -1.68
                                       -1.68; -0.77 0.77 -0.77 0.77], ...
                                   'frontal_drag_coefficient', 0.25, ...
                                   'side_drag_coefficient', 0.5, ...
                                   'tire_friction_coefficient', 0.01, ...
                                   'tire_radius', 0.4572, ...
                                   'engine_torque', 0.4572*200, ...
                                   'rotational_inertia', 2443.26, ...
                                   'rolling_resistance_coefficients', [0.013
                                       6.5e-6], ...
                                   'height_automobile', 2/0.77, ...
                                   'side_and_frontal_automobile_dimensions',
                                       [1.17+1.68 2*0.77]);

% Make the other cars identical
d.car(2) = d.car(1);
d.car(3) = d.car(1);
d.car(4) = d.car(1);
nAuto    = length(d.car);

% Velocity set points for cars 1-3. Car 4 will be passing
vSet               = [12 13 14];

% Time step setup
dT    = 0.1;
tEnd  = 300;
n     = ceil(tEnd/dT);

% Car initial state
x   = [140; 0;12;0;0;0;...
       30; 3;14;0;0;0;...
       0;-3;15;0;0;0;...
       0; 0;11;0;0;0];

% Radar
m                  = length(x)-1;
dRadar.kR          = [7:6:m;8:6:m];
dRadar.kV          = [9:6:m;10:6:m];
dRadar.kT          = 11:6:m;
dRadar.noise       = [0.1;0.01;0.01]; % [range; range rate; azimuth]
dRadar.fOV         = pi/4;
dRadar.maxRange    = 800;
dRadar.noLimits    = 0;

figure('name','Radar_FOV')
range = tan(dRadar.fOV)*5;
fill([x(1) x(1)+range*[1 1]],[x(2) x(2)+5*[1 -1]],'y')
iX = [1 7 13 19];
l = plot([[0;0;0;0] x(iX)]',(x(iX+1)*[1 1])','-');
hold on
for k = 1:length(l)
```

```
    plot(x(iX(k)),x(iX(k)+1)','*','color',get(l(k),'color'));
end
set(gca,'ylim',[-5 5]);
grid
range = tan(dRadar.fOV)*5;
fill([x(1) x(1)+range*[1 1]],[x(2) x(2)+5*[1 -1]],'y')
legend(l,'Auto_1','Auto_2', 'Auto_3', 'Auto_4');
title('Initial_Conditions_and_Radar_FOV')

% Plotting
yP = zeros(3*(nAuto-1),n);
vP = zeros(nAuto-1,n);
xP = zeros(length(x)+2*nAuto,n);
s  = 1:6*nAuto;

%% Simulate
t                   = (0:(n-1))*dT;

fprintf(1,'\nRunning_the_simulation...');
for k = 1:n

  % Plotting
  xP(s,k)      = x;
  j            = s(end)+1;

  for i = 1:nAuto
    p            = 6*i-5;
    d.car(i).x   = x(p:p+5);
    xP(j:j+1,k)  = [d.car(i).delta;d.car(i).torque];
    j            = j + 2;
  end

  % Get radar measurements
  dRadar.theta        = d.car(1).x(5);
  dRadar.t            = t(k);
  dRadar.xR           = x(1:2);
  dRadar.vR           = x(3:4);
  [yP(:,k), vP(:,k)]     = AutoRadar( x, dRadar );

  % Implement Control

  % For all but the passing car control the velocity
  for j = 1:3
      d.car(j).torque = -10*(d.car(j).x(3) - vSet(j));
  end

  % The passing car
  d.car(4)      = AutomobilePassing( d.car(4), d.car(1), 3, 1.3, 10 );

  % Integrate
  x             = RungeKutta(@RHSAutomobile, 0, x, dT, d );
```

```
end
fprintf(1,'DONE.\n');

% The state of the radar host car
xRadar = xP(1:6,:);

% Plot the simulation results
figure('name','Auto')
kX = 1:6:length(x);
kY = 2:6:length(x);
c  = 'bgrcmyk';
j  = floor(linspace(1,n,20));
[t, tL] = TimeLabel( t );
for k = 1:nAuto
    plot(xP(kX(k),j),xP(kY(k),j),[c(k) '.']);
    hold on
end
legend('Auto 1','Auto 2', 'Auto 3', 'Auto 4');

for k = 1:nAuto
    plot(xP(kX(k),:),xP(kY(k),:),c(k));
end
xlabel('x (m)');
ylabel('y (m)');
set(gca,'ylim',[-5 5]);
grid

kV = [19:24 31 32];
yL = {'x (m)' 'y (m)' 'v_x (m/s)' 'v_y (m/s)' '\theta (rad)' '\omega (rad/s)
    ' '\delta (rad)' 'T (Nm)'};
PlotSet( t,xP(kV,:), 'x label',tL, 'y label', yL,'figure title','Passing car
    ');

% Plot the radar results but ignore cars that are not observed
for k = 1:nAuto-1
        j   = 3*k-2:3*k;
        sL  = sprintf('Radar: Observed Auto %d',k);
        b   = mean(yP(j(1),:));
        if( b ~= 0 )
    PlotSet(t,[yP(j,:);vP(k,:)],'x label',tL,'y label', {'Range (m)' 'Range
        Rate (m/s)' 'Azimuth (rad)' 'Valid'},'figure title',sL);
        end
end


%% Implement MHT

% Covariances
r0      = dRadar.noise.^2;           % Measurement 1-sigma
q0      = [1e-7;1e-7;.1;.1];         % The baseline plant covariance diagonal
p0      = [5;0.4;1;0.01].^2;         % Initial state covariance matrix diagonal

% Adjust the radar data structure for the new state
```

315

```
dRadar.noise   = [0;0;0];
dRadar.kR      = [1;2];
dRadar.kV      = [3;4];
dRadar.noLimits = 1;

ukf         = KFInitialize('ukf','x',xRadar(1:4,1),'f',@RHSAutomobileXY,...
                           'h', {@AutoRadarUKF},'hData',{dRadar},'alpha'
                             ,1,...
                           'kappa',2,'beta',2,'dT',dT,'fData',[],'p',diag(p0
                             ),...
                           'q',diag(q0),'m',xRadar(1:4,1),'r',{diag(r0)});
ukf         = UKFWeight( ukf );

[mhtData, trk] = MHTInitialize( 'probability_false_alarm', 0.01,...
                           'probability_of_signal_if_target_present',
                             1,...
                           'probability_of_signal_if_target_absent',
                             0.01,...
                           'probability_of_detection', 1, ...
                           'measurement_volume', 1.0, ...
                           'number_of_scans', 5, ...
                           'gate', 20,...
                           'm_best', 2,...
                           'number_of_tracks', 1,...
                           'scan_to_track_function',@ScanToTrackAuto
                             ,...
                           'scan_to_track_data',dRadar,...
                           'distance_function',@MHTDistanceUKF,...
                           'hypothesis_scan_last', 0,...
                           'remove_duplicate_tracks_across_all_trees'
                             ,1,...
                           'average_score_history_weight',0.01,...
                           'prune_tracks', 1,...
                           'create_track', 1,...
                           'filter_type','ukf',...
                           'filter_data', ukf);

% Size arrays
%------------
m        = zeros(5,n);
p        = zeros(5,n);
scan     = cell(1,n);
b        = MHTTrkToB( trk );

t        = 0;

% Parameter data structure for the measurements
sParam = struct( 'hFun', @AutoRadarUKF, 'hData', dRadar, 'r', diag(r0) );

TOMHTTreeAnimation( 'initialize', trk );
MHTGUI;
MLog('init')
MLog('name','MHT_Automobile_Tracking_Demo')
```

```matlab
fprintf(1,'Running_the_MHT...');
for k = 1:n

  % Assemble the measurements
        zScan = [];
  for j = 1:size(vP,1)
    if( vP(j,k) == 1 )
      tJ      = 3*j;
      zScan      = AddScan( yP(tJ-2:tJ,k), [], [], sParam, zScan );
    end
  end

  % Add state data for the radar car
  mhtData.fScanToTrackData.xR      = xRadar(1:2,k);
  mhtData.fScanToTrackData.vR      = xRadar(3:4,k);
  mhtData.fScanToTrackData.theta         = xRadar(5,k);

  % Manage the tracks
  [b, trk, sol, hyp, mhtData] = MHTTrackMgmt( b, trk, zScan, mhtData, k, t )
      ;

  % A guess for the initial velocity of any new track
  for j = 1:length(trk)
    mhtData.fScanToTrackData.x =  xRadar(:,k);
  end

  % Update MHTGUI display
  if( ~isempty(zScan) && graphicsOn )
    if (treeAnimationOn)
      TOMHTTreeAnimation( 'update', trk );
    end
    if( ~isempty(trk) )
      MHTGUI(trk,sol,'hide');
    end
    drawnow
  end

  % Update time
  t = t + dT;
end
fprintf(1,'DONE.\n');

% Show the final GUI
if (~treeAnimationOn)
  TOMHTTreeAnimation( 'update', trk );
end
if (~graphicsOn)
  MHTGUI(trk,sol,'hide');
end
MHTGUI;

PlotTracks(trk)
```

317

Figure 12.10: Automobile demo car trajectories.

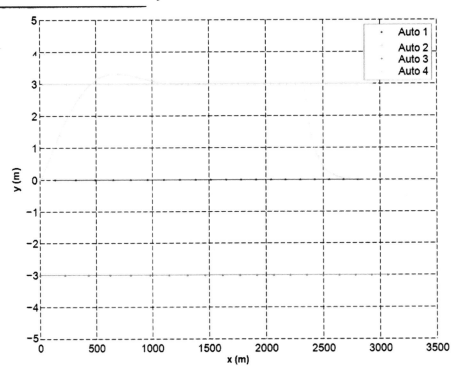

Figure 12.11 shows the radar measurement for car 3 which is the last car tracked. The MHT system handles vehicle acquisition well.

The MHT graphical user interface (GUI) in Figure 12.12 shows a hypothesis with three tracks at the end of the simulation. This is the expected result.

Figure 12.13 shows the final tree. There are several redundant tracks. These tracks can be removed since they are clones of other tracks. This does not impact the hypothesis generation.

Figure 12.11: Automobile demo radar measurement for car 3.

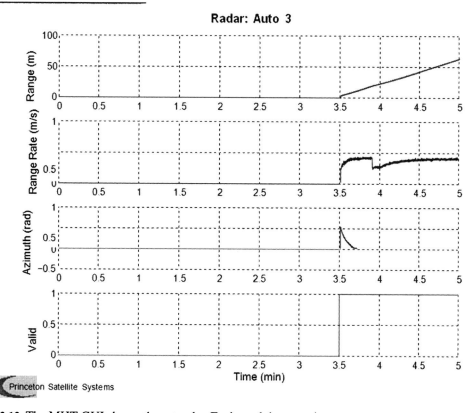

Figure 12.12: The MHT GUI shows three tracks. Each track has consistent measurements.

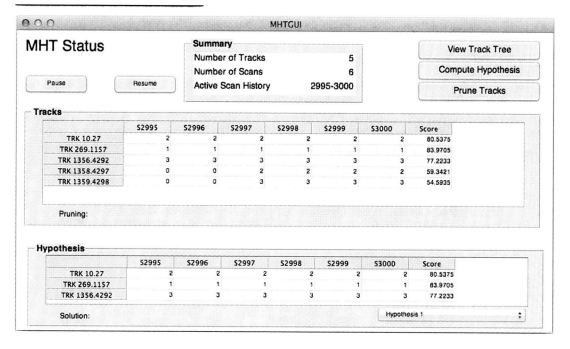

Figure 12.13: The final tree for the automobile demo.

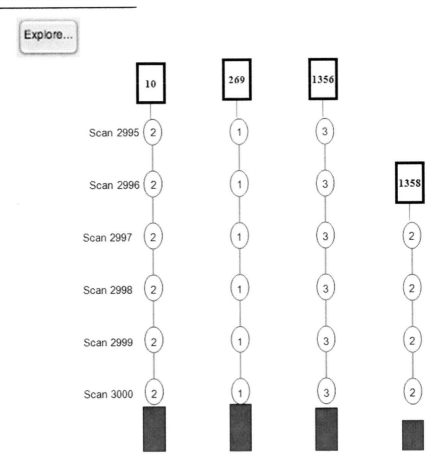

Summary

This chapter has demonstrated an automobile tracking problem. The automobile has a radar system that detects cars in its field of view. The system accurately assigns measurements to tracks and successfully learns the path of each neighboring car. You started by building a UKF to model the motion of an automobile and to incorporate measurements from a radar system. The UKF is demonstrated in a simulation script. You then build a script that incorporates track-oriented MHT to assign measurements taken by the radar of multiple automobiles. This allows our radar system to autonomously and reliably track multiple cars.

You also learned how to make simple automobile controllers. The two controllers steer the automobiles and allow them to pass other cars. Table 12.2 lists the code used in this chapter.

Table 12.2: Chapter Code Listing

File	Description
AddScan	Add a scan to the data
AutoRadar	Automobile radar model for simulation
AutoRadarUKF	Automobile radar model for the UKF
AutomobileInitialize	Initialize the automobile data structure
AutomobileLaneChange	Automobile control algorithm for lane changes
AutomobilePassing	Automobile control algorithm for passing
CheckForDuplicateTracks	Look through the recorded tracks for duplicates
MHTAutomobileDemo	Demonstrate the use of MHT for automobile radar systems
MHTDistanceUKF	Compute the MHT distance
MHTGUI.fig	Saved layout data for the MHT GUI
MHTGUI	GUI for the MHT software
MHTHypothesisDisplay	Display hypotheses in a GUI
MHTInitialize	Initialize the MHT algorithm
MHTInitializeTrk	Initialize a track
MHTLLRUpdate	Update the log-likelihood ratio
MHTMatrixSortRows	Sort rows in the MHT
MHTMatrixTreeConvert	Convert to and from a tree format for the MHT data
MHTTrackMerging	Merge MHT tracks
MHTTrackMgmt	Manage MHT tracks
MHTTrackScore	Compute the total score for the track
MHTTrackScoreKinematic	Compute the kinematic portion of the track score
MHTTrackScoreSignal	Compute the signal portion of the track score
MHTTreeDiagram	Draw an MHT tree diagram
MHTTrkToB	Convert tracks to a b matrix
PlotTracks	Plot object tracks
Residual	Compute the residual
RHSAutomobile	Automobile dynamical model for simulation
RHSAutomobileXY	Automobile dynamical model for the UKF
ScanToTrackAuto	Assign a scan to a track for the automobile problem
TOMHTTreeAnimation	Track-oriented MHT tree diagram animation
TOMHTAssignment	Assign a scan to a track
TOMHTPruneTracks	Prune the tracks
UKFAutomobileDemo	Demonstrate the UKF for an automobile

References

[1] A. Amditis, G. Thomaidis, P. Maroudis, P. Lytrivis, and G. Karaseitanidis. Multiple hypothesis tracking implementation. www.intechopen.com, 2016.

[2] S. S. Blackman. Multiple hypothesis tracking for multiple target tracking. *Aerospace and Electronic Systems Magazine, IEEE*, 19(1):5–18, Jan. 2004.

[3] S. S. Blackman and R. F. Popoli. *Design and Analysis of Modern Tracking Systems*. Artech House, 1999.

[4] S. S. Blackman, R. J. Dempster, M. T. Busch, and R. F. Popoli. Multiple hypothesis tracking for multiple target tracking. *IEEE Transactions on Aerospace and Electronic Systems*, 35(2):730–738, April 1999.

[5] D. B. Reid. An algorithm for tracking multiple targets. *IEEE Transactions on Automatic Control*, AC=24(6):843–854, December 1979.

[6] L. D. Stone, C. A. Barlow, and T. L. Corwin. *Bayesian Multiple Target Tracking*. Artech House, 1999.

[7] Matthew G. Villella. *Nonlinear Modeling and Control of Automobiles with Dynamic Wheel-Road Friction and Wheel Torque Inputs*. PhD thesis, Georgia Institute of Technology, April 2004.

Index

Get the eBook for only $4.99!

Why limit yourself?

Now you can take the weightless companion with you wherever you go and access your content on your PC, phone, tablet, or reader.

Since you've purchased this print book, we are happy to offer you the eBook for just $4.99.

Convenient and fully searchable, the PDF version enables you to easily find and copy code—or perform examples by quickly toggling between instructions and applications.

To learn more, go to http://www.apress.com/us/shop/companion or contact support@apress.com.

CPSIA information can be obtained
at www.ICGtesting.com
Printed in the USA
LVOW09s1606270217
525559LV00004B/6/P

9 781484 222492